W I L D

STORIES OF SURVIVAL FROM THE
WORLD'S MOST DANGEROUS PLACES

W I L D

STORIES OF SURVIVAL FROM THE
WORLD'S MOST DANGEROUS PLACES

EDITED BY CLINT WILLIS

MAINSTREAM
PUBLISHING

EDINBURGH AND LONDON

Adrenaline ™ and the Adrenaline™ logo are trademarks of
Balliett & Fitzgerald Inc. New York, NY

An Adrenaline Book™

First published in Great Britain in 2000 by
MAINSTREAM PUBLISHING COMPANY (EDINBURGH) LTD
7 Albany Street
Edinburgh EH1 3UG

ISBN 1 84018 316 0

First published in the United States by
Thunder's Mouth Press
841 Broadway, 4th Floor
New York, NY 10003

and

Balliett & Fitzgerald Inc.
66 West Broadway, Suite 602
New York, NY 10007

Series Editor: Clint Willis
Book design: Sue Canavan
Frontispiece photo: © D. L. Mazur

Printed and bound in Great Britain by Butler and Tanner Ltd, Frome and London

For Harper Willis, who knows the way.

c o n t e n t s

photographs   8

introduction   9

from *In Trouble Again*
**by Redmond
O'Hanlon**   15

from *Savages*
by Joe Kane   39

Down the River
by Edward Abbey   67

from *Deborah: A Wilderness
Narrative*
by David Roberts   115

Pearyland
by Barry Lopez   129

from *Young Men & Fire*
by Norman Maclean   139

from *Arabian Sands*
**by Sir Wilfred
Thesiger**   169

from *The Sea and the Jungle*
by H. M. Tomlinson   191

from *A Walk in the Woods*
by Bill Bryson   211

from *Deliverance*
by James Dickey   231

To Build a Fire
by Jack London   239

The Willows
**by Algernon
Blackwood**   259

The Man Who Liked Dickens
by Evelyn Waugh   311

acknowledgments   329

bibliography   332

photographs

15   Piranha, mouth open
      © Vera Storman/Tony Stone
      Images

39   Amazon Basin
      © Frans Lanting/Tony Stone
      Images

67   Colorado River gorge
      © Chad Ehlers/Tony Stone
      Images

115   Climber in crevasse
      © D. L. Mazur

129   Caribou running
      © Pal Hermansen/Tony Stone
      Images

139   Mann Gulch grave marker
      courtesy of U.S. Forest Service

169   Bedouins and camels
      © Lorne Resnick/Tony Stone
      Images

191   Rain forest in mist
      © Frans Lanting/Tony
      Stone Images

211   Hikers on the trail
      © Paul Harris/Tony Stone
      Images

231   Chattooga River
      courtesy of U.S.D.A. Forest
      Service

239   Fingers with match
      © Vera Storman/Tony
      Stone Images

259   Mist-shrouded river
      © David Meunch/Corbis

311   Amazon tributary in
      Amazonas
      © Will & Deni McIntyre/
      Tony Stone Images

Introduction

What are we afraid of?

I went to summer camp 30 years ago. I had lived 11 years in a place flat and appallingly hot. I understood that summer camp had mountains, cool air in the evenings. Not swamps and highways but lakes and dirt roads, not cars and powerboats but trucks and sailboats and canoes. I arrived and signed up for a three-day cross-country hike. My sister had advised me to sign up for everything.

The hikers turned out to be older boys led by two college kids. No one had much to say to me. I was equipped with a shapeless and too-small Boy Scout knapsack and an army poncho (to double as rain gear and my half of a pup tent) and a heavy canteen: gear like a World War II soldier's. I remember struggling across a hillside in the sun the first afternoon and along a ridge in the semishade; then making camp in a dark piney forest in a haze of sweaty worry and fatigue.

I knew that I had made a terrible mistake. These people didn't know me, didn't seem responsible for me. I suddenly knew I was going to cry—it was like needing to throw up—so I wandered into the woods. I stayed there while the woods got darker, looking around me and seeing the shadows form: just trees and dirt. I was alone in a new way. The woods wouldn't protect me. But I didn't think they would hurt me.

• • •

Edward Abbey embarks on a raft trip down a canyon that is soon to be destroyed (and Abbey knows it). He watches a distant stranger shout and gesticulate—a warning? A farewell? Abbey doesn't care; he is filled with "the delirious exhilaration of independence . . . the freedom to commit murder and get away with it scot-free. . ."

> My *God*! I'm thinking, what incredible *shit* we put up with most of our lives . . . the stupid and useless and degrading jobs, the *insufferable* arrogance of elected officials, the crafty *cheating* and the *slimy* advertising of the businessmen, the tedious wars in which we kill our buddies instead of our *real* enemies back home in the capital, the foul, diseased and *hideous* cities and towns we live in, the constant petty tyranny of automatic washers and automobiles and TV machines and telephones! ah, *Christ*!, I'm thinking at the same time that I'm waving goodby to that hollering idiot on the shore, what *intolerable* garbage and what *useless crap* we bury ourselves in day by day. . .

In the wilderness we can be alone.

Or can we? We go to the wilderness to escape, to be apart, to be by ourselves. Yet the wilderness reminds us that we are not apart in any real sense. We aren't anybody in particular; our everyday selves are fake, manufactured out of fear and other oddments. We imagine the wilderness is a place to find ourselves; it's more a place to lose ourselves. A passage from Algernon Blackwood's "The Willows" reminds me of a summer's day I spent two years ago, walking alone in a canyon: "Midway in my delight of the wild beauty, there crept, unbidden and unexplained, a curious feeling of disquietude, almost alarm."

I thought I was worried about bears. There is something disturbing about the idea of being eaten, being used that way (the way we use the wilderness, as fuel for our oddly aimless purposes). Yet people are eaten in the wilderness. But it wasn't bears that frightened me. I was afraid of the place. It didn't need me, didn't notice me. That hurt my feelings.

Civilization offers us tools that make us powerful: We push buttons and lights come on; we press pedals and travel at high speeds; we tap keys and words appear on a screen a thousand miles away; we speak into plastic and our voices cross oceans.

Without our tools, what are we? If we leave our cell phones at home, the wilderness may offer answers—but we won't always like them.

Listen, we're very confused about wilderness: There is nothing but wilderness; we're lost in it, we're never getting out. Read some of the stories in this collection and you may be glad that you're safe at home, comfortable, secure. But you're not safe at all: *The New York Times* informs me and its 1.5 million other readers that scientists now believe in an infinite number of universes.

So it's all wilderness, and maybe that's not so bad. The wilderness does things to the people who live there; it can make them admirable, sometimes enviable. Men and women from cities and towns visit people in the wilderness and often admire those people's independence, their generosity, their toughness and élan, even their flashes of absolute without-a-clueness.

Wilfred Thesiger traveled with Bedu tribesmen in their harsh desert country more than half a century back. He cherished the bond that united him with his companions; it was, he wrote, "as sacred as the bond between host and guest, transcending tribal and family loyalties. Because I was their companion on the road, they would fight in my defense even against their brothers and they would expect me to do the same."

Of course: When you travel in the desert or in any wilderness, you must be able to count upon your companions. But you can't always. Joe Kane, traveling in the Amazonian jungle with members of the Huaorani tribe, is in their hands entirely; when the group becomes lost, Kane, very hungry, concludes that he probably is going to die. The Indians have long since eaten his food:

"Shouldn't we save some for later?" I asked . . .

"Later?" Quemperi said. "What is later?"

A worldview that omits the concept of later seems to us impractical—and may be supremely so; it may cause the death of the person who owns it. But aren't you at all jealous? Don't you wish even a little that you'd never heard of "later"? Or wish that you could trust your companions on any random journey—or find yourself the object of such a promiscuous trust—as a matter of course?

These are gifts often denied to people who live in civilized places. We must, if we can, find other ways to keep our dignity. This takes practice and is difficult—living in this world is perhaps no easier than living in the wild—and we sometimes fail.

Here is Thesiger leaving the Bedu:

> I shall always remember how often I was humbled by those illiterate herdsmen who possessed, in so much greater measure than I, generosity and courage, endurance, patience, and light-hearted gallantry. Among no other people have I ever felt the same sense of personal inferiority.

Imagine what happens to a Bedu or a Huaorani when his wilderness is gone.

When Redmond O'Hanlon was four years old, a bird dropped an empty eggshell next to him. He remembers the moment:

> Being unaware, at the time, of the empty cosmos, of the unfeelingness of causal connections, I concluded that this message of brown and purple blotches on a background of browny-white had been intended just for me.

We all think that: The world I see and inhabit is a gift to me, not something to share. But this illusion, if such it is, is hard to maintain in a crowd. In solitude or something like it, we may find it easier to believe that all of it—sky, leaf, birdcall, water sounds, sunlight, shade, night—

is for us; that we own it, know it. In so pretending we can hold ourselves apart from the wilderness for a while; we can fend it off the way we fend off one another.

Or we may become afraid. Perhaps the wilderness is not for us; perhaps we are for the wilderness. Edward Abbey, looking for grizzlies, quotes a friend: "It ain't wilderness unless there's a critter out there that can kill you and eat you."

The writer H. M. Tomlinson and a companion walk into the Amazonian jungle for a single day. He is struck by its stillness, which he sees is something else:

> If time had been accelerated, if the movements in that war of phantoms had been speeded, we should have seen what really was there, the greater trees running upwards to starve the weak of light and food, and heard the continuous collapse of the failures, and have seen the lianas writhing and constricting, manifestly like serpents, throttling and eating their hosts. We did see the dead everywhere, shells with the worms at them. Yet it was not easy to be sure that we saw anything at all, for these were not trees, but shapes in a region below the day, a world sunk abysmally from the land of living things, to which light but thinly percolated down to two travelers moving over its floor, trying to get out to their own place.

It's like going swimming in the ocean in Maine in June: You want to get in, you get in, you want to get out. You get out, you want to get back in. The wilderness is our home. That makes us glad and afraid.

But linger in a manifestly wild place for any time at all, and you may quiet your fear; you may learn what some of its inhabitants seem to know: There is no later; we live now or not at all. The bird's egg belongs to us; we belong to it; each belongs to itself. Whatever is wild is in us already. It may be that whatever is in us is wild.

—*Clint Willis*

from In Trouble Again
by Redmond O'Hanlon

Naturalist and explorer Redmond O'Hanlon (born 1947) seeks out the world's most difficult places, dragging with him the most unlikely companions. He is fiercely alert to the attractions of the wild (particularly its birds) as well as its manifold perils (virtually everything that moves). Here, he prepares for a trip to a swampy wilderness near the Amazon.

Having spent two months travelling in the primary rain forests of Borneo, a four-month journey in the country between the Orinoco and the Amazon would pose, I thought, no particular problem.

I re-read my nineteenth-century heroes: the seven volumes of Alexander von Humboldt's *Personal narrative of travels to the equinoctial regions of the New Continent during the years 1799–1804* (trans. Helen Maria Williams, 1814–29); William H. Edwards' *A Voyage up the River Amazon* (1847); Alfred Russel Wallace's *A Narrative of Travels on the Amazon and Rio Negro* (1853); Henry Walter Bates's *The Naturalist on the River Amazons* (2 vols., 1863); and Richard Spruce's *Notes of a Botanist on the Amazon and Andes* (edited by Wallace, 2 vols., 1908).

There are no leeches that go for you in the Amazon jungles, an absence which would represent, I felt, a great improvement on life in Borneo. But then there *are* much the same amoebic and bacillary dysenteries, yellow and blackwater and dengue fevers, malaria, cholera, typhoid, rabies, hepatitis and tuberculosis—plus one or two very special extras.

There is Chagas' disease, for instance, produced by a protozoon,

Tripanozoma crusii, and carried by various species of Assassin bugs which bite you on the face or neck and then, gorged, defecate next to the puncture. When you scratch the resulting itch you rub the droppings and their cargo of protozoa into your bloodstream; between one and twenty years later you begin to die from incurable damage to the heart and brain. Then there is onchocerciasis, river-blindness, transmitted by blackfly and caused by worms which migrate to the eyeball; leishmaniasis, which is a bit like leprosy and is produced by a parasite carried by sandflies (it infects eighty percent of Brazilian troops on exercise in the jungle in the rainy season): unless treated quickly, it eats away the warm extremities. And then there is the odd exotic, like the fever which erupted in the state of Pará in the 1960s, killing seventy-one people, including the research unit sent in to identify it.

The big animals are supposed to be much friendlier than you might imagine. The jaguar kills you with a bite to the head, but only in exceptional circumstances. Two vipers, the fer-de-lance (up to seven and a half feet long) and the bushmaster (up to twelve feet, the largest in the world), only kill you if you step on them. The anaconda is known to tighten its grip only when you breathe out; the electric eel can only deliver its 640 volts before its breakfast; the piranha only rips you to bits if you are already bleeding, and the Giant catfish merely has a penchant for taking your feet off at the ankle as you do the crawl.

The smaller animals are, on the whole, much more annoying—the mosquitoes, blackfly, tapir-fly, chiggers, ticks, scabies-producing Tunga penetrans and Dermatobia hominis, the human botfly, whose larvae bore into the skin, eat modest amounts of you for forty days, and emerge as inch-long maggots.

But it was the candiru, the toothpick-fish, a tiny catfish adapted for a parasitic life in the gills and cloaca of bigger fish, which swam most persistently into my dreams on troubled nights.

In Borneo, when staying in the longhouses, I learned that going down to the river in the early morning is the polite thing to do—you know you are swimming in the socially correct patch of muddy river when fish nuzzle your pants, wanting you to take them down and produce their breakfast. In the Amazons, on the other hand, should you have too much to drink, say, and inadvertently urinate as you swim, any homeless candiru, attracted by the smell, will take you for a big fish and swim excitedly up your stream of uric acid, enter your urethra like a worm into its burrow and, raising its gill-covers, stick out a set of retrorse spines. Nothing can be done. The pain, apparently, is spectacular. You must get to a hospital before your bladder bursts; you must ask a surgeon to cut off your penis.

In consultation with my friend at the Radcliffe Hospital in Oxford, Donald Hopkins, the inventor of the haemorrhoid gun, I designed an anti-candiru device: we took a cricket-box, cut out the front panel, and replaced it with a tea-strainer.

Released so brilliantly from this particular fear, I began, in earnest, to panic. Alfred Russel Wallace's resolution seemed the only one possible. Attacked by fever in his dugout on the Rio Negro in 1851, 'I began taking doses of quinine,' he tells us,

> and drinking plentifully cream of tartar water, though I was so weak and apathetic that at times I could hardly muster resolution to move myself to prepare them. It is at such times that one feels the want of a friend . . . for of course it is impossible to get the Indians to do those little things without so much explanation and showing as would require more exertion than doing them oneself . . . during two days and nights I hardly cared if we sank or swam. While in that apathetic state I was constantly half-thinking, half-dreaming, of all my past life and future hopes, and that they were perhaps all doomed to end here on the Rio Negro. . . . But with resuming health those gloomy thoughts passed away, and I again went on, rejoicing in this my last voyage, and looking forward with firm hope to home, sweet home! I however made an inward vow never to travel again in such wild, unpeopled districts without some civilized companion or attendant.

That was the answer: I would persuade the civilised companion of my

Borneo journey, the poet James Fenton, to visit the Venezuelan Amazons with me. He would be flattered to be asked. He would be delighted to come.

After supper at the long table in James's kitchen (a map of Borneo still hung on the wall), halfway through a bottle of Glenmorangie, I judged the time was ripe.

'James,' I said, 'you are looking ill. You are working far too hard writing all these reviews. You need a break. Why don't you come to the Amazon with me?"

'Are you listening seriously?'

'Yes.'

'Are you sitting comfortably?'

'Yes.'

'Then I want you to know,' said James, shutting his eyes and pressing his palms up over his face and the top of his bald head, *'that I would not come with you to High Wycombe.'*

I asked everyone I knew. I went to see the poet Craig Raine. 'It will increase your stock of metaphors,' I said.

'It will increase my stock of parasites,' said Craig.

I rang the photographer Don McCullin.

'To be frank with you', said Don, 'I thought you might get round to me sooner or later. You've come to the right man. It makes sense. Look, I don't want to be rude or anything, Redmond, but I've looked at a lot of pictures in my time, and well, frankly, *yours are the worst I've ever seen.* But I'm not interested. I've done it all. I cleaned up on the Xingu for Norman Lewis, and that was enough for me. Just at the moment, just for now, I want to get drunk a lot. And I also want to make love to Lorraine a lot—and where you're going you can't do either.'

And then I thought of Simon Stockton, a friend of my early twenties. Born in Cambridge, the high point of his education had been sharing a school classroom with the future novelist Martin Amis, an experience so demoralising it had decided him against any further study whatever, and sent him off to run his own discotheques. He had set up a nightclub in Hamburg and there, some time later, his partner had been found by the police one day, through no fault of Simon's, lying on a park bench with a bullet through his head. Simon's passport was stamped 'UNDESIRABLE ALIEN' and he was deported.

He started again as a croupier, worked his way up from club to club, and now helped to run the Kensington Sovereign. He would be a push-over. His secret ambition, I knew, was to abandon his wild, professional night-life and become something really peaceful, like a war photographer. I gave him a ring. It would be my first visit to a casino.

Simon, in his mid-thirties, suave in a dark suit, met me by the guard at the reception desk.

'Come on through and try to keep calm,' he said. 'We've got big punt-ers tonight. Everyone's tense.'

We sat at the bar. Simon clicked his fingers and a Malay brought a bottle of claret. The dim red table and wall lights cast reflections along the rows of bottles, threw up warm, shiny patches on the oak panelling, reproduced themselves whole in the corner mirrors and hung trans-parent in the large, zig-zag glass partition. Through it we could watch the players hunched round the roulette and blackjack tables, and one or two wives or mistresses, sitting on stools behind their husbands or lovers, anxious, chain-smoking.

'So you're coming?'

'Of course I'm coming. It's the biggest opportunity of my life. I've bought a 500-millimetre mirror lens for the birds. I wouldn't miss it for the world. And besides, after fifteen years in this joint, it's the Amazon or the bin for me.'

'And there again,' he added à propos of nothing in particular, 'I'm good on the violence. See that?' He lifted the hair off his forehead to reveal a long, recently healed scar. 'Eight stitches. Some maniac lost all he'd got and thought I'd put the hex on him. Smashed me over the head with an ashtray. The doorman butted him in the stomach and we did him for assault.' Simon nodded at a waiter and a tray of oriental dishes arrived.

'What do they generally do,' I asked, 'when they lose everything?'

'They go home and top themselves,' said Simon, his mouth full of monkfish. 'We get a lot of that—but it's not our fault—it's just that we happen to be at the end of the line.'

'You'll be bored in the jungle.'

'I can handle it,' said Simon, turning round briefly to scan the tables. 'There's nothing much I can't handle. Why, we had three Iraqis in here only last week. Some Arab gangster thought we were cheating and these boys were his minders. So I promised them everything—my Aunt Sally, the cat, the piggy-bank, *everything*—while the car-jockey called the police. When the Old Bill rolled them we found their pockets were just wide slits: they'd got the hardware strapped down their thighs, eighteen inches long and curved at the ends. *It was the dimensions.* Right out of order, in my opinion.'

I was staring through the glass partition, admiring the half-naked girl croupiers by the dull lights above the green baize, when an elderly Japanese scowled, beckoned to a flunkey, muttered something and despatched him to Simon.

'Fatso,' said Simon, 'you just got yourself thrown out.'

'Thrown out?'

'For smiling.'

'Smiling?'

'Yeah. You were smiling at the girls. You upset Mr Yamamoto there. He thinks you put the jinx on him. You are interfering with his astral powers. You'll have to go. They're *gamblers*, you see. They come here to *gamble*. It's called a *casino*. If you want girls you go to something called a *brothel*.'

Outside on the pavement, with the lorries and cars and taxis soughing past in the drizzle, we stood and looked at Waterhouse's masterpiece, the great Victorian Romanesque façade of the Natural History Museum, its cleaned blue and cream brick, its window arches and mullions, its pinnacles and towers shining in the beams of floodlights: a secular cathedral sheltering the very collections (then housed at the British Museum at Bloomsbury) which Bates and Wallace and Spruce had visited before setting out for the Amazons.

'Isn't it beautiful?' I said. 'Don't you think it's the most tempting building on earth? Do you often slip over there when you're on a day shift?'

'Frankly,' said Simon, turning to go back down the steps past the uniformed doorman, 'I've never set foot in the place.'

I stood in the rain, unable to move, and continued staring at the celestial building across the road, a palace of disturbed yearnings.

And I imagined myself back on the late spring lawn of my Vicarage childhood. When I was about four and three-quarter years old, a mistlethrush which had been clearing out its nest flew high over my head and dropped one half of an empty eggshell in front of me, close by the sundial. Being unaware, at the time, of the empty cosmos, of the unfeelingness of causal connections, I concluded that this message of brown and purple blotches on a background of browny-white had been intended just for me.

I began an egg collection and kept it in a box on top of the chest of drawers in my little bedroom, whose window looked out over the kitchen-garden, across the small fields and thick hedges and woods of the cheese country, to the distant scarp of the Wiltshire downs. I took one blackbird's egg from a clutch of five in their rough cup lined with dried grass hidden in a thicket by the laburnum tree. I found a thrush's egg in its mud-rounded nest in a bush by the pond. I raided the nest of a fly-catcher that returned each year to rear its young on a ledge against the mellow ochre Bath-stone front of the house, where it was shielded from the sun by ivy leaves. With a teaspoon I scooped out the white, brown-speckled egg of a wren from its dome of dead leaves built into the leaf-litter behind an old wall-pinioned greengage tree. One day, sitting in the front of my father's two-seater canvas canoe on Bowood lake (which was part of his parish) I lifted the covering from a floating mound of weed moored in a lily-bed and removed the chalky egg of a Great crested grebe. It was the pride of my collection.

When I was seven, on the day I was sent away to board at a prep school in Dorset, my father gave me the two volumes of T. A. Coward's *The Birds of the British Isles and their Eggs*, my first proper books, which he had been given by *his* father, who used to watch birds and geologise with Coward all over Cheshire in the early 1900s. To go with them he gave me T. A. Coward's own custom-built binoculars which Coward had left to my grandfather: in fact a pair of matching telescopes, slim, black, brass tubes through which, one day, I hoped to see all the birds that

Coward had seen, as mysterious in their marsh and coastland, on their moors and mountains and forests, as Thorburn had depicted them in his tempera plates.

On the first week of the school holiday I persuaded my father to take me to the Natural History Museum. It was all different then: you could actually go to the mahogany egg cabinets and pull out the drawers. And there were all the eggs of all the birds in the British Isles, thousands of them, lying in whole clutches, on their beds of cotton wool in the wood partitions under the glass. It was the guillemots' eggs that really astonished me—they had a whole cabinet to themselves: they were white or yellow or blue or green or purple or red or brown; and they were smeared or lined or blotched or spotted with all kinds of different colours. If these were the eggs of just one species, how could you ever hope to know enough? It was all variety and surprise and difference; and each egg looked so fine in itself. Perhaps it was *that* feeling, I now thought, standing in the rain on the Cromwell Road, which I had really been searching for—and which I had found—in the primary rainforest in the heart of Borneo, that sudden, passing, incandescent moment when you are not even sure if the something that is flying across the river in front of you is a bat or a bird or a butterfly. And it was that feeling which I vowed to experience again, if I could, in the vaster forests of the northern Amazons.

There was a hand on my shoulder.

'Are you all right, sir?' It was the doorman. He had a compassionate look on his craggy face. He had seen it all before.

'Not want to go home? Is that it? Listen to me, sir—it's always best to go straight home when you've had a spot of bad luck. You'll feel better in the morning. If you haven't the money for a cab, sir—if you don't mind my saying—the Kensington Sovereign will lend it to you. It's the policy.'

Over the next two months I made an unerring selection from different camping shops of seriously defective equipment. Having searched without success, I eventually found two pairs of heavy-duty-plastic 'campaign-tested' water bottles which fastened to belts; I took them home and filled one with water: it was so designed that when you screwed the lid home the bottle split down the sides.

Exasperated, I once again invoked the talismanic name of my uncle, Colonel Egerton-Mott, who had run Special Operations Executive in Borneo against the Japanese during the war, and I went to see the sponsors of our Borneo journey, 22 SAS.

At their Headquarters near Hereford I was absurdly pleased to see that I had been promoted, from Training Wing to Regular Stores.

'Well done, lad,' said the Quartermaster as we walked from his office to the equipment shed. 'I liked your book on Borneo. You made us sound almost human.'

Then I got that wrong, too, I thought, as we passed a platoon of young soldiers on the apron making a last check on their bergen packs before jumping into two parked lories. They were fit and lean and possessed by a ferocious energy. They didn't even *look* human.

In the stores I had a reunion with Ernie and Eddie and signed for two complete sets of the jungle equipment I had taken to Borneo, plus an outfit of special lightweight jungle fatigues (large) and a floppy camouflage hat (it had two pairs of large airholes set above the brim, covered with wire mesh fine enough to keep out blackfly). Over-excited, I put on the clothes. I felt tough at once. I was ready for anything.

'We can't let him go like that,' said Ernie, sounding genuinely distressed.

'Why not?' I said. 'Am I missing something?'

'No,' said Ernie, in an agonised voice, 'it's just that you're a disgrace to the Regiment. You look like Benny Hill.'

A week later, I took Simon's share of the equipment down to his house in a suburb of West Drayton. It was easy enough to find. The villa was dramatically distinguished from the row of look-alikes because Simon had painted it purple all over, and an enormous blown-up photograph of his head entirely blocked off the left upstairs window.

It was three in the afternoon and Simon came to the door in his flannel dressing gown.

'Hi, Fatso. Brought the kit? Lob it in here,' he said, helping me carry the bergen into the room on the right. Against one wall, there was a stack of tuners, amplifiers, record and tape decks topped with shelves of records. An outsize television and several video machines stood by the window. In the corner, a wooden girl, her big wooden breasts painted cream, held out an ashtray. We spread the olive-drab basha-top, the canvas hammock, the mosquito net and the pole-bed across the carpet on top of one pair of small, red dancing shoes, one pair of black fishnet stockings, one black suspender belt, and one black G-string with a tiny, scarlet silk heart sewn onto the front.

'It's okay,' said Simon. 'She's asleep upstairs. She wears anything I ask her to, comes on a Thursday night, and goes away again on Friday. She *never* gives me any aggravation. Want a tour of the house? Stocky's maximum-pleasure dream-machine?'

We walked across the corridor.

'This is the front room', said Simon. 'We take tea in here when very special guests, like Mother, come to pay their respects. We eat cucumber sandwiches and little cakes.'

The floor was fully occupied with a large work-bench. The walls were covered with a comprehensive collection of tools in hanging rows which stretched right round the room, their categories marked in an index of fluorescent red paint beside the light switch, 'CHISELS, HAMMERS, DRILLS, SAWS, PLANES AND MISCELLANEOUS'.

On our way upstairs we climbed past an even larger inscription: 'REMEMBER REMEMBER THE FIFTH OF NOVEMBER'.

'What's this? Did you forget the fireworks?'

'No,' said Simon, 'it's the day my wife left me.'

'I'm not surprised she went,' I said.

'I'll never forgive her,' said Simon.

I looked out of the landing window, to take the air.

An old plum tree was growing in the middle of the lawn. From its lowest branch there hung a bedraggled outsize Snoopy, a riding-hat on its head, a much-holed target pinned to its chest. It swayed, slightly, in the breeze.

'What's that?'

'That,' said Simon, 'is an *image*. It's my ex-wife. That's her crash helmet. She had a *horse*. Whenever I get depressed I take my crossbow, lean out, and bolt her one.'

'And this,' he said, flinging open a door marked 'DANGER, HIGH VOLTAGE OVERHEAD CABLES', 'is the master bedroom. This is where the maid brings me my croissant and I read the *Financial Times* every morning.'

He switched on a red light. It was a darkroom, the window obscured by black shutters and a light proof ventilator. Tables ran round the edge of the room, with filing cabinets beneath them. There were two big Durst enlargers, a set of developing and fixing trays and three plumbed-in washing sinks. The cameras and lenses were neatly arranged on a shelf. A set of Bowens flashlights stood half-rigged in a corner, their heads on tripods, their folded umbrellas and barn-door, cone and bowl reflectors piled beside them. But the chief glory of the room was the girls. They pouted from Simon's sofa in soft-focus black and white. They sat naked in full Cibachrome on Simon's flower-bed. They perched in sepia on the knob of his banisters and giggled; they sprawled long and languorous on his carpet; they were caught by remote-control on the bed, with the master himself undressing them.

'Good, eh?' said Simon.

'They look surprisingly happy about it,' I said. 'They must actually like you.'

'Of course they do,' said Simon, 'it's only natural. They love me to death. But it's wham, bam and thank you mam with me, I'm afraid. Not like you. How long you been married? Fifty years?'

'Eighteen,' I said.

'Eighteen!' said Simon, walking across the passage and easing open another door. 'Eighteen! Well, if we ever come out of the jungle you might make it to your silver wedding—if Belinda's fool enough to wait for you—and I could give you a round fat teapot with a quarter-inch spout.'

We peered round the door.

'This is the romper-room,' said Simon.

A very young girl lay asleep on the double bed; she was half-covered by a duvet, curled in the foetal position. Three Siamese cats snuggled together, pressed into the hollow between her buttocks and the back of her thighs. Her yellow hair fell forward across the pillow.

'She's lovely,' I said, as we went downstairs.

'Lovely cats,' said Simon.

'Aren't you *very* fond of her?'

'Look here,' said Simon, 'don't you get heavy with me. She works in the casino. I'm in charge of personnel. I'm not kidding, Redmond, I'm *exhausted* with pretty girls. I'm *manhandled* by them. There are days when I can hardly call my dick my own.'

We sat down at the table in the appliance-choked spaceship of a kitchen.

'You're a lucky man,' I said.

'It's just a problem I have,' said Simon, reaching over to a wine-rack and pulling out a bottle of Châteauneuf du Pape, 'I wanted someone to come here properly and look after me, so I put a notice up in the local newsagent. "*Unbelievably* ugly charlady wanted," it said. "Top rates for real old bag. No one under sixty need apply." I interviewed for *two weeks*; and chose a right old horror. Mrs T. She does for me. My Mrs Treasure. She's the best. I think I'm falling in love. In fact, one of these days, I'll have to give her one.'

'What's in the other rooms?' I said, as Simon filled up two half-pint-sized wine glasses.

'Nah. They were my wife's; I hardly go in them; I haven't colonised them yet. There's a full set of Encyclopaedia Britannica's *Great Books of the World* in the garden room. I bought them for her. They're still in their shrink-wrap. Bloody dire. Which reminds me—when we're on this trip, when we're stuck in the old jungle—you've got to educate me.'

'Educate you?'

'Yeah. I want to change my life. I really do. You tell me what books to read—and, come to that, why are we going on this trip, anyway? Why aren't you still teaching in Oxford, you fat berk? *That's* the life. Free port, as much as you want, laid down *hundreds* of years ago. Old codgers handing you expensive lardy-dahs all day. Young students all over you.'

'I was only on trial,' I said. 'And I taught my undergraduates the wrong century, just before their exams. It was terrible.'

'Shit a brick,' said Simon, looking seriously alarmed. 'I thought you were safe to go with; I thought I could trust you.'

'They made the same mistake. It wasn't their fault.'

'Jesus,' said Simon, uncorking another bottle.

'It's all right,' I said. 'We're going to take a nineteenth-century route.

And that *is* my period. I thought we'd follow Humboldt up the Orinoco and through the Casiquiare; pick up Spruce and Wallace on the Rio Negro; go down to Manaus and join Bates, and then maybe go up the Purus. I've been wobbling round our local wood every morning. I'm fitter than I used to be.'

'Are you hell,' said Simon, pouring himself another glass. 'You drink too much.'

'And as for changing your life,' I said, 'with your through-put, sooner or later you're bound to find the right woman. That's the way to change your life.'

Simon relaxed and leant back in his chair.

'Well, as it happens, I *may* have found the right woman, scumbag. And it might just have something to do with you. I think she likes it— Stockton the explorer and photographer. Yeah. She doesn't know I've hardly seen daylight in my working life, let alone a jungle. She's a genuine schoolteacher-lady. Her husband died. She's got three lovely kids. I like kids. I might just go for her in a big way. In fact, as far as I'm concerned, she's angel-drawers.'

'But you've only got two weeks.'

'Easy-peezy. Lemon squeezy,' said Simon, 'she's coming to see me off. And if it comes to that—you're a monster.'

'What do you mean?'

'How can you do it?' said Simon, looking suddenly wild about the eyes. 'How can you leave your wife and daughter? Belinda just out of hospital. Puffin two weeks old. You ought to be shot. Just for thinking of it.'

'It was planned a year ago,' I said, looking away, focusing on a photograph in a stand-up frame on the table. 'I didn't know it would be like this. It's now or next year. We have to catch the rainy season. We may want to go up some very small rivers.'

'Spoken like a psychopath,' said Simon.

'Who *is* this girl?' I said, picking up the photograph. Simon stared out of the picture, carrying a silver cane and wearing a blazer, a boater, a high collar, a silk shirt with ruffles and a silk cravat. On his arm was a dark-haired girl in a 1920s dress and a wide-brimmed hat with ostrich feathers, carrying a furled umbrella.

'The Mr Cool in the boater is me,' said Simon, 'and the sexy bit in the dress is me. It's my last year's Christmas card. Good, eh? Don't you ever slip into a pair of knicks?'

• • •

That evening, as I was driving back to Oxford, it gradually dawned on me that it was too late to change anything: I was not just going to the jungle, I was going to the jungle with Simon.

I left Simon reading *Pride and Prejudice* in the flat I had rented in the centre of Caracas and took a taxi to the Country Club to meet Charlie Brewer-Carias.

Charlie, the great explorer and photographer of Venezuela, is a man whose hobby is dropping by helicopter onto jungle mountains like the Autana or Sarisarinama, and then abseiling into their caves and sink-holes; an ex-dentist who has now written six illustrated books about the mountains and plants of his country, he has led so many scientific expeditions into the interior that thirteen new species and one genus of plant, one new species and one new sub-species of bird and one aquatic insect (*Tepuidessus brewer, Spangler*, 1981) now bear his name. A popular hero, every taxi driver in Caracas likes to tell you about his term of office as Minister of Youth. To draw attention to the lands that Venezuela claims from the former British Guiana, now Guyana, Charlie gathered a band of young admirers and invaded the territory. Guyana mobilised her army and airforce. Charlie unscrewed a brass nameplate proclaiming 'British Guiana' on a frontier post, and withdrew. The Communist government of Guyana was not amused. The democratic government of Venezuela was not amused. Charlie lost his job.

I found him sitting at a table in the cloister of the central, flowerfilled quadrangle, sipping a glass of water.

'Care for a session in the gym?' said Charlie, stroking his enormous drooping moustache.

'Certainly not,' I said, panicking. 'Couldn't we talk over a bottle or two?'

'That would be very bad for you. A very bad idea. You must stay away from drink altogether. The Indians have not adapted to it. You must not take it with you. The Amazonas, Redmond, is not a kind place.'

'Look here—I haven't been to a gym since school.'

'Now's the time,' said Charlie, getting up. 'You must fight that belly. Everyone should go to a gym.'

He picked up an athlete's bag from the paving stones, swung it on to his muscled shoulders, and pointed to a leather pouch on the table.

'Bring that,' said Charlie, 'and give it to me if there's trouble. Come on. We can get in a full hour before lunch.'

The pouch was extraordinarily heavy. I half-undid the zip and looked inside. It was a large, black Browning automatic.

'Jesus,' I said.

'Everyone out there,' said Charlie, 'wants to kill me. From the government of Guyana to the lowliest nut. Only last month some drug-crazed lunatic in a suburb came up to my car at some traffic lights and said he'd wanted to shoot me every day for years, but that his doctor had just talked him out of it. "Yeah. Thanks. Wild news," I said. "Just let me know if you change your mind."'

In the locker room Charlie changed into shorts, socks and gym shoes. I took off my shirt and shoes but held my trousers firmly in place by taking in another notch of my belt. We collected two towels and entered the gym.

A huge man was lying flat on his back on a small bench and lifting above his chest a bar whose weights seemed about equivalent to that of three buses on one side and half a small house on the other. It was just possible to make out his head amongst the muscles. Every time he drew in a breath it sounded like a jet taking off.

'Nobody else here can do this,' said Charlie, hoisting himself up and down between the parallel bars and kissing his knees. He nodded at the young men upside-down on wall bars and flying through the air on a succession of trapezes. 'I'm forty-six. But they just don't have the strength *and* the flexibility.'

'So what do you think of my route?' I said, my feet numb under a pair of leg irons I found impossible to move.

'Not now,' said Charlie, 'don't talk to me when I'm doing my exercises. I concentrate on a different set of muscles every day. If I throw a rope to a man who is drowning in a rapid, Redmond, I *must* be strong enough to pull him to the bank.'

'I shouldn't talk to *him*, anyway,' said a glistening hulk next to me with a super-signal wink (you probably train your eyelids, too, I thought). He was undulating his biceps with weights like bogeys from a railway truck. 'You need to get, ah, *strong*. I'm a surgeon myself, but I see plenty of jungle diseases at the hospital. If you take my advice, you'll stay in Caracas.'

'It's a *ridiculous* plan,' called Charlie from the cold shower next to mine.

'Next stage,' he said, ushering me into the dry-heat room. We joined a line of men sitting sweating and joking in front of directional heaters. It's just that I am not yet used to this climate, I told myself; there is no need to feel so outclassed by the mere bulk of dicks flopped along this bench.

'Those rivers,' said Charlie, 'I've been thinking about it. They're as big as the sea. What could be more boring? People have done it *in a hovercraft*. But I like you. You're bizarre. You're helpless here. You give me your old volumes of Spruce and Wallace—I've never even seen those books bound up—and I'll make you photocopies and I'll give you a little project all of my own, something that has not been attempted since the seventeenth century.'

'It's a deal,' I said, sweating.

'Then let's go next door,' said Charlie, 'it's the Club rainforest.'

In the steamroom my glasses misted up. Charlie, pacing up and down, went in and out of focus in the swirling murk.

'There's no point following Humboldt and Bonpland down the Casiquiare,' said his disembodied voice. 'You won't find your birds and animals. But there's another river that connects the Orinoco and the Rio Negro, the Maturaca—it's marked on the maps but it rises in a dendritic delta, an inland swamp to the south-west of Neblina. We don't know exactly where. You must go and find out; but it's wild country—the trees meet overhead all the way, the streams are criss-crossed with fallen trunks, you must cut your own way through; the last people to try—the Border Commission officers—were lost in there for two months in 1972 and gave up; the country is so remote that Neblina itself, the highest mountain in South America outside the Andes, was not discovered until 1953.'

We took another cold shower.

'You will come to my apartment,' shouted Charlie from his stall. 'I have low-level radar and high-level NASA infra-red satellite maps of the area. It is a small obsession of mine.'

In his eight-cylinder Chevrolet, Charlie told his driver to take us to the flat. One wall was hung with assorted blow-pipes, another obscured by a map-drawer cabinet and files of photographs. Books and papers lay everywhere. An adjoining room, furnished with metal shelves, contained a Sten gun, a Hasselblad, a combined .22 rifle and .410 shot-gun, a 7 × 8 Pentax with a wooden carrying handle, a 12-bore shotgun, a Linhof panoramic, a 16-bore shotgun, a pair of Olympuses and a case of lenses. On the floor stood a large radio transmitter. On a spare piece of table various bits of a knife and its accompanying plans were spread.

'This is the Brewer Explorer Survival Knife,' said Charlie, taking a complete model out of a drawer, '6¼–inch stainless steel blade, Rockwell Hardness 56–58; 2¾-inch saw extending from the handle towards the point; on the left here a 180-degree clinometer for calculating the height of mountains; on the right instructions for five ground-to-air signals and a six-centimetre ruler. This small hole in the blade is of course for sighting when you use it as a signalling reflector; this large rectangular hole converts it into wire cutters when engaged with this T-type fitting on the tip of the sheath. It can also be made into a harpoon with another special device of mine. This end-cap screws off like this and, inside the hollow handle, here's a compass and a waterproof container with the morse code printed on its sides: holding six fish hooks, a monofilament nylon fishing line, two lead sinkers, one float, an exacto blade, two sewing needles, three matches, a flint stick and a suture needle with suture material attached. It's made by Marto of Toledo and imported into the US by Gutman at $150. But you and Simon can have one. It's good for skinning alligators. And when the Yanomami have had a go at you you can sew each other up round the arrow holes.'

'The Yanomami?'

'Yeah. The most violent people on earth. Some anthropologists think they were the first peoples to reach South America from the

North. They have very fair skins, occasionally green eyes. They are the largest untouched group of Indians left in the rainforest. The other Indians are terrfied of them. My friend Napoleon Chagnon called his book on them *The Fierce People*—I'll give you a copy, and Jacques Lizot's too, *Tales of the Yanomami*. It's all perfectly understandable—they grow a few plantains, but basically they're hunter-gatherers and there's not much food in these forests. So when times are hard they kill the new-born girls; so there are never enough women to go round; so they fight over them. Within the tribe, in formalised duels, they hit each other over the head with ten-foot long clubs. Outside the tribe they raid each other's settlements for women and kill the enemy men with six-foot-long arrows tipped with curare. And on top of all that they've no concept of natural death, so if anyone dies from a fever it's the result of malign magic worked by an enemy shaman. Each death must be avenged.'

I stood there stupidly, holding the enormous Brewer Explorer knife.

'And this still goes on?' I said, shaken.

'They are killing each other,' said Charlie, *'right now.'*

He pulled open a map-drawer, took out a 20 × 16 photograph and spread it on the carpet. On a deep red background were patches of white and long black squiggles.

'This is the infra-red picture on a good day with minimal cloud. You will charter a light aircraft in Puerto Ayacucho on the Orinoco and fly south onto the map—to here'—a tiny white cross and blob, the only sign of settlement in the whole area, beside the biggest of the squiggles—'San Carlos on the Rio Negro.'

Charlie's callused, muscly forefinger tapped emphatically at the spot. He was getting excited.

'There you will employ my men. It will be their only job this year. You will pay the Indians eight dollars a day and Galvis, the radio-operator and cook, ten. Half in advance. You start when they sober up. Allow a week. Chimo is an old motorman of vast experience, and he claims to know this route. Valentine is an old prow-man. Pablo is very strong and good with an axe. I am giving you the best crew in Venezuela. You will hire my two outboard motors and two of Chimo's dugouts. I will call San Carlos on the radio tonight, atmospheric conditions permitting.'

'Two dugouts?'

'Redmond, you are going to one of the most isolated places on earth. If you break a boat, running it over tree trunks, you could *never* walk out of that swamp.'

'Do you think we're up to it?'

'That's your affair,' said Charlie, with an annoyed shake of the head. 'You will travel north up the Rio Negro, turn east into the Casiquiare; and then swing south down the Pasimoni which narrows into the Baria' (the squiggle grew faint) 'just after the Yatua joins it from the east. Almost at once you will begin to see all kinds of monkeys, two species of otter, sloth, anacondas, tapir, peccaries, jaguar, deer, ocelot, everything. And here' (Charlie spread out his fingers and set them travelling south-east) 'the river divides into a thousand tributaries. It disappears entirely beneath the red, the forest. You can say goodbye to the sunlight. Believe me—I've flown over bits of it in a helicopter and you can't see the streams from the air. But you'll be going in the wet season. There'll be plenty of water. You should be able to get through to Brazil.'

'So why don't you want to do it?' I said, suspicious.

'I'm fully occupied with this,' said Charlie, tapping a mass of cliffs and ridges ringed with cloud in the south-east corner of the picture. 'I lead expeditions to Neblina for the American Museum of Natural History and the Venezuelan Foundation for the Development of Science. We go in by helicopter to my base camp and then by helicopter to the summit. There's a 250-square-kilometre lost world up there— 98% of the plants are new species: Neblinaria, for instance, like an artichoke; new orchids; bromeliads; mosses. The tepuis are islands of life, cut off from each other by the jungle and from the jungle by 3000-metre-high cliffs. They're remnants of the Guyana shield, 100-million-year-old blocks of sandstone that pre-date the drifting apart of Africa and South America. We have so many results, so many new species to describe, that I'm setting up a new journal with the Smithsonian. I'm a very busy man.'

Charlie put the photograph away. We heated up a cheese and tomato pizza in the kitchen. Charlie's wife-to-be, Fanny, came home just long enough to collect some books, a passionate kiss and a piece of pizza. Small, dark and beautiful, still at university, she was in training for a place in the rhythmic gymnastics team that Venezuela would be sending to the Olympics.

'She is also studying for her exams,' said Charlie, 'and so, at the moment, she only adorns me with her presence by night.'

He made a guava juice.

'Come to that—you could try and reach Neblina by the Baria. Just follow the strongest current and you'll get there eventually. You could rest in my base camp and then go up the canyon. You'd be the first people to reach it by the Baria route. Bassett Maguire and William and Kathy Phelps went by the Siapa in 1953.'

'And where are the Yanomami?'

'Oh, *them*,' said Charlie, grinning. 'You won't meet them around Neblina. It's entirely uninhabited and probably always has been—*they* won't kill you until you're halfway down the Maturaca.'

'So what do we do now?' I said, trying to look calm.

'You stop panicking,' said Charlie, flexing his huge shoulders and massaging the back of his neck with his right hand. 'In Brazil on the south of their range they do knock off the odd fur-trapper or gold-panner, but it's not systematic. I actually did some work down there with my friend Julian Steyermark in 1975. We wanted to find out which plants go into yoppo.'

'What the hell's that?'

'It's a drug they blast up each others' noses through a metre-long tube. It produces peripheral vision colour disturbances and enables the shamans to summon their *hekura*, their tutelary spirits. It also produces severe shock in the ear, nose and throat system and the pain blows your head off: Julian and I never tried it. The other Indians swear it causes brain damage. But it's probably harmless. You must have a go if you get the chance.'

Charlie strode over to a different filing cabinet.

'Here, you can have an offprint of our joint paper from *Economic Botany*. Our particular Yanomami used Justicia pectoralis, Virola elongate, and the bark from the tree Elizabetha princeps.'

I picked up the knives and took my second Venezuelan gift, a small green pamphlet entitled '*Hallucinogenic Snuff Drugs of the Yanomamo Caburiwe-Teri in the Cauaburi River, Brazil*'.

'Now I must kick you out,' said Charlie, seeing me to the door, 'I have work to do. Tomorrow morning I will collect you at your flat at ten o'clock sharp. We must visit three different Ministers. You will need a whole sheaf of official letters to the Regional Military Governor. With me, it will take a week, maybe two. Without me, you would never get in there. Not a chance. The entire area is restricted. The Guardia will think you're a spy or a gold prospector. However, it so happens that I am a Special Adviser to the Venezuelan Army on all its jungle training. I will pull rank on any soldier who bothers you. But remember, Redmond, the frontier posts are there for a reason. It doesn't matter a damn about you. But it's bad for the Indians if they kill you. It's bad for public opinion. You can't have just anybody going in there and getting themselves stuck full of arrows like a porcupine.'

Back in the flat, Simon was curled up on the sofa, watching a football match on the television, *Men Only* spread open on his knees. A glass and a half-empty bottle of Chilean wine were on the table beside him and a further empty bottle lay discarded on the floor, together with three empty packets of Marlboro cigarettes, *Playboy, Penthouse, Fiesta* and *Pride and Prejudice.*

'GooooAAAA!' yelled Simon. 'When there's a goal, they say GooooAAAA!'

'I thought you were meant to be educating yourself,' I said.

'I am,' said Simon, not taking his eyes off the match. 'I've been reading a lot of new stuff here about the G-spot. Find the G-spot. Drive them *wild.*'

'What about Jane Austen?'

'She's great. I love it. I'm saving her up. Just when you think you've sussed it all out you find it's really someone else's second cousin who wants to get the leg over.'

'There's been a small change of plan,' I said.

'Yeah,' said Simon, still watching, 'I've been thinking about all this. When your old friend asks you to the country by the Caribbean, don't pack your bikini, that's what I say.'

I took one of Charlie's knives out of its black metal sheath and laid it on the sofa beside him. Its thick, highly polished blade with the jagged saw-top and engraved reminders for helicopter signals (v ASSISTANCE + MEDICAL) glinted in the table-light.

'Oh god,' said Simon, looking down, 'that's *horrible*. That would give *Hitler* the screaming ab-dabs.'

'It's a present from Charlie,' I said, sitting on a chair. 'This change of plan—we're going to try to be the first people to reach Neblina, the highest mountain in South America outside the Andes, via the vast Baria swamp. Then we'll be going down a river that nobody's been down since the seventeenth century, to try and find a fierce people called the Yanomami. Apparently they hit each other over the head in duels with ten-foot-long clubs and they hunt each other with six-foot-long arrows.'

'Oh, thanks,' said Simon, concentrating at last, kicking out with his legs on the floor and pushing himself hard back into the angle of the sofa. 'Out of sight. Thanks a bundle for telling me in London. I've *always* wanted to be slammed up the arse with an arrow and then whacked on the nut with a pole.'

from Savages
by Joe Kane

Joe Kane went to the Ecuadorian Amazon in the early 1990s to report on the conflict between economic development (led by energy companies) and the Huaorani Indians, ". . . a small but fearsome nation of hunter-gatherers who have lived in isolation so long that they speak a language unrelated to any other on earth." Kane is frightened by the Indians' ways—and with good cause: "What they are known for is killing."

To my eye the only sign that we had reached Quemperi's settlement was the sudden appearance of a long, silent line of Huaorani standing in a clearing on the right-hand side of a broad bend in the Cononaco River. There might have been thirty of them. Some held spears; some were naked. They neither waved nor spoke; they simply stared. They stood atop a bank about fifteen feet high, but it felt as if they were studying us from a much greater height.

After Enqueri and I climbed up through the mud, a short, potbellied old man with a single tooth in the middle of his upper gum walked over to me, indicated that I should open my mouth, then tapped my teeth one by one. He said something in Huaorani, and a roar of laughter went up.

"Quemperi says welcome," Enqueri said. "He wants to know if you will give him your teeth."

At a nod from Quemperi a gaggle of small boys slid down the bank and began hauling up our gear, which they deposited at the shaded edge of an otherwise barren, sun-broiled stretch of open ground a few yards from the river—an airstrip, or *pista*, as it was known. For years

Quemperi and his clan had roamed widely between the Cononaco River and the Yasuní, to the north, changing homesites every few months, alternating among half a dozen manioc gardens. About 1991, however, they settled more or less permanently around the *pista*, which the Company built during the seismic testing of the region and then abandoned. The *pista* was intended to be temporary, but the Huaorani were fastidious about keeping it free of brush. It was the only significant patch of open ground for miles in any direction. From their point of view, it was a kind of trap, really, which from time to time caught missionaries, tourists, or the Company. The *cowode* didn't come often, but when they did they always brought gifts. Most Huaorani had never seen a car, a horse, or a bicycle, but the airplane had become as integral a part of their world as the blowgun, the banana, and the boa. They would have identified the make of an inbound craft long before a visitor could hear it coming ("Cessna!" they would yell, racing for the *pista*), and when the plane revved up to leave, the young Huaorani men would plant themselves behind the tail and bare their chests to the fusillade of rock and dirt blasted their way by the prop wash.

Enqueri and I spent eleven days with Quemperi, much of the time ducking in and out of the ten houses that had been built around the *pista*. Most of them were of the traditional, thatched-A-frame design, with the roofs extending to dirt floors, and they were cool and pleasant. When the Huaorani were not out hunting or gardening, or when it was raining, which was often (the first Huaorani phrase I learned was "It is wet around here"), they passed many hours in their hammocks. Sometimes they were resting, but usually they were working— sharpening a spear, perhaps, or braiding palm leaf into cord, or chewing manioc, which would be left to ferment into a drink called *chicha*. They talked constantly. Their material goods were few: A typical house had a couple of machetes, a shotgun, some spears and blowguns, two or three cooking pots, and several hammocks.

Inside each hut a small fire burned most of the day, and there was always something for a visitor—*chicha*, banana juice, a piece of boiled manioc, a smoked monkey arm. Some of the men, many of the women, and all the children went naked, or wore a thin strap about the groin. In older times the entire clan had slept in one big house, but now each household slept around its own fire. During the night one or more of the adults would awaken and sing. The songs, rendered in a haunting three-note scale, and finished with a short, invigorating yodel, told of hunting, travel, the history of the clan, war, love. A hairy-legged cannibal was welcome to sing his songs, too.

Despite the *pista*, in other words, Quemperi and his clan seemed to live much as the Huaorani had lived for centuries. They might drink banana juice from aluminum pots, but they still drank banana juice. They might hunt woolly monkeys with shotguns, but they still hunted woolly monkeys. Turkey, monkey, caiman, and peccary were plentiful, and so was material for spears, blowguns, hammocks, and string bags. They had long ago developed treatments for the illnesses indigenous to the area, and though scabies and skin funguses were common, and phlegm-larded, tubercular hacks often split the night air, they had only sporadic contact with the Company and had avoided many of the viral infections that in the last twenty years had become the major cause of Huaorani death.

Nevertheless, life was often brutal. At twenty-five Enqueri had already reached middle age. Typically, the body of an adult Huao displayed half a dozen major scars, from staph infection, shotgun and outboard-motor accidents, falls, animal and snake bites. Many Huaorani were missing pieces of fingers and toes and large chunks of flesh, and in the entire adult population there was probably not a single full set of teeth. Still, as Quemperi was quick to assert, life along the Cononaco was superior to life in the protectorate, which was crowded and sedentary, and it was infinitely better than life along the Vía Auca— a life of, at best, canned tuna and Coca-Cola.

Quemperi had a gentle disposition and a generous nature: When he hunted he usually brought some grandkids along for instruction, and he always chuckled to himself while doing such quotidian tasks as making blowgun darts, weaving fresh leaves into his roof, and hauling firewood. But it would have been foolish to think Quemperi anything less than a warrior. Around the fire he spoke of killing Ecuadorian soldiers for their machetes, Peruvian soldiers for their boots, oil workers for their food and T-shirts, Quichua for daring to cross the Napo into Huaorani land. Smiling, he told the story of Toña, one of the first

Huaorani converted by Rachel Saint. Toña traveled to the Cononaco to preach to Quemperi, and brought with him an evil so strong that it killed a child. Quemperi asked Toña to help him make spears. When the spears were ready, Quemperi said, he and seven other Huaorani men turned on Toña and, one by one, thrust them home. Quemperi went last, using a spear that Toña himself had made.

Quemperi usually sat beside the fire when we spoke, but when I asked his thoughts on the Conoco road, he stood up and declaimed loudly and forcefully, sometimes stamping his feet for emphasis. It was the only time I saw him angry—indeed, it was the only time I saw any Huao angry—and the display was a frightening one. The ninety-mile road that Conoco proposed to build, and along which it would develop all its 120 wells, would terminate in the heart of Quemperi's traditional hunting territory. By then it would have traversed the territory of the five or six clans that inhabit the area north of Quemperi, and it would have opened up to petroleum exploitation—by Conoco and the growing list of companies counting on the infrastructure Conoco would build—the homelands of the Tagaeri, the Taromenga, and, if they exist, the Oñamenane and the Huiñatare. The dangers the road posed for the Huaorani were, of course, complex and immense—exposure to a simple flu, for example, could wipe out the uncontacted groups—but Quemperi's analysis was direct: A road means bad hunting. Game won't cross it. Colonists will come and cut down the forest and kill the animals. A road, in other words, meant hunger. It meant the end of abundance, and the end of the self-reliance and independence the Huaorani value above all else.

Enqueri went about his work in Cononaco with diligence. He kept his census in a small spiral notebook, in a neat schoolboy script. He visited each household and, slowly and carefully, wrote down the name of each member and his or her birth date, or an approximation: "In the season of the palm fruit" became February. Many of the younger people knew what year they had been born in, but few of the elders did, and Enqueri had to dead reckon. Quemperi found this exercise hilarious. "I am eighty!" he said at one point, then, "I am forty!" and, still later, "I am six!" What these numbers actually meant to Quemperi was anybody's guess. The only number that really meant anything was "enough," which you either had or had not. The world in which he had been raised had been so contained, in fact, that a typical Huao would have lived his entire life without laying eyes on more than seventy or eighty people, almost all of whom he would know by name.

Quemperi's clan numbered about thirty-five. I knew this not from Enqueri's census but because whenever Quemperi or his daughter was preparing food for me, almost every member of the clan descended on the hut. I would see them running across the *pista*, yelling to one another. They would jam up at the door and elbow their way in, then stand along the wall, splay into hammocks, sprawl on the dirt floor. Once inside they were dead silent. The children would snuggle up next to me, and because smell and touch are still principal means by which the Huaorani gather information, I constantly felt little fingers running up my shirt or beneath my arms or along the back of my neck or, now and then, inside the waistband of my shorts.

I was allowed to eat first, using my fingers to scoop food from a small plastic bowl I had brought with me. Thirty-five pairs of eyes followed every move I made, because when I finished eating I was expected to pass along the leftovers. I was also expected to provide enough for everyone, and I quickly learned that if there is one thing a Huao can do well, it is eat. Their eating took them beyond the demands of hunger, beyond simple gluttony, into a whole other zone of engorgement the likes of which I had never seen before. They ate everything in sight. Afterward, it was all they could do to wobble back to their huts and collapse in bloated discomfort.

Enqueri and I had brought supplies that we thought would last three weeks. They were gone in four days.

"Shouldn't we save some for later?" I asked him, and he passed this along to Quemperi.

"Later?" Quemperi said. "What is 'later'?"

Fortunately, we had prepared one sack of emergency food—rice, chocolate bars, canned tuna—which Enqueri kept in his care, so that we would have something for our long trek. But once our main supplies vanished I was onto a Huaorani diet. This meant I went hungry for three days, until I learned that I had to ask to be fed. Then there was the problem of getting the food down. What is revolting about monkey, for example, isn't the taste but the smell. A good eating monkey runs twenty to thirty pounds, or roughly the size of a three-year-old child. The carcass is thrown on the fire whole. First the hair burns off; burning, it smells exactly like human hair. Then the skin chars, and as it shrinks back from the skull the lips shrivel up over the teeth. About then—if you are tired and hungry and feeling a bit out of your element—it is easy to imagine that you are watching a hideously grinning dwarf being burned alive. Later an arm is cut off and you eat it holding it by the wrist, cupping the dainty, shriveled fingers.

Of course, there is always *chicha*, which is made by wives and by elder women. They masticate raw manioc, spit it into a pot, and leave it to ferment. Later—a day, two days, or, if it is time for a fiesta and a stronger brew is required, a week or longer—it is diluted with water and drunk from a bowl in long drafts. (No matter how diluted the *chicha*, it retains a certain slobbery essence: Imagine corn kernels drenched in raw egg.) *Chicha* is said to be quite nutritious, and, carried in a damp but undiluted form and mixed with water as needed, it is often the principal sustenance during treks of a week or more. At home it is ubiquitous—it is taken with all meals and offered whenever there is a visitor. As the Huaorani term for "happiness" has it, "another serving of *chicha* we laugh happily."

Even when left to ferment completely, *chicha* never gets much stronger than very weak beer. However, like all American Indians, the Huaorani lack an enzyme critical to metabolizing alcohol, and a typical house *chicha* draped even a stalwart young buck like Enqueri in rosy good cheer. Leaning back in a hammock, sipping *chicha* steadily from a deep bowl, spinning tales of all that he had seen across the Napo, where the sky met the ground and the world was thought to end, he would hold the other Huaorani in thrall through an entire evening. Late into the night I would hear his voice drifting across the *pista*, by turns frenetic and singsong, broken up by peals of laughter.

One night, as Enqueri and I sat around the fire talking to Quemperi, I said, "Enqueri, please ask Quemperi if the Huaorani still kill people."

Enqueri had a long exchange with Quemperi, who punctuated his reply with much shouting and finger-pointing and deep grunting. Then Enqueri turned to me. "He says no."

"When did they stop?"

Another long exchange: shrieks, howls, stamping of feet.

"He says September."

"September of what year?"

"This year."

This conversation took place in July.

I came to learn that the Huaorani are highly egalitarian: Though work is divided by gender—men hunt, women garden—neither is considered more worthy than the other. I learned, too, that in their self- reliance they display a clear-eyed pragmatism, and that they strive for family harmony. But the Huaorani are not known for these qualities. What they are known for is killing.

The Huaorani kill outsiders for obvious reasons: to fend them off, or to steal their goods. But when it comes to killing their own—who, until quite recently at least, they killed as often as they killed anyone else—the Huaorani follow fairly strict rules. Almost always such killing is a matter of revenge, usually for the death of a child. The Huaorani consider all human deaths to have been caused by other humans, and require all to be avenged. A Huao does not kill alone; he must persuade other men in his clan to assist him. Each man makes a half dozen or more spears and personalizes them with carvings and feathers. Spearing is performed on moonless nights; rain is considered a good sign. The killing must be done face to face, and for several weeks afterward the killers must not hunt, eat meat, or sleep indoors.

Mercy killings of both the newborn and the aged were common in the past and probably continue today among the groups with the least exposure to missionaries. Because self-sufficiency means so much to the Huaorani, the dependency that comes with old age is unacceptable, and the aged often asked to be killed rather than become a burden on their offspring. The very young children of dying parents—the terminally ill, say, or someone mortally wounded in a raid—were sometimes buried alive with their parents, and unwanted infants were killed at birth, usually by choking. (The clan as a whole could suggest this, but the final decision was the birth mother's. However, another clan member could intervene to save the child if he or she took responsibility for raising it.)

Although it is rare today, spear killing is still practiced. In May of 1994 a Huaorani clan spear-killed a Quichua and two Shuar, and severely wounded two others, in a revenge attack triggered by the death of a Huaorani child. In any case spear killing remains a central fact of how the Huaorani see themselves. Many adults carry, and proudly display, spear scars from the battles of their youths, and the old people still chant killing songs:

• • •

You are not from here.
You are different.
I will hunt you like a wild pig.
I will plunge my spear into your body many times.
It will not break.
Down you will go.
You will never leave.
You are quick like a monkey, running through the treetops,
but now you will die. . . .
I have no fear.
My enemies hunt for me.
Their spears may come tonight, or the next night.
They will pierce my body again and again.
When I die I will make no sound.

I am like the jaguar.
I have no fear.

Firsthand experience of spear killing is rare among younger Huaorani, but it remains a source of both pride and fear—which is why Enqueri was not entirely comfortable in Cononaco. One day he told me that the Huaorani who lived there were "uncivilized."

"What do you mean?" I asked.

"They have no radio," he said, "and they do not play volleyball."

What he actually meant was that he was afraid. Raised on radio and volleyball and El Señor (the Christian God), the Condorito now found himself immersed in what the missionaries had taught him was the dark and demonic side of the Huaorani culture. As traditional as it appeared, Quemperi's clan was the most acculturated wing of what the missionary literature refers to as the "ridge group"—those Huaorani, small in number but fierce in reputation, who lived far downriver from the evangelical protectorate and who for the most part had eluded its influence. "Ridge" refers to a divide between the Cononaco and Yasuní basins, which Enqueri and I intended to cross on foot. It was said to be inhabited by three clans. While it is probably true that no Huaorani have escaped at least some influence by the missionaries—among even the most remote clans, one occasionally spots a Maidenform bra—contact with the ridge group had been minimal, and our proposed trek caused Enqueri no small anxiety (which, in Huaorani, is the same as the word for "kill"). Visitation rights among the Huaorani are determined by a complex system of familial ties, and anyone lacking them, even a Huao, is considered an enemy.

The first clan we were likely to encounter was that of Quemperi's cousin Menga. There was no way to gauge how Menga would receive us, and as a precautionary measure, Enqueri had arranged for us to be accompanied by Quemperi's son-in-law, Miñiwa. Among the younger Cononaco men, Miñiwa had experienced the least contact with the outside, and he retained the appearance and bearing of the elders: He had drooping, perforated earlobes, long, black hair, shoulders a yard wide, and, because he spent as much time walking in the treetops as he did on the forest floor, feet deformed into crescents. He lived to hunt.

Rare was the day when I did not see him striding across the *pista* with the carcass of a woolly monkey slung across his back, its arms locked around his neck in rigor mortis. Quemperi said that when Miñiwa was still a boy they had raided a military camp and butchered five soldiers for their axes.

Miñiwa spoke no Spanish, but he was, as near as I could tell, absolutely without fear. His gaze was so penetrating, so intense, that whenever it came to settle on me I felt very much as if he intended to "hunt you like a wild pig." He rifled through my pack at will, and though he took nothing, he experimented with everything—even, mimicking me, my dental floss, for which he had no apparent use. Often when I sat in Quemperi's hut making notes, Miñiwa would kneel right behind me and rest his chin on my shoulder. One day he reached down, yanked my pen out of my hand, and, gripping it like an ice pick, drew on the page. He made a series of half circles, opening first one way, then the opposite way, back and forth. When he finished he pointed to one of them and said a whole lot of things, of which I caught only one word: Menga. It would be weeks before I understood that Miñiwa had drawn a map. The half circles represented watersheds, with creeks and rivers running one way, then another. In the middle, at the biggest divide, we would find Menga: still on the ridge, still, for all intents and purposes, beyond contact.

One day, shortly after dawn, Enqueri appeared at Quemperi's hut and announced that he was ready to hit the trail. He was wearing only a camouflage baseball hat, a faux Yves Saint Laurent belt cinched up over his navel, a pair of men's underpants, and a pair of rubber boots. He was also wearing, proudly, the backpack he had asked me to buy for him, but it was little more than an ornament. We had almost nothing left to carry. Most of our emergency stores had been looted, along with my Swiss Army knife, my long pants, a roll of duct tape, and my extra socks. When I explained this to Enqueri, he hooted with laughter. "The Huaorani," he said, "they are the *worst*."

Still, we were to travel with Miñiwa, which meant we would find food along the way. Or so I'd thought. Standing there in his BVDs, however, Enqueri suddenly informed me that Miñiwa had decided to stay home. Instead, we would be accompanied by three boys. Two were teenagers, one a twelve-year-old. We had no radio, so we could not call a plane, and we had no gas, so we could not go back upriver to the Vía Auca by boat. The only way out was north to the Yasuní, on foot, across seventy-five miles of steaming, unmapped wilderness, and the prospect of making that journey without an experienced guide and hunter was more than I could handle, to say the least. "We need men, not children!" I shouted at Enqueri. "How will we eat? How will we find the trail?"

"The boys know the way," he said, but he would not look me in the eye. Then he added, strongly, "My people can travel ten days without food."

"Maybe they can," I said, "but *I* can't, and neither can you." Compared with the muscular young hunters in Quemperi's clan, Enqueri was a city slicker, no more likely to kill a monkey than I was.

Rummaging in my pack, however, I came up with five shotgun shells, and these gifts persuaded Miñiwa to accompany us. As for my tantrum, it hadn't lasted long, but by the time I finished we were surrounded by pretty much the whole clan. No one spoke. I had witnessed almost no public anger among the Huaorani. Surely my outburst shocked them, and it left me unsettled.

I turned and walked toward the river as calmly as I could, trying to show no fear, but when I reached the high, muddy bank I misstepped and tripped and slid down it face first and into the water, coming to a soggy stop beneath the canoe. Spitting mud, I looked up to find most of the clan standing along the bank. Some of them were pointing at me, and some were mimicking my fall. Others were so convulsed by laughter that they had to lean on one another for support.

Giggling, one of Quemperi's granddaughters knelt in the bow of the canoe and poled us across the Cononaco. One by one, we climbed the north bank and ducked into the dark forest.

We picked up a faint hunting trail and hiked all day in single file, as the Huaorani always do, and we did not stop for the lunch we did not carry. At ground level the bush was thin, but the canopy was dense as a circus tent, revealing neither sun nor sky. The forest was surprisingly quiet, and we walked in silence. The twelve-year-old, Yohue, led the way, Enqueri followed him, I followed Enqueri, and the two teenagers, Quimonca and Awa, followed me, herding me like sheepdogs ("Psssst, psssst"). Miñiwa took up the rear with his five-year-old son, who kept pace with no apparent difficulty.

As we walked I wondered whether there had been malice in the Huaorani's sudden change of plans. Having helped themselves to what valuables I carried, were they now ready to abandon me to the forest? On the other hand, I thought, the matter might well be as simple as it appeared: No one in the clan but the three boys had felt like traveling. This was an adventure for them—they intended to accompany Enqueri all the way to his home on the far side of the territory, a journey none of them had made before. It would take them at least two weeks to get there, and yet they carried nothing but the shirts on their backs, their shorts, and their cheap rubber boots. In fact, young Yohue lacked even these. His left foot was bare, and on his right he wore only a cotton sock, which slapped the soggy trail like a beaver's tail.

Suddenly, Yohue stopped short, his way blocked by a brown-and-orange snake about five feet long and thick as a man's arm.

"Boa," Enqueri said. I couldn't tell for certain what it was, and *boa* appeared to be the only Spanish word the Huaorani had for snakes. Still, fear stopped each one of us in his tracks. The Huaorani have an extraordinarily high incidence of death from snakebite. Most adults have been bitten at least once, and many have suffered multiple bites. In fact, the snake represents the most evil force in the Huaorani cosmology, and the magic of a boa *curandero*, or witch doctor, as the evangelical ministry has it, is especially feared. Killing any snake, poisonous or not, is a powerful and pragmatic taboo. Enqueri hacked a detour well away from this one, and we hustled past it as quietly as we could.

A few minutes later Miñiwa announced that his son had malaria, and that he would bring him back to the *pista*, then catch up with us on the trail. Naively, I believed him. As it turned out, I would never see him again. It would be some time before I realized that the snake had been an omen so evil that it had frightened Miñiwa away from our journey.

Now and then came the squawking of invisible parrots, and once a rustling of shrubs that Enqueri identified as peccary. Twice we flushed turkeys, two of them easy kills if we'd had a weapon.

I made this point to Enqueri.

He stopped dead and turned around and faced me with a look as cool as a river rock.

"Give me your pack," he said.

He shouldered it quickly, along with his own, and took the lead, hacking forcefully through the bush with his machete—driven, it seemed to me, by anger and wounded pride.

By now the trail had disintegrated into a slimy mess of rotting tree trunks, clotted undergrowth, thick mud, and spiny vines. Despite these obstacles Enqueri moved so swiftly that I had to jog to keep up with him. Often the only sign in what looked to me like a wall of green was a few stubby branches cut long ago. Mostly Enqueri spotted them without missing a step.

When Enqueri did lose the trail, it was Yohue who found it, again and again, without hesitation. "There," he would say, and there it was. It was soon clear that I had badly underestimated him, and the other two boys as well. Awa—handsome, dark, and disdainful—was the younger and more impulsive of the two, given to sprinting away through the forest and disappearing for an hour at a time. Quimonca was sturdier and quieter, and though, like Awa, he spoke no Spanish beyond *Sí*, any comment directed his way elicited a broad, shy smile. He refused to pass me on the trail, and once, when I pitched headlong off an improvised sapling bridge into a creek—the sort of bridge the Huaorani cross without so much as a downward glance—he sprang to my rescue, an effort that caused him to laugh so uncontrollably that both of us had to sit on the bank for a minute to collect our wits, such as they were.

By midafternoon it was clear that I had slowed us down even more than Enqueri had anticipated I would, and that night would fall long before we could reach the ridge where we expected to find Menga encamped with his clan. However, Enqueri said that we were not far from another hut. Quemperi's clan had abandoned it six months earlier, when a man and woman died there of malaria.

"Who were they?" I asked.

"They were the parents of Quimonca and Awa."

If Quimonca and Awa were at all affected by this, they did not show it. Indeed, toward dark they raced ahead of us, and when we arrived at the hut we found them gorging on sugarcane picked from the abandoned gardens. The hut itself was strikingly different from those at the *pista*. For one thing, it was ten times larger; the entire clan had lived in it. Whereas the *pista* was flat and open, and the homes exposed, here the forest was dense and the hut almost hidden. I hadn't seen it until it was three feet in front of me. There was no barren ground at all—the gardens grew right up to the thatch walls.

The hut itself was pitched on the spine of the high, narrow ridge. The Huaorani had lived in this manner—hidden, isolated, protected—until a few decades ago, when the Company arrived and they took to settling along the rivers and traveling in canoes and raiding the oil camps. I couldn't see five feet in any direction except when I stood at the hut's entrance, which had been placed right above the ridge's steepest slope. From there, however, I could see for miles, down and across a sweeping sea of green. Without a doubt it was the most spectacular view of the Amazon that I had ever come across.

Once inside the hut I collapsed on the dirt floor. By my estimate we had walked from twelve to fourteen hours. We might have come five miles, or twenty. My clothes were in shreds, and I was covered with blood, mud, sweat, and slime. The Huaorani looked as fresh as the moment we left the river. Even their feet were clean.

We sucked on sugarcane, and Enqueri cooked up the handful of rice we had left. Each of us got about a cup. During the night it rained ferociously, and the roof leaked, and now and then rainwater splashed me awake. Once I was startled awake by the deep, constant hacking of Awa, a cough that was surely tubercular. It was so fierce and uncontrollable that it sounded as if he'd hack up his very guts, there in the place where his parents had died.

In the morning we went in search of Menga and his clan, counting on a meal when we found them. We located their hut within a couple of hours, but it was abandoned. What little was left had been neatly packed up and hung from the pole rafters, secured by lengths of electric cord pilfered from the Company. Several spears were tied to the walls, along with some shirts and blankets. A dozen aluminum pots hung from poles shoved vertically into the dirt floor. Inside one of these pots Yohue found a plastic tub of palm-oil lard, which he ate by the handful.

Menga had moved on, Enqueri said, and no one could know for certain where he had gone or when he would return. It could be days; it could be months. I began to appreciate the absurdity of conducting a census among nomads. Menga and his clan had hidden themselves so thoroughly that even their fellow Huaorani couldn't find them. They might be yards away, watching us from the trees; they might be in Peru. They were just out there, gone, independent, self-contained, unaccountable and unaccounted for.

After we raided a manioc garden near the hut, Enqueri announced that we would walk until "five minutes after five." This puzzled me—it was true that he wore a watch, but it didn't work. In any case we walked for perhaps ten hours, during which I fell, slid, and stumbled and got stung, bit, and branch-whipped so often that by the time Enqueri announced, "Five minutes after five," I had no idea of direction or distance, of where we were or even where we were going. I was aware only of my pain and fatigue. I collapsed right there on the muddy forest floor. Immediately, a line of biting ants marched up my left leg, but I was too tired to brush them off. Removing my leather hiking boots, or what was left of them, I saw that I'd broken the nails of both big toes.

Meanwhile, Enqueri built a lean-to of vines and saplings, and Yohue, Awa, and Quimonca fetched broad palm leaves and wove them into a roof. More palm leaves were laid to form a soft, mud-tight floor. The entire operation took about fifteen minutes.

It was raining by then—at that point, who cared?—but Enqueri found yet another palm, one with wood so hard that water couldn't penetrate its core, and succeeded in cutting and splitting several branches. Then he held a candle to them and started a fire, and the boys lay down next to the fire, curled themselves into a bundle, and went right to sleep. I managed to hang a mosquito net and wrap myself in a blanket. Enqueri watched me without saying a word.

During the night it rained furiously. I was sure the lean-to would collapse, but it didn't so much as leak. At one point, awakened by rustling near the fire, I saw Quimonca take our kitchen knife and lance a golfball-size infection on his left shoulder. It gushed pus and blood, and the pain must have been tremendous, but he betrayed no emotion at all.

Later the air turned sharply cold, and despite the blanket I shivered through what was left of the night.

We awoke to silence and darkness—in that dense bush there was no "dawn" as such—and ate the last of our food, a thin gruel of rice, chocolate, and tuna. Like me, the Huaorani shook with cold.

As we set out on foot, Enqueri announced, in all sincerity, that we would reach an upper tributary of the Yasuní in "one hour and forty-two minutes." Six or seven or eight hours later, he adjusted that claim to "an hour and a half." By then he had a bewildered look in his eye, and Yohue passed him on the trail and took the lead again, the steady slapping of his muddy sock the only sound in the forest. Still later—I had by then lost all sense of time—we did in fact achieve the bank of a small river, though when I asked Enqueri whether it was the tributary we were looking for, he mumbled only an unconvincing "Of course." But there was enough light to execute a quick turn and flourish in the shallows, and to share a bar of soap. Ivory, to be specific. "It floats," Enqueri said. Time and again the little bar jiggled off downstream like a tippy canoe, a display the Huaorani found sidesplitting.

Awa had collected a small turtle on the trail. Enqueri boiled it. No sooner had the three boys inhaled their meager portions and dropped their empty bowls than they were asleep next to the fire, curled up like puppies.

Later, when I again asked Enqueri if we had reached the correct river, he launched into a long and complicated monologue that began with him fighting three soldiers in a bar in Coca, a battle he was on the verge of losing until he called "Time out" and downed a Coca-Cola, after which he prevailed. Somehow this story segued into a story of how a jaguar and an eagle mated to spawn the Huaorani. Then Enqueri said, "Last night I had a dream. We were in an airplane, and it crashed in the forest. I grabbed you right before you fell out."

"Really?"

"Yes, but we died anyway."

"That is a terrible dream."

"No, it is a very good dream. If you fall out of an airplane, it means good luck."

There was no way out of the forest except with the Huaorani. No way to call for help; no one to call if there were. My life was in Enqueri's hands. I fell asleep thinking that I liked him very much but that I did not trust him at all.

In the morning we waded the river, sinking buck naked and chest deep in the cool, slow-moving current, then dressed and shambled into the forest in search of an abandoned well called Amo Dos, one in a string of exploratory wells Conoco had drilled inside Block Sixteen. Enqueri said that Amo Dos was near the tributary we were seeking, and that once we found the well we'd be able to set course for the Yasuní. However, after a couple of hours we had found no evidence of oil work. Even Yohue seemed confused, and we retreated back across the river. This time, wet, hungry, exhausted, and unable to see the sky, I did not bother to remove my clothes, which in any case were not going to dry out anytime soon, if ever. Enqueri, for his part, would not admit that we were lost. ("Where *are* we?" I asked, to which he replied, with an absolutely straight face, "We are in the *jungle*.")

Several hours later Enqueri stopped before a ceiba tree, affixed to which was a piece of red metal about two inches square. CONOCO, it said, and Enqueri announced, "Block Sixteen."

• • •

"Green wall" is a phrase often used to describe Amazonian bush, but in all my wanderings in the Amazon I've never seen anything quite so wall-like as what now confronted us. Two or three years earlier great chunks of the forest had been cleared for seismic lines and helicopter pads, and the new understory had grown back so densely that it was impassable even with the aid of a machete. It was a visceral demonstration of the impact, largely ignored but difficult to overstate, that seismic exploration can have on a forest. At intervals of approximately one mile, ten-foot-wide trails are cut across the concession. Dynamite is detonated every 300 yards along each of these trails, producing seismic waves that can be analyzed to determine the geological profile under the forest floor. Within a typical concession, at least 800 miles of trails are cut, as well as some 1,500 helicopter pads, deforesting up to 2,000 acres. Noise from cutting and blasting scares away much of the wildlife, and the new understory growth inhibits its return. Fructivores—toucans, monkeys, turkeys—won't move into cleared areas, and their absence means not only a loss of game but diminished regeneration of the forest, because these species distribute the seeds of the large fruiting trees.

Enqueri and I sat in front of the ceiba tree and drank water. If we were not exactly found—there was no telling just where along the Block Sixteen boundary we were—we were not quite so lost as we had thought. I expected some reaction from Enqueri—elation, righteousness, whatever—but he seemed completely blank. Then, after a while, he began to speak.

Like many Huaorani men, Enqueri had once worked on a seismic crew; he had, in fact, worked on a crew that had explored Block Sixteen. Cutting seismic trails is the hardest, dirtiest, and worst-paying work in the exploration process, and the Company usually hires Indians to do it. "I needed money," Enqueri said. "When we are sick, the *evangelistas* take us to their hospital. They make us pay them, and once when I was

gone on a trip my sister went to the hospital." When Enqueri got home
he learned that he owed the hospital the equivalent of about $180, or
roughly six months' pay at the prevailing national minimum wage. He
went to work for the Company. "I had a ninety-day contract," he said.
"I worked from six in the morning until six at night, cutting the forest.
I worked seven days a week. The Company gave us a machete and boots,
and the helicopter would drop rice and beans. After work, we cut a
clearing and put up a tarp. I worked with other Huaorani; we all slept
together. There was a lot of malaria, and someone was always getting
hurt—cutting off a finger or getting chopped by a machete or ax. But if
you didn't work you didn't get paid. When we asked for better
treatment, the Company said we didn't deserve it, because we were
uncivilized."

Looking around, I could see the massive sawn trunks of mahoganies,
ceibas, and palms littered through the forest. Awa, Quimonca, and
Yohue were sitting on a flat stump that was at least fifteen feet in
diameter. They were talking with uncharacteristic animation—angered,
I imagined, by the heedless destruction of their lands.

"What are they saying?" I asked Enqueri.

"They are saying that if the Company was still here, it might give us
something to eat."

We thrashed through the forest until midday, when Yohue yelled, "Amo
Dos!" and bolted ahead of us. Ten minutes later I stepped onto the slick
bank of a broad, brown river. After three and a half days under the forest
canopy, the sudden openness of the river—the long vistas upstream and
down, the vast gray sky overhead—struck me with a kind of vertigo, and
I felt dizzy and weak-kneed. Seconds later the sky burst with a ferocity
that I hadn't yet experienced in the Oriente. Despite this Enqueri and
the boys waded across the river to see if they could find the well. I stood
on the bank and got pounded.

After a couple of minutes it hit me that we were not necessarily lost,
and in a rush of hope I ate the one candy bar I'd hidden deep in my
pack. It is impossible to describe how delicious it tasted. Overall, I had

eaten very little in the eleven days with Quemperi, and during our trek I had hiked perhaps seventy miles on the equivalent of two full meals. I was hungrier than I could ever remember being. It dawned on me that I might well be starving.

I sat in the rain for about an hour, staring at my feet, until I heard an ominous roar and looked up to see a fifty-foot balsa tree toppling into the river from the far bank. A few minutes later Yohue appeared on the bank dragging long coils of vine. A second tree fell, and then Awa and Quimonca scrambled from the bush and, kicking and pushing, rolled the two trunks into the water. Enqueri ran out of the forest behind them and waded into the river waist deep. Chipping frantically with his machete, the rain streaming down his body into the river, he hacked the trunks into logs about ten feet long and bound them with vine to make two rafts. Then he trimmed a couple of saplings for paddles and, wearing a serious expression, maneuvered across the river to pick me up.

"I saw where the well is," he said. "It was very far away, so we did not try to reach it." But he was mumbling and glancing up and down the river and looking everywhere but at me, and I did not believe a word of it.

In any case our next step was clear: We were going to float the river. If it did not join the Yasuní, then in all likelihood it was bound for Peru, and we had no hope of coming across help for weeks, at best. I did not think I would live that long, and after I stepped onto the raft, I was overcome with a panic so consuming that the simple act of sitting down required every bit of will I could muster.

I shared a raft with Quimonca. I sat amidships, facing him, and he sat at the stern and directed the raft with his paddle. If our predicament offered any saving grace, it was that we were no longer on foot. In almost no other way was it possible to see the raft as an improvement. It was slow, drifting with the river, permanently awash, and profoundly uncomfortable—the middle log, poorly secured, bounced like a seesaw, and at the top of each arc whacked me in the tailbone. Every so often Quimonca would glance my way to be sure I was still in place, considering me with neither more nor less interest that he would, say, a turkey.

Submerged to their hips, silent, Enqueri, Awa, and Yohue drifted ahead of us. In other circumstances I probably would have appreciated the surroundings. Like most of the Amazonian rivers in Ecuador—the notable exceptions being the Napo and, farther north, the Aguarico—this one was no more than ten yards wide. Moss and vine hung like drapery from the tall trees, walling off the river. The humid air smelled of rot and mud, and aside from the occasional whistle of a bird and the gentle purling of the current, silence reigned. It was a world more concealed than exposed, all darkness and shadows. It was small wonder that the Huaorani had remained hidden for so long.

The rain let up for a few hours, until we hit a snag and had to wade into the river and work the rafts through by hand. About then the temperature suddenly dropped a good ten degrees, and seconds later the skies burst. All at once I was shivering so with cold that I could not stop—right there in the heart of the Amazon, one degree of latitude off the equator. My teeth chattered violently. If I wasn't yet hypothermic, I was getting there fast.

Enqueri, Quimonca, Awa, and Yohue appeared no better off. They were shaking with cold, their muscles jerking under the skin. There was a small plastic tarp in my pack, and we wrapped ourselves in it and stood on the bank for the next half hour, until the rain abated. We made camp right there. The business of hauling our gear up from the raft and building a shelter helped steady my nerves, but not much. The Huaorani, too, looked lost and worried, though Enqueri managed to get a fire going.

"What river is this, Enqueri?" I asked.

"I do not know."

"What does that mean?"

"It means we are lost."

"And what does that mean?"

"It means we might die."

It was a simple statement of fact, and that night, though I tried to rest, every time I dozed off I shocked myself awake. My hunger had become physically painful—my stomach burned and had begun to cramp—and it seemed to have deepened into something else entirely, a bitter stew of frustration, despair, and anger at my own foolishness. I knew, as surely as I had ever known anything, that I was going to die. I would leave behind a pregnant wife; I would never know my child. And there really wasn't a damn thing I could do about it.

It was true that we had a machete and could, in theory, carve hunting spears, and surely the canopy held many edible nuts and fruits. But "hunting and gathering" is not so simple as it sounds. Traveling between communities was one thing, but if our focus were to become food gathering, we would have had to make a base camp, find materials for weapons, fashion the weapons, then begin the arduous process of stalking game in unfamiliar territory. A spear for killing peccaries can be made in an afternoon, but peccaries are fast and wily, and tracking and killing them can take several days. A monkey can be killed in a day, but you need a blowgun; making a good one—straight and airtight—is a week's work. You have to make darts, too, and find and prepare poison for the tips. Usually, monkeys are high in the canopy, so you must drive a dart a hundred feet or more with enough force to pierce hair and skin. To help achieve this force, the Huaorani wrap their darts in a kind of cotton gasket, to build up pressure inside the blowgun. But only one species of tree provides this fiber, and it is not always easy to find. Likewise for the species of palm—the one among the 150 or so that grow in the forest—that provides the right wood for darts.

Once you've made your weapons, of course, you have to go and do some hunting. It takes three or four darts to kill a monkey, and even a good hunter will hit with only, say, one shot in five. Once you wound a monkey, and send it fleeing for its life along the canopy, you have to somehow keep your eyes on it while hauling your nine-foot, five-pound blowgun through more or less impenetrable forest. When, finally, you do kill the monkey, more likely than not you'll have to climb into the canopy to retrieve it.

Hunting, in other words, is very hard work, and long-term planning is not what the Huaorani do well, or, for that matter, at all. I could suggest whatever I wanted to, but they wouldn't start to think about hunting until they noticed that they were starving, which didn't appear to be anytime soon. As for what they thought of my problems—well, hey, there were plenty more *cowode* where I came from.

Far better than hunting would be to find some friends who had already been hunting and hit them up for something to eat. This, at least, was what Enqueri had in mind.

Meanwhile, I was slowly dying of hunger, and if nothing else, I was coming to understand that for the Huaorani, hunger defines life. You are hungry or you are not; all else flows from that. From this point of view, I could see why the Huaorani so value self-reliance, and why their culture revolves around food, ritual sharing, feast and famine. However illusory it might be at times, the notion of *abundancia*—of the forest as ever fruitful and providing—is absolutely critical to their ability to survive. Without such faith, one would feel terrified by the forest, terrified to the point of paralysis. It was easy to see, too, why all the money in the world could never compensate them for the destruction of their land.

Light came early and hard to the exposed bank, raising a voracious insect hatch. The air buzzed, and mosquitoes attacked in dense thickets. But the river was up a couple of feet and moving more quickly, which had to be read as a good sign. If we were heading toward the Yasuní, we would probably find a Huaorani camp within a few days. And if we weren't? I tried not to think about that.

Soon after we put in, however, the sky turned a woolly gray, and the air suddenly chilled—signs of impending rain that were, to me, immensely frightening, for I believed that a serious rain was likely to kill me. I was not at all sure, by then, that I had the strength left to withstand even a common cold.

To the extent that I had any strategy for survival, it was to rip a hole in the plastic tarp and wear it like a poncho, and I sat athwart the stoic Quimonca looking for all the world like a human tent. Once in a while our eyes would meet and he would smile, then turn intently back to the river. He was nineteen years old. His parents were dead. He was off to the land of the cannibals armed with only a T-shirt, shorts, and boots. What did he expect, if anything at all?

The morning passed with no indication of what river we were on. The sky darkened, but the rain held off. It was probably midafternoon when I heard a sound like that of a branch snapping. It was both distant and too sharp, but only when it came a second time did I begin to think it might be something else—something manmade, perhaps; perhaps a gunshot. Yohue heard it, too, and jumped to his feet. Moments later there came the thin, low hum of an outboard motor, and then, around a bend in the river, the prow of a canoe.

Our rescuer proved to be a grinning young friend of Enqueri named Araba. He was accompanied by two clansmen, Bainca and Anaento. They had been on the river three days, and the hunting had been good. The canoe was piled high with bananas and manioc, and under a tarp in the stern were a couple of dead turkeys, a couple of monkeys, and a great pile of charred meat—hindquarters, hooves, snouts, guts. They had come upon four peccaries, that much was clear, but beyond that each man had his own story. Each version was delivered in what to my ear sounded like an absolute frenzy, high-pitched and manic, and though each man appeared to agree enthusiastically with whatever version was being told, no two versions were the same. It was at any rate a big kill, and at each telling of the tale all the Huaorani howled with delight.

As for me, I boarded Araba's canoe cautiously, not so much from fatigue—though that certainly was one reason—as from awe and disbelief. I had so convinced myself that I was going to die that for a few long moments it was difficult for me to accept without question that Araba and his friends and their canoe and their heaps of food were real.

Somebody handed me a chunk of boiled manioc. I nibbled at it; it was soft, almost tasteless, and utterly exquisite. That broke the spell, and then it was off to the races. For the next hour we ate pig like pigs, until we reached the hunting camp, where Bainca boiled up manioc and bananas and turkey and monkey and we ate some more. Toward dusk we unloaded the canoe and washed out the blood and put back into the river. The evening was unusually clear, and by the light of the setting sun Bainca motored us slowly downstream and Enqueri leaned back against the meat pile and, not for the first time, told the story of our journey. Wielding a bowl of *chicha* in one hand and a chunk of meat in the other, he pointed at me and made as if to fall out of the boat, rocking it wildly—that was me plunging off the sapling bridge. The other Huaorani were in stitches. I didn't mind at all. My belly was full, and I was thankful to be alive. I sat against my pack and stretched my legs out in front of me and stared at the sky for what seemed forever, until my reverie was broken by the sound of my own laughter.

Down the River
by Edward Abbey

The wilderness gives curmudgeons like Edward Abbey (1927–1989) space to recover from encounters with their exasperating fellow humans: the foolish, the blind, the destructive. Abbey showed his gratitude to the wild by becoming its protector. He couldn't save Glen Canyon, though. He rafted the canyon just months before its destruction and wrote this elegy to it. No misanthrope, he loves us all: It's just that we're such idiots.

T he beavers had to go and build another goddamned dam on the Colorado. Not satisfied with the enormous silt trap and evaporation tank called Lake Mead (back of Boulder Dam) they have created another even bigger, even more destructive, in Glen Canyon. This reservoir of stagnant water will not irrigate a single square foot of land or supply water for a single village; its only justification is the generation of cash through electricity for the indirect subsidy of various real estate speculators, cottongrowers and sugarbeet magnates in Arizona, Utah and Colorado; also, of course, to keep the engineers and managers of the Reclamation Bureau off the streets and out of trouble.

The impounded waters form an artificial lake named Powell, supposedly to honor but actually to dishonor the memory, spirit and vision of Major John Wesley Powell, first American to make a systematic exploration of the Colorado River and its environs. Where he and his brave men once lined the rapids and glided through silent canyons two thousand feet deep the motorboats now smoke and whine, scumming the water with cigarette butts, beer cans and oil, dragging the water skiers on their endless rounds, clockwise.

PLAY SAFE, read the official signboards; SKI ONLY IN CLOCKWISE DIRECTION; LET'S ALL HAVE FUN TOGETHER! With regulations enforced by water cops in government uniforms. Sold. Down the river.

Once it was different there. I know, for I was one of the lucky few (there could have been thousands more) who saw Glen Canyon before it was drowned. In fact I saw only a part of it but enough to realize that here was an Eden, a portion of the earth's original paradise. To grasp the nature of the crime that was committed imagine the Taj Mahal or Chartres Cathedral buried in mud until only the spires remain visible. With this difference: those man-made celebrations of human aspiration could conceivably be reconstructed while Glen Canyon was a living thing, irreplaceable, which can never be recovered through any human agency.

(Now, as I write these words, the very same coalition of persons and avarice which destroyed Glen Canyon is preparing a like fate for parts of the Grand Canyon.)

What follows is the record of a last voyage through a place we knew, even then, was doomed.

One day in late June Ralph Newcomb and I arrive on the shore of the Colorado River at a site known variously as Hite, White Canyon or Dandy Crossing, about one hundred and fifty miles upriver from the new dam already under construction. In my pickup truck, badly shaken by a long drive down one of the roughest roads in Utah, we carry camping gear, enough grub for two weeks, and two little rubber boats folded up in suitcase-size cartons.

We spend half a day on the shore, preparing our boats and ourselves for the journey. The river looks terribly immense and powerful, swollen with snow-melt from the western slope of the Rockies and from the Wind River Range in Wyoming, a veritable Mississippi of a river rolling between red rock walls. Our rubber boats, after we inflate them, seem gaudy, flimsy and much too small. Inevitably we've forgotten a few things, among them life jackets, and I can't help thinking that maybe we should make the trip some other time. One of the things that worries me, besides the missing life jackets and the obvious fragility of our Made-in-Japan vessels, is the fact that Ralph has only one good leg. He can walk but not hike; he can swim but not very far.

However, I keep my cowardly doubts to myself, waiting for Ralph to speak of them first. But he doesn't. Imperturbable as the river itself, tranquil as the sky overhead, he puffs on his corncob pipe, limping back and forth between the truck and the launching point with canned goods and bedrolls.

We divide our supplies, mostly bacon and beans, into equal parts, bind them in canvas and rope, and stow them under the bow seats; in case one boat is lost we will still have survival rations left in the other. Ralph has also had sense enough to bring along a bit of line and a few fishhooks—the river is lively with catfish, as we'll soon discover. We expect to spend about ten days on the river and will not see any human habitation, after Hite, until we reach the dam site a hundred and fifty miles downstream.

At last we're ready. I push my boat onto the water of an inlet and climb aboard. The floor of the boat is nothing but a single layer of rubberized canvas and sags like jelly beneath my weight. Sitting there I can feel the coolness of the water through the canvas and my blue jeans. But it floats, this toy boat, and I can find no more excuses for delay. Since Ralph has a camera and wants pictures of the launching I am obliged to go first. I paddle out of the quiet inlet and onto the brown silt-rich bosom of the Colorado.

This is my first experience with a rubber boat and I discover at once that a single canoe-type paddle is not appropriate. The shallow-drafted almost weightless boat tends to turn in circles, pivoting beneath my seat; in order to make any headway I have to shift the paddle quickly from side to side, an awkward and tiring procedure. Staying clear of the main current, drifting slowly past the shore, I paddle in circles and wait for Ralph to catch up.

He comes alongside. We lash the boats together, side by side, which makes not only for better companionship and ease of conversation but also improves the maneuverability: Ralph paddles on one side, I on the other, giving us some control over our direction.

We paddle our double craft into the current, ship paddles, lean back against the stern seats, which make good backrests and nothing much else, and smoke and talk. My anxieties have vanished and I feel instead a sense of cradlelike security, of achievement and joy, a pleasure almost equivalent to that first entrance—from the outside—into the neck of the womb.

We are indeed enjoying a very intimate relation with the river: only a layer of fabric between our bodies and the water. I let my arm dangle over the side and trail my hand in the flow. Something dreamlike and remembered, that sensation called *déjà vu*—when was I here before? A moment of groping back through the maze, following the thread of a unique emotion, and then I discover the beginning. I am fulfilling at last a dream of childhood and one as powerful as the erotic dreams of adolescence—*floating down the river*. Mark Twain, Major Powell, every man that has ever put forth on flowing water knows what I mean.

A human shout reaches our ears from the west shore. A man is waving at us from the landing of old Hite's ferry. A warning? A farewell? He shouts once more but his words are unintelligible. Cheerfully waving back, we drift past him and beyond his ken without the faintest intimation of regret. We shall not see another of the tool-making breed for a long time and we could not care less.

Misanthropy? Shakespeare could say

> Man delights not me,
> No, nor woman neither. . . .

And Raleigh, too,

> I wish I loved the human race,
> I wish I loved its silly face.

And Jeffers:

> Be in nothing so moderate
> as in love of man.

But no, this is not at all what we feel at this moment, not at all what I mean. In these hours and days of dual solitude on the river we hope to discover something quite different, to renew our affection for ourselves and the human kind in general by a temporary, legal separation from the mass. And in what other way is it possible for those not saints? And who wants to be a saint? Are saints human?

Cutting the bloody cord, that's what we feel, the delirious exhilaration of independence, a rebirth backward in time and into primeval liberty, into freedom in the most simple, literal, primitive meaning of the word, the only meaning that really counts. The freedom, for example, to commit murder and get away with it scot-free, with no other burden than the jaunty halo of conscience. I look at my old comrade Newcomb in a new light and feel a wave of love for him; I am not going to kill him and he—I trust—is not going to kill me.

(My *God*! I'm thinking, what incredible *shit* we put up with most of our lives—the *domestic* routine (same old wife *every* night), the stupid and useless and degrading *jobs*, the *insufferable* arrogance of elected officials, the crafty *cheating* and the *slimy* advertising of the business-man, the tedious wars in which we kill our buddies instead of our *real* enemies back home in the capital, the foul, diseased and *hideous* cities and towns we live in, the constant *petty* tyranny of automatic washers and automobiles and TV machines and telephones—! ah *Christ*!, I'm thinking, at the same time that I'm waving goodby to that hollering idiot on the shore, what *intolerable* garbage and what utterly *useless crap* we bury ourselves in day by day, while patiently enduring at the same time the creeping strangulation of the clean white *collar* and the rich but *modest* four-in-hand garrote!)

Such are my—you wouldn't call them thoughts, would you?—such are my feelings, a mixture of revulsion and delight, as we float away on the river, leaving behind for a while all that we most heartily and joyfully detest. That's what the first taste of the wild does to a man, after having been too long penned up in the city. No wonder the Authorities are so anxious to smother the wilderness under asphalt and reservoirs. They know what they're doing; their lives depend on it, and all their rotten institutions. Play safe. Ski only in clockwise direction. Let's all have fun together.

We drift on; the current seems to accelerate a bit as the mighty river squeezes between great red walls of sandstone rising on either side to heights of a thousand feet or more, cliffs so sheer and smooth even a bird could find no perch there. One little white cloud of dubious substantiality hovers above in the strip of blue between the canyon walls. Gazing up at it I think I hear, as in a dream, a confused rumble and roar, the sound of a freight train highballing down a mountain grade. Rapids.

Actually there are not supposed to be true rapids in Glen Canyon— only "riffles." But it's been a dry winter, the river is low, the rocks high. To us these foamy waves *look* like rapids.

"White water ahead," says Ralph quietly, with a sort of complacent satisfaction, as if he had invented the phenomenon all by himself. And instead of doing anything about it he reloads his cheap pipe.

We're rounding the first major bend in the canyon. From ahead comes the sound of the rapids—toneless vibrations growing stronger, what acoustical specialists call "white noise." Like the sound of a waterfall. Supposedly a blissful and sleep-inducing impression on edgy nerves.

"I didn't know we'd hit rapids so soon," I say to Ralph. I open up my map, the only one we've brought with us, a Texaco road map of the state of Utah, and study the tributaries of the Colorado. "That must be where Trachyte Creek comes in," I explain; "if we had life jackets with us it might be a good idea to put them on now."

Actually our ignorance and carelessness are more deliberate than accidental; we are entering Glen Canyon without having learned much about it beforehand because we wish to see it as Powell and his party had seen it, not knowing what to expect, making anew the discoveries of others. If the first rapids are a surprise to us it is simply because we had never inquired if there were any on this stretch of the river.

Anyway, there's no turning back now. After the entrance, the inescapable spasm. Between narrowing walls the river rushes at increasing speed. Our little boats bounce over choppy waves toward the whitecaps that now are visible, churning to foam around glistening wet boulders strewn across our course, boulders which seem to rise and fall as we race toward them on the bounding current.

There is no longer time enough to be frightened. I have a glimpse of the willows on the shore sweeping past, the only available gauge of our velocity, before we grab the paddles, settle deep into the boats and go to work trying to keep our bows headed into the waves.

Not that it makes much difference. The spray hits our faces and closes vision, the waves come aboard, in a moment we are soaking wet and spinning through the heart of the turmoil, bouncing off one rock and into the next. A great shining boulder looms before us, unavoidable; Ralph's boat slams upon it and hangs there for a second or two until my boat, still roped to his, swings round in the spillway and pulls his free. Paddling furiously we right the boats and face the next obstacle, skin past it safely, bounce in and out of a few more troughs and suddenly find ourselves in the clear.

The waves smooth off as the river broadens through a wider channel, resuming its serene and steady flow. We've run our first rapids and are still alive. The boats are drifting along half full of water and we are drenched but the pipe in Ralph's teeth is still burning, so quickly did it all happen.

Happy, exultant, we rest for a while in the foggy boats before bailing them out. If this is the worst Glen Canyon has to offer, we agree, give us more of the same.

In a few minutes the river obliges; a second group of rapids appears, wild as the first. Forewarned and overcautious this time, despite ourselves, we paddle too far out of the main current and end up aground in the shallows. We have to climb out of the boats and drag them over a pebble-covered bar until we again reach deep water. Hard work for game-legged Newcomb but he makes no complaint.

Back in the boats, sprawled out comfortably on our baggage, nothing lost but the road map—and there are no gas stations in Glen Canyon anyhow—we drift onward without further effort, paddles inboard and at rest. The surface of the river is wide and gleaming, slick as glass; an immaculate stillness pervades the canyon, pointed up deftly now and then by a gurgling eddy near the shore, the call of a bird.

Smoking peacefully, we watch the golden light of afternoon climb the eastern wall as the sun goes down beyond the rim to the west. An early evening breeze rustles through the willows ashore and we hear again the tinkling music of canyon wrens—like little silver bells falling across a glockenspiel—no, like wilderness lorelei—calling down to us from the rimrock, sweetest of all bird songs in the canyon country.

Other voices also speak: queer squawks and honkings from the thickets, sounds we cannot identify until we see, a little later, a great blue heron flap its wings among the lavender plumes of a tamarisk tree.

"Ralph Newcomb," I say, "do you believe in God?"

"Who?" he says.

"Who?"

"Who."

"You said it," I say.

An owl. Ravens. More canyon wrens. The splash of fish breaking the surface. Lizards palpitating on the rocks. And once we see, between us and the far shore, something sleek and dark following its nose upstream—a beaver. The same that lured the mountain men—Robidoux, Jim Bridger, Jedediah Smith—into these parts more than a century ago.

The river bears us quietly along, the canyon fills with shadow and coolness. The sky above turns a deeper darker blue as the last of the sunlight glows on the domes and turrets and elephant-backs of the Navajo sandstone above the Wingate cliffs. We begin to think about food and a camp for the night.

When a beach of white sand comes in sight, backed with a stand of green young willows, we get out the paddles and work toward it, paddling strenuously across the current. As will usually happen, we are on the wrong side of the river when we want to make a landing. And it's a wide river this time of the year. And with Ralph on the upstream side of our double boat, I have to paddle twice as hard as he does just to keep even.

Closing in on the beach, I jump out and wade ashore, towing the boats onto the sand. We tether them to a clump of willows, unload and prepare to camp. My bedroll is a little wet but everything else, well wrapped in tarpaulins, is dry, and our feelings of pleasure and satisfaction are as great as our appetite for supper.

It is a beauteous evening, calm and free. We build a small fire of dead willow branches and propitiate the gods of river and canyon with the incense of woodsmoke, an offering with which, being intangible beings, they are content; we the worshipers, of baser stuff, fry and eat the actual beans, corned beef and eggs. A crude meal, no doubt, but the best of all sauces is hunger. To us it seems a shade better than anything available at Sardi's or Delmonico's. What's more we aren't raveled for leg room.

We make the coffee with river water, dipping a canful from among the rocks and letting it set for a time until the silt settles to the bottom. For entertainment we have the murmur of the river, the drone of cicada and amphibians, the show of nighthawks plunging through the evening gulping bugs. Afterwards we sit by the fire until the fire gives out, listening, smoking, analyzing socioeconomic problems:

"Look here, Newcomb," I say, "do you think it's fitting that you and I should be here in the wilds, risking our lives amidst untold hardships, while our wives and loved ones lounge at their ease back in Albuquerque, enjoying the multifold comforts, benefits and luxuries of modern contemporary twentieth century American urban civilization?"

"Yes," he says.

I rebuild the fire and drape my sleeping bag above it on a willow bough, smoking it good and proper. When it's ready I scoop two shallow holes in the sand, one for the hipbones and one for the shoulder blades, lay out the sleeping bag and turn in. Ralph, peaceful as a hanging judge, is already sound asleep. For myself I choose to listen to the river for a while, thinking river thoughts, before joining the night and the stars.

Morning on the river: up with the dawn, before the sun, Ralph still sleeping, strange invisible birds calling and croaking from the bush, I wash last night's dishes in the muddy river. And why not? That same force which corraded a gorge five thousand feet deep through the Kaibab Plateau will also serve to scour the grease from the tin plates of the Abbey-Newcomb Expedition. The Colorado has no false pride.

Then breakfast: bacon and eggs, fried potatoes, coffee. The unknown birds continue to creak and chirrup. Some I begin to recognize—a mockingbird, killdeer, Mexican finches. Also the usual and prevalent canyon wrens and a few magpies and ravens.

Ralph awakes, stirred to life by the aroma of food, takes a bath in the river, combs and pomades his hair, his long black evil sheepherder's beard. We eat.

Afterwards as we pack and load the boats, sun coming up over the rim, we begin to feel the familiar terrible desert thirst. We drink the last of the spring water in our canteens and, still thirsty, look to the river, that sombre flow the color of burnt sienna, raw umber, *muy colorado*, too thin to plow—as the Mormons say—and too thick to drink. But we drink it; we'll drink plenty of it before this voyage is over.

The sun rises higher, fierce on our faces; the western wall blazes like hot iron. We shove off, keeping to the shady side of the canyon, and commence the second day of our journey.

Why, we ask ourselves, floating onward in effortless peace deeper into Eden, why not go on like this forever? True, there are no women here (a blessing in disguise?), no concert halls, no books, bars, galleries, theaters or playing fields, no cathedrals of learning or high towers of finance, no wars, elections, traffic jams or other amusements, none of the multinefarious delights of what Ralph calls syphilization. But on the other hand most anything else a man could desire is here in abundance: catfish in the main stream and venison in the side canyons, cottonwoods for shade and shelter, juniper for fuel, mossy springs (not always accessible) for thirst, and the ever-changing splendor of sky, cliffs, mesas and river for the needs of the spirit.

If necessary, we agree, a man could live out his life in this place, once he had adjusted his nervous system to the awful quietude, the fearful tranquillity. The silence—meaning here not the total absence of sound, for the river and its canyons are bright with a native music— but rather the total absence of confusion and clamor, that would be the problem. What Churchill spoke of as *"bloody peace"*—could we bear it for very long? Yet having known this, how could we ever return to the other?

"Newcomb," I say, "you're condemned. You are doomed."

"So are you," he says.

"Let's drink to that. Where's that rum we were going to bring along?"

"Stowed with the life jackets."

"And the case of beer we were going to tow instead of a dinghy?"

"We drank it all back in Albuquerque."

The thirst. I dip a can in the river under my elbow and place it on the gunwale (so to speak) of my little rubber boat, giving the mud in the water time to settle out. The river at this point is so steady and serene that the can of drinking water hardly trembles, though it's balanced on a rounded surface.

The current carries us on its back smoothly south and west toward the Gulf of California, the Sea of Cortez, but with many a wonderful meander on the way. Occasionally we lay a paddle over the side, drop the blade in the water and with the slightest, most infinitesimal of exertions turn the double boat for a view in a different direction, saving ourselves the trouble—somewhat greater—of turning our heads or craning our necks.

In this dreamlike voyage any unnecessary effort seems foolish. Even vulgar, one might say. The river itself sets the tone: utterly relaxed, completely at ease, it fulfills its mighty purpose without aim or effort. Only the slow swing of the canyon walls overhead and the illusory upstream flow of willows, tamarisk and boulders on the shore reveal and indicate the sureness of our progress to the sea.

We pass an opening in the eastern wall, the mouth of a tributary stream. Red Canyon Creek? There's no telling and it certainly doesn't matter. No rapids here; only a subtle roiling of the water, ripples corresponding to the ripples on the river's sandy bed. Beyond the side canyon the walls rise up again, slick and monolithic, in color a blend of pink, buff, yellow, orange, overlaid in part with a glaze of "desert varnish" (iron oxide) or streaked in certain places with vertical draperies of black organic stains, the residue from plant life beyond the rim and from the hanging gardens that flourish in the deep grottoes high on the walls. Some of those alcoves are like great amphitheatres, large as the Hollywood Bowl, big enough for God's own symphony orchestra.

When the sun stands noon-high between the walls we take our lunch, on board and under way, of raisins and oranges and beef jerky and the cool cloudy river water with its rich content of iron and minerals, of radium, uranium, vanadium and who knows what else. We have no fear of human pollution, for the nearest upstream town is Moab, pop. 5000, one hundred miles away. (Blessed Utah!)

In any case, when a man must be afraid to drink freely from his country's rivers and streams that country is no longer fit to live in. Time then to move on, to find another country or—in the name of Jefferson—to *make* another country. "The tree of liberty is nourished by the blood of tyrants."

(Or Bakunin: "There are times when creation can be achieved only through destruction. The urge to destroy is then a creative urge.")

After lunch we paddle hard across the current again to the west side of the river, seeking shade. Shade as precious as water. Without shade, in the middle of the river, we must cower beneath our hats, hammered by sun and by the reflected heat and blaze from the mirrorlike sheen of the river, the hot red walls of the canyon. Once in the shade we can rest, expand, unsquint our eyes, and see.

All afternoon we glide onward, running a few slight rapids (slight compared to those of Cataract Canyon and Grand Canyon), smoking our tobacco, drinking the river, talking of anything and everything which comes to our heads, enjoying the delirium of bliss.

"Newcomb, for *godsake* where do we come from?"

"Who knows."

"Where are we going?"

"Who cares."

"Who?"

"Who."

Words fail. I draw the rusty harmonica from my shirt pocket and play old folksongs and little tunes from the big symphonies—a thin sweet music that floats for a while like smoke in the vastness all around us before fading into the silence, becoming forever a part of the wilderness. Yielding to nostalgia, I play the Sunday-morning songs out of my boyhood: *What a friend we have in Jesus . . . . Leaning, leaning, leaning on the everlasting arms. . . .* (diatonics for the soul) and:

> We shall gather by the river,
> The beautiful the beautiful-ah river . . .
> We shall gather by the river
> That flows (from?) the throne of the Lord. . . .

We make our second river camp this evening on another sandy beach near the mouth of a small creek which enters the main canyon from the northwest. Hall's Creek? Bullfrog Creek? Sometimes I regret not having brought a decent map. Not far below are what look and sound like the most ferocious of rapids, far worse than those we'd encountered on the first day. But tomorrow we'll worry.

We eat a good, simple, sandy supper of onion soup, beef and beans, tinned fruit and coffee. With the coffee we each have a pipeful of Newcomb's Mixture—half Bull Durham and half Prince Albert, the first for flavor and the second for bulk. Good cheap workingman's tobacco.

After the meal, while Ralph washes the dishes, I take the canteens and walk up the creek to get some spring water if possible. In the sand I see the prints of deer and coyote and bobcat, also a few cattle tracks, strays perhaps, fairly fresh. I find no spring within a reasonable distance and return to camp with empty canteens; there is water in the creek, of course, but we'd rather drink from the river than downstream from a Hereford cow.

Dark when I return, with only the light of Ralph's fire to guide me. As I brush away sticks and stones on the ground, making a place for my sleeping bag, I see a scorpion scuttle off, tail up and stinger ready. Newcomb and I meditate upon the red coals of the fire before turning in. Watching the sky I see shooting stars, blue-green and vivid, course across the narrow band of sky between the canyon walls. From downriver, as I fall asleep, comes the deep dull roar of the rapids, a sound which haunts the background of my dreams all night long.

We get up too late in the morning and have to cook breakfast in the awful heat of the sun. I burn the bacon and the wind blows sand in the pancake batter. But we're getting accustomed to sand—sand in our food and drink, in our teeth and eyes and whiskers, in our bedrolls and underwear. Sand becomes a part of our existence which, like breathing, we take for granted.

Boats loaded, we launch them into the river, still roped together side by side for the sake of comfort, conversation and safety. The rapids that worried my dreams turn out in daylight to be little more than a stretch of choppy waves and a few eroded boulders past which our boats slip without difficulty. If it were not so late in June, following a dry winter, the river consequently lower than usual, we would probably not notice these trivial ripples at all.

Down the river we drift in a kind of waking dream, gliding beneath

the great curving cliffs with their tapestries of water stains, the golden
alcoves, the hanging gardens, the seeps, the springs where no man will
ever drink, the royal arches in high relief and the amphitheatres shaped
like seashells. A sculptured landscape mostly bare of vegetation—earth
in the nude.

We try the walls for echo values—

HELLO. . . .

Hello. . . .

hello. . . .

—and the sounds that come back to us, far off and fading, are so strange
and lovely, transmuted by distance, that we fall into silence, enchanted.

We pass sandbars where stands of white-plumed cane and the lacy
blossoms of young tamarisk wave in the breeze among driftwood logs
aged to a silver finish by sun and wind and water. In the lateral canyons
we sometimes see thickets of Gambel oak and occasional cottonwoods
with gray elephantine trunks and bright clear-green leaves, delicately
suspended, trembling in the air.

We pass too many of these marvelous side canyons, to my everlasting
regret, for most of them will never again be wholly accessible to human
eyes or feet. Their living marvels must remain forever unknown, to be
drowned beneath the dead water of the coming reservoir, buried for
centuries under mud.

Here we become aware of the chief disadvantage of our cheap little
rubber boats: far too often, when we see some place that demands
unhurried exploration, the strong current will carry us past before we
can paddle our awkward craft to the shore. You might think we could
make a landing anyway and walk back up river on the bank but in Glen
Canyon, where the sandstone walls often rise straight up out of the
water, this is sometimes impossible.

Furthermore we are lazy, indolent animals, Newcomb and I, half-
mesmerized by the idyllic ease of our voyage; neither of us can seriously
believe that very soon the beauty we are passing through will be lost.
Instinctively we expect a miracle: the dam will never be completed,
they'll run out of cement or slide rules, the engineers will all be
shipped to Upper Volta. Or if these fail some unknown hero with a
rucksack full of dynamite strapped to his back will descend into the

bowels of the dam; there he will hide his high explosives where they'll do the most good, attach blasting caps to the lot and with angelic ingenuity link the caps to the official dam wiring system in such a way that when the time comes for the grand opening ceremony, when the President and the Secretary of the Interior and the governors of the Four-Corner states are all in full regalia assembled, the button which the President pushes will ignite the loveliest explosion ever seen by man, reducing the great dam to a heap of rubble in the path of the river. The splendid new rapids thus created we will name Floyd E. Dominy Falls, in honor of the chief of the Reclamation Bureau; a more suitable memorial could hardly be devised for such an esteemed and loyal public servant.

Idle, foolish, futile daydreams. While we dream and drift on the magic river the busy little men with their gargantuan appliances are hard at work, day and night, racing against the time when the people of America might possibly awake to discover something precious and irreplaceable about to be destroyed.

> . . . Nature's polluted,
> There's man in every secret corner of her
> Doing damned, wicked deeds.

The ravens mock us as we float by. Unidentifiable birds call to us from the dark depths of the willow thickets—solitary calls from the wild. We see a second beaver, again like the first swimming upstream. All of our furred and feathered and hairy-hided cousins who depend for their existence upon the river and the lower canyons—the deer, the beaver, the coyotes, the wildcats and cougars, most of the birds and smaller animals—will soon be compelled to find new homes. If they can. For there is no land in the canyon country not already fully occupied, to the limit of the range, by their own kind. There are no vacant lots in nature.

At four or five miles per hour—much too fast—we glide on through the golden light, the heat, the crystalline quiet. At times, almost beneath us, the river stirs with sudden odd uproars as the silty bed below alters in its conformations. Then comfortably readjusted, the river flows on and the only noise, aside from that of scattered birds, is the ripple of the water, the gurgling eddies off the sandspits, the sound of Newcomb puffing on his old pipe.

We are deep in the wild now, deep in the lonely, sweet, remote, primeval world, far far from anywhere familiar to men and women. The nearest town from where we are would be Blanding in southeast Utah, close to the Colorado line, or maybe Hanksville in south-central Utah, north of the Henry Mountains, either place about a hundred miles away by foot and both on the far side of an uninhabited wilderness of canyons, mesas, clay hills, slickrock domes, sand flats, pinyon and juniper forests.

Wilderness. The word itself is music.

Wilderness, wilderness . . . . We scarcely know what we mean by the term, though the sound of it draws all whose nerves and emotions have not yet been irreparably stunned, deadened, numbed by the caterwauling of commerce, the sweating scramble for profit and domination.

Why such allure in the very word? What does it really mean? Can wilderness be defined in the words of government officialdom as simply "A minimum of not less than 5000 contiguous acres of roadless area"? This much may be essential in attempting a definition but it is not sufficient; something more is involved.

Suppose we say that wilderness invokes nostalgia, a justified not merely sentimental nostalgia for the lost America our forefathers knew. The word suggests the past and the unknown, the womb of earth from which we all emerged. It means something lost and something still present, something remote and at the same time intimate, something buried in our blood and nerves, something beyond us and without limit. Romance—but not to be dismissed on that account. The romantic view, while not the whole of truth, is a necessary part of the whole truth.

But the love of wilderness is more than a hunger for what is always beyond reach; it is also an expression of loyalty to the earth, the earth which bore us and sustains us, the only home we shall ever know, the only paradise we ever need—if only we had the eyes to see. Original sin, the true original sin, is the blind destruction for the sake of greed of this natural paradise which lies all around us—if only we were worthy of it.

Now when I write of paradise I mean *Paradise*, not the banal Heaven of the saints. When I write "paradise" I mean not only apple trees and golden women but also scorpions and tarantulas and flies, rattlesnakes and Gila monsters, sandstorms, volcanos and earthquakes, bacteria and bear, cactus, yucca, bladderweed, ocotillo and mesquite, flash floods and quicksand, and yes—disease and death and the rotting of the flesh.

Paradise is not a garden of bliss and changeless perfection where the lions lie down like lambs (what would they eat?) and the angels and cherubim and seraphim rotate in endless idiotic circles, like clockwork, about an equally inane and ludicrous—however roseate—Unmoved Mover. (Play safe; worship only in clockwise direction; let's all have fun together.) That particular painted fantasy of a realm beyond time and space which Aristotle and the Church Fathers tried to palm off on us has met, in modern times, only neglect and indifference, passing on into the oblivion it so richly deserved, while the Paradise of which I write and wish to praise is with us yet, the here and now, the actual, tangible, dogmatically real earth on which we stand.

Some people who think of themselves as hard-headed realists would tell us that the cult of the wild is possible only in an atmosphere of comfort and safety and was therefore unknown to the pioneers who subdued half a continent with their guns and plows and barbed wire. Is this true? Consider the sentiments of Charles Marion Russell, the cowboy artist, as quoted in John Hutchens' *One Man's Montana*:

"I have been called a pioneer. In my book a pioneer is a man who comes to virgin country, traps off all the fur, kills off all the wild meat, cuts down all the trees, grazes off all the grass, plows the roots up and strings ten million miles of wire. A pioneer destroys things and calls it civilization."

Others who endured hardships and privations no less severe than those of the frontiersmen were John Muir, H. D. Thoreau, John James Audubon and the painter George Catlin, all of whom wandered on foot over much of our country and found in it something more than merely raw material for pecuniary exploitation.

A sixth example and my favorite is, of course, Major J. Wesley Powell, one-armed veteran of the Civil War, sitting in a chair lashed to the deck of the small wooden boat with which he led his brave party into the unknown canyons of the Green, Grand and Colorado rivers. From the railroad town of Green River, Wyoming, to the mouth of the Grand Canyon in what is now Lake Mead, Powell's first journey took three months. Within that time he and his men withstood a variety of unpleasant experiences, including the loss of a boat, the hard toil of lowering their boats by rope down the worst of the rapids, moldy flour and shortages of meat, extremes of heat and cold, illness, and the constant fear of the unknown, the uncertainty of success, the ever-present possibility that around the next bend of the canyon they might encounter hazards worse than any they had so far overcome. This psychological pressure eventually proved too much for three of Powell's men; near the end of the voyage these three left the expedition and tried to make their way overland back to civilization—and were all killed by Indians. Powell knew the inner gorge of the Grand Canyon as a terrible and gloomy underworld, scene of much physical and mental suffering for himself and his men, but despite this and despite all that had happened in his explorations, he would write of the canyon as a whole in panegyric accent:

"The glories and the beauties of form, color and sound unite in the Grand Canyon—forms unrivaled even by the mountains, colors that vie with sunsets, and sounds that span the diapason from tempest to tinkling raindrop, from cataract to bubbling fountain. . . .

"You cannot see the Grand Canyon in one view, as if it were a changeless spectacle from which a curtain might be lifted, but to see it you have to toil from month to month through its labyrinths. It is a region more difficult to traverse than the Alps or the Himalayas, but if strength and courage are sufficient for the task, by a year's toil a concept of sublimity can be obtained never again to be equaled on the hither side of Paradise."

No, wilderness is not a luxury but a necessity of the human spirit, and as vital to our lives as water and good bread. A civilization which destroys what little remains of the wild, the spare, the original, is cutting itself off from its origins and betraying the principle of civilization itself.

If industrial man continues to multiply his numbers and expand his operations he will succeed in his apparent intention, to seal himself off from the natural and isolate himself within a synthetic prison of his own making. He will make himself an exile from the earth and then will know at last, if he is still capable of feeling anything, the pain and agony of final loss. He will understand what the captive Zia Indians meant when they made a song out of their sickness for home:

> My home over there,
> Now I remember it;
> And when I see that mountain far away,
> Why then I weep,
> Why then I weep,
> Remembering my home.

Down the river. Our boats turn slowly in the drift, we see through a break in the canyon walls a part of the Henry Mountains retreating to the northwest, last range in the United States to be named and explored and mapped. Mount Ellsworth, one of the lower peaks, is the one we see, rising sharp and craggy against the sky, a laccolithic dome of varicolored sedimentary and igneous rock (part of the intrusion now exposed by erosion) furred over with a growth of pinyon pine, juniper and jackpine at the highest elevations. The flowers we cannot see but easily imagine will also be blooming up there in the cool—larkspur, lupine, Indian paintbrush, the Sego lily, perhaps a few columbines.

The boats continue to turn, and facing downriver now we see to the southwest, far beyond the opening in the cliffs, a kind of convulsed hump in the earth's stony crust. It is the southern end of the Waterpocket Fold, a fifty-mile-long monocline or ridge of warped sandstone, eroded along its base into triangular studs of naked rock that look, from here, like the teeth of a mowing machine. This will be our only glimpse of a weird area that is sure to be, someday, another national park complete with police, administrators, paved highways, automobile nature trails, official scenic viewpoints, designated campgrounds, Laundromats, cafeterias, Coke machines, flush toilets and admission fees. If you wish to see it as it should be seen, don't wait—there's little time. How do you get there? Well, I couldn't tell you.

A little after noon, when the surface of the river is gleaming under the sun like molten amber, we see an abandoned mining camp ahead of us on the eastern shore. We paddle hard to port and beach our craft on a steep arid slippery mud bank, tethering it to a stout willow tree.

While Ralph makes himself comfortable in the shade, happy to take a siesta—he is one of those fortunates who can sleep at will or stay up talking and drinking till dawn, like Socrates, if he prefers—I go on up beyond the vegetated shore to the ledge of barren redrock on which the camp is situated.

Here I find the familiar fascinating semimelancholy debris of free enterprise: rusted tin cans, a roofless frame shack, the rags of tents and broken canvas cots, rusty shovels, a blunted old iron bullprick, rotting rat-bitten steel-toed boots, dynamite boxes, battered hard hats, two sticks of blasting powder (but no caps), sheaves of legal documents pertaining to mining claims and production agreements (rather interesting reading), a couple of withered sun-bleached topographical maps, and an astonishing heap of tattered magazines of the All-Man He-Male type—*True* (false), *Male* (a little queer), *Stag* (full of ragged does blasting Japs with machine guns), *Saga* (fairy tales), *Real* (quite phoney) and others of the *genre*, all of them badly chewed up by rodents, barely readable, with the best pictures torn out by some scoundrel. These fellows must have spent a lot of time reading; no wonder they failed to find whatever they'd been looking for—gold? God? uranium?—and had to leave.

I climb the hill behind this ghost camp, up mountainous dunes of copper-colored sand, and find the trace of a jeep trail winding off to the east into a never-never land of black buttes, salt domes and prehistoric plateaus inhabited only by mule deer and mountain lions. Perhaps this track leads to the mine; there are no diggings of any kind in the vicinity of the camp. The prospectors or miners had no doubt established their camp near the river so they'd have a reliable water supply. Everything else they needed, from boots to beans, perhaps even the jeep, must have been brought in by way of the river, for this camp is a long long way from any road known to the mapmakers.

The climb gives me some comprehension of the fact that we are *down inside* the mantle of the earth. For though I stand on the summit of a considerable hill, at least a thousand feet above the river, I can see no more than ten miles in any direction. On all points the view is cut off, near or far, by the unscalable walls of buttes, mesas and plateaus far higher than the hill beneath my feet. They are ranged in bench or terrace fashion, up from the river, forming an almost horizontal skyline all around me which obstructs any sight of the mountains that I know are out there—the Henry Mountains to the northwest, the La Sal Mountains to the northeast, the Blue Mountains to the east, Navajo Mountain somewhere on the south, and Kaiparowits on the west or southwest.

In all of this vast well of space enclosed by mesa and plateau, a great irregular arena of right angles and sheer rock in which the entire population and all the works of—Manhattan, say—could easily be hidden, there is no sign whatever, anywhere, of human or animal life. Nothing, not even a soaring buzzard. In the heat and stillness nothing moves, nothing stirs. The silence is complete.

It is a strange fact that in the canyon country the closer you get to the river which is the living artery of the entire area, the drier, more barren, less habitable the land becomes. In this respect the desert of the Colorado is opposite to that of the Nile in Egypt or the Rio Grande in New Mexico where, in both cases, life, men and the cities are gathered along the shores of the rivers. Along the Colorado River there is no town from Moab in Utah to Needles in California, a distance of over a thousand miles (if we except the two small, improvised, completely artificial company towns connected with the building and operation of Glen Canyon Dam and Boulder Dam).

What is true of human life is true also of plant life: except for the comparatively lush growth along the very banks of the river and on the floors of the many narrow side canyons, life in all forms diminishes in quantity as you approach the Colorado. The mountains are covered with forest; the plateaus are also forested, at the higher elevations with aspen and yellowpine and farther down with pinyon and juniper; but as you descend through the lateral canyons toward the great river the pinyon and juniper yield to sagebrush and other shrubs; from that to yucca, prickly pear and ephedra; and from that, nearing the river, to almost nothing but scattered clumps of saltbush and blackbrush and the fragile annuals—snakeweed, mule-ear sunflowers, and other widely dispersed rain-dependent growths, separated from each other by open spaces of nothing but sand and rock.

The reason for this apparent anomaly is twofold. First, though all of the plateau and canyon province must be classified as an arid or semiarid region, the higher tablelands naturally receive a little more rainfall, on the average, than the lower areas. Second, the Colorado River carries its great volume of water swiftly seaward well *below* the general level of the surrounding land, through deep and largely impassable gorges (such as the Grand Canyon), and therefore does not and cannot water the desert through which it passes. Not until the river reaches the open country beyond the canyons is its water utilizable for agriculture and there, as we know, California and Arizona and Mexico have been fighting each other for half a century over the division of the precious liquid. (Each additional dam that is built on the Colorado, incidentally, reduces the quantity of usable water, because of unavoidable losses through evaporation and percolation into the porous sandstone containing the reservoirs.)

The sun is beginning to give me a headache. I glissade down the slopes of sand, copper-gold and coral-pink, past isolated clusters of sunflowers, scarlet penstemon and purple asters, to the shade of the willows and the life of the river. Here I take a swim and drink my fill of the cool muddy water—both at the same time.

We eat lunch, Ralph and I, and lie for another hour or two in the willow glade until the bright inferno in the sky has edged far enough westward to let the cliffs shade part of the river. Then we launch off, in the middle of the afternoon, and paddle across the current to the shady side, abandoning ourselves once more to the noiseless effortless powerful slide of the Colorado through its burnished chute of stone.

Although we are voyaging blind and ignorant, without map or compass or guide, I know (from Powell's book and hearsay) that sometime soon we should reach the mouth of the Escalante River, another small tributary. This I wish to explore for I have heard that back in its meandering depths are natural bridges and arches, cliff dwellings and hanging gardens and other spontaneous marvels.

As the sun goes down and we drift on through the smoky-blue twilight and the birdcalls I keep the Escalante in mind, one eye skinned for the likely *debouchment*. Reluctantly I allow to pass the intriguing slits and dark deep defiles which promise much but seem improbable; then we see not far ahead and on the correct, starboard shore the opening of a big canyon, full of shadows and cottonwoods. I feel at once with a thrill of certainty that here is one we must not pass. We head for shore.

But already the current is pulling us to the middle of the river and everything is further away than it looks. We work desperately toward the riverside and the mouth of the big side canyon but we've started too late, the river sweeps us by and we're going to miss it.

This has happened to us several times before and each time, spoiled by the wonders still lying ahead, we have surrendered to the river, given up and floated on. This time, however, we resolve not to give up; we keep paddling till we hit the shore and then work our way upstream, along the bank, with the aid of the willows at the water's edge. We reach an eddy and backwater, paddle around a giant boulder and find ourselves at last safe in the quiet, warm, green floodwater of the canyon's entrance. Nearly exhausted, we rest for a while in the boats before paddling slowly into the dark canyon.

The sun has been down for an hour, the moon will not clear the rimrock for another hour. The great canyon we have entered is as dark as a cave. We move deeper inside until we see in the dimness what looks like a white beach attached precariously to the foot of a sheer wall. We make for it, land, secure the boats, find a little dead wood and start a fire.

The heat in this deep and narrow canyon seems dense, stifling, almost sickening after a day on the wide and breezy expanse of the river. We make tea but have no appetite for any supper but a tin of fruit each. After the necessary soporific smoke and a weary conversation we unroll our sleeping bags and go to bed.

I sleep uneasily, haunted by the persistent dream of rising water and the drifting away of our boats. Near midnight, the waxing half-moon overhead, I wake up to the noise of wind and splashing water. The water is lapping at the sand less than a foot from my sleeping bag. I roll out of the bag, make sure the boats are still securely tied to the willows, and am about to wake up Ralph. Hesitating, I realize that the cause of the high water is not what I'd been half-consciously fearing all along, a flash flood from the world above us, but simply a strong wind blowing waves into the canyon from the river.

The wind has freshened the air and cooled it. Naked in the moonlight, I enjoy the change, and listen for a time to the hoodoo voice of a great horned owl up on the rim somewhere. Then I go back to sleep and this time sleep well, lullabied by wind and water.

In the morning before breakfast we dump our gear loosely into the boats and paddle on up the canyon until we reach shallow water. We are now around a bend and out of sight of the river. Here I get out and tow the boats farther through the still backwaters, wading on till we come to the place where a broad shallow stream of clear water enters and merges with the dead water of the flood. This stream is about six inches deep and six feet wide, with a fast steady flow—undoubtedly the Escalante "River." The water is fresh and clean, almost cool; without bothering this time to look for cattle tracks we each take a long and satisfying drink.

Feeling much better now, our appetites returning, we make breakfast, eating the last of our bacon, the last of the eggs and the last of the canned fruit. From now on we must subsist on our dehydrated food supplies—survival rations—or on whatever we can forage from the land.

As I prepare for a day's hike up the Escalante I can hear Ralph muttering something about channel cat; I pay no attention. Bouillon cubes and raisins are good enough for me, so long as they are seasoned with plenty of sun and storm and adventure, but Newcomb, somewhat of a gourmet, has different ideas. Lacing my boots I see him attach a fragment of moldy salami to a fishhook and toss it—with a line, of course—into the deep and muddy water below the stream.

"You got a license, bud?" I demand.

For reply he clenches his right hand, extends the middle finger rigidly and thrusts it heavenward. Invoking the Deity?

I take off but before I'm out of earshot I hear a curious thumping noise. I look back and there's Newcomb beating a giant catfish on the head with his canoe paddle, putting it quickly out of its misery. God provides.

What little I can see of the sky between the high and almost interlocking walls of the canyon looks cloudy, promising rain. Rain or sun it's all one to me. Burdened only with canteen, a stick and a lunch of raisins and chipped beef I march up the firm wet sand of the canyon floor, reading the register: many deer, one coyote, the three-toed track of a big bird, many killdeer or sandpipers, many lizards, the winding trail of a snake, no cattle, no horses, no people.

All of the prints look fresh, none more than a few days old. With good reason. The damp sand, the wet rushes crushed riverward under a layer of silt, the dust-free polish of pebbles and stones, the general appearance of neatness and tidiness all indicate that the canyon has quite recently been flushed out with a vigorous torrent.

I look at the perpendicular walls rising slick and unbroken on both sides; in case a flood should now appear, what could I do? Nothing. I'd float with the tide back to Newcomb and the boats, eat catfish for lunch.

The walk gets wet. The channel of the stream meanders from one wall to the opposite and within the first mile I have to wade it a dozen times. Hard on boots. Impossible to outflank these meanders, for they swing hard against and undercut the cliff first on one side and then the other. Should have brought tennis shoes. Since I have no tennis shoes I take off the boots and sling them over my shoulder, proceeding barefoot. I walk lightly across shoals of quicksand and ford the river when necessary, but over the pebbled and rocky stretches the going is hard and slow.

Another half mile and I come to a "dripping spring." This is a seep high on the canyon wall, two hundred feet above my head, where ground water breaks out between beds of sandstone and slides over the contours of the cliff, nourishing the typical delicate greenery of moss, fern, columbine and monkeyflower. Below the garden the cliff curves deeply inward, forming an overhang that would shelter a house; at this point the water is released from the draw of surface tension and falls free through the air in a misty, wavy spray down to the canyon floor where I stand, as in a fine shower, filling my canteen and soaking myself and drinking all at the same time.

I go on. The clouds have disappeared, the sun is still beyond the rim. Under a wine-dark sky I walk through light reflected and rereflected from the walls and floor of the canyon, a radiant golden light that glows on rock and stream, sand and leaf in varied hues of amber, honey, whiskey—the light that never was is here, now, in the storm-sculptured gorge of the Escalante.

That crystal water flows toward me in shimmering S-curves, looping quietly over shining pebbles, buff-colored stone and the long sleek bars and reefs of rich red sand, in which glitter grains of mica and pyrite—fool's gold. The canyon twists and turns, serpentine as its stream, and with each turn comes a dramatic and novel view of tapestried walls five hundred—a thousand?—feet high, of silvery driftwood wedged between boulders, of mysterious and inviting subcanyons to the side, within which I can see living stands of grass, cane, salt cedar, and sometimes the delicious magical green of a young cottonwood with its ten thousand exquisite leaves vibrating like spangles in the vivid air. The only sound is the whisper of the running water, the touch of my bare feet on the sand, and once or twice, out of the stillness, the clear song of a canyon wren.

Is this at last the *locus Dei*? There are enough cathedrals and temples and altars here for a Hindu pantheon of divinities. Each time I look up one of the secretive little side canyons I half expect to see not only the cottonwood tree rising over its tiny spring—the leafy god, the desert's liquid eye—but also a rainbow-colored corona of blazing light, pure spirit, pure being, pure disembodied intelligence, *about to speak my name.*

If a man's imagination were not so weak, so easily tired, if his capacity for wonder not so limited, he would abandon forever such fantasies of the supernal. He would learn to perceive in water, leaves and silence more than sufficient of the absolute and marvelous, more than enough to console him for the loss of the ancient dreams.

Walking up the Escalante is like penetrating a surrealist corridor in a Tamayo dream: all is curved and rounded, the course of the mainstream and canyon as indirect as a sidewinder, winding upon itself like the intestines of a giant. The canyon floor averages about fifty feet in width but the curving walls are at least five times that high, without benches or ledges, sheer, monolithic and smooth as if carved in butter, paralleling each other in a sort of loosely jointed ball-and-socket fashion, each concavity matched by a corresponding convexity on the opposite wall. And all this inspired by the little stream that swings through the rock and the centuries—truly a perfect example of what geologists call an entrenched meander.

Others have been here before. On a mural wall I find petroglyphs— the images of bighorn sheep, snakes, mule deer, sun and raincloud symbols, men with lances. The old people, the Anasazi.

I come to a second dripping spring, water seeping from a fissure far above, falling in spray upon a massive slab of rock at the foot of the wall. On the flat surface of this tilted slab somebody, maybe a Mormon cowboy fifty years ago, maybe an Indian eight hundred years ago, has chiseled two converging grooves which catch some of the falling water and conduct it to a carved spout at the lower edge. The grooves are well worn, smooth as a pebble to the touch.

As I sit there drinking water from cupped hands, I happen to look up and see on the opposite wall, a hundred feet above the floor of the canyon, the ruins of three tiny stone houses in a shallow cave. As is the case with many cliff dwellings, the erosion of eight centuries has removed whole blocks of rock which formerly must have supported ladders and handholds, making the ghost village now inaccessible.

I am content, however, to view the remains from below. Neither a souvenir collector nor an archeologist, I have no desire to stir the ancient dust for the sake of removing from their setting a few potsherds, a few corncobs, a child's straw sandal, an arrow point, perhaps a broken skull.

What interests me is the quality of that pre-Columbian life, the feel of it, the *atmosphere*. We know enough of the homely details: the cultivation of maize, beans, melons; the hunting of rabbit and deer; the manufacture of pottery, baskets, ornaments of coral and bone; the construction of the fortlike homes—for apparently, like some twentieth century Americans, the Anasazi lived under a cloud of fear.

Fear: is that the key to their lives? What persistent and devilish enemies they must have had, or thought they had, when even here in the intricate heart of a desert labyrinth a hundred foot-miles from the nearest grassland, forest and mountains they felt constrained to make their homes, as swallows do, in niches high on the face of a cliff.

Their manner of life was constricted, conservative, cautious; perhaps only the pervading fear could keep such a community together. Where all think alike there is little danger of innovation. Every child in this quiet place would have learned, along with his language and games, the legends of old battles and massacres, flights and migrations. He would be taught that the danger of attack was always present, that in any hour of the day or night, from up or down the canyon or over the rim, the Enemy might appear—cruel, devious, hungry, terrible—perhaps in the shape of those red-horned, hollow-eyed, wide-shouldered monsters painted on the walls of Sego Canyon north of Moab.

Long ago the cliff dwellings were abandoned. Were the inhabitants actually destroyed by the enemies they had always dreaded? Or were they reduced and driven out by disease, by something as undramatic as bad sanitation, pollution of their water and air? Or could it have been, finally, simply their own fears which poisoned their lives beyond hope of recovery and drove them into exile and extinction?

As I walk on, miles beyond Ralph and the river, the canyon changes a little in character, in places growing wider, less deep, with breaks in the wall and steeply pitched ravines that seem to suggest the possibility of an exit to the world above. I make two attempts to climb out of the canyon but the first route dead-ends at the foot of another vertical cliff and the second at a deep, stagnant plunge-pool swarming with tadpoles and dragonflies. Above this pool is an overhanging drop-off down the center of which a thousand years of intermittent drainage has scooped out a pothole and then drilled clear through it, creating a long polished chute and a window in the rock. But there are many of these Moore-like formations, hundreds of them, in the canyon country.

Late in the evening, the sun already down, I find what looks like a deer path leading up over an alluvial hill toward the southwest rim. I am tempted to take it and see where it goes but I am also hungry, tired, and a bit sore-footed; my raisins are all gone and the canyon grows dark; sadly I turn and start the long walk back.

Long before I come again to the second of the dripping springs night has covered the desert world. I sit down on a driftwood log, build a small fire with shreds of its bark, wait for moonrise. I put the boots back on; water or no water, my feet have suffered enough.

The new moon finally comes, edging above the rimrock, bright as a silver shield. Through moonlight and darkness, as the moon is revealed, then concealed, by the turning of the canyon walls, I continue the march toward camp. For company on the way I have my thoughts and the flutterings and cries of a great horned owl that chooses, for reasons of its own, to follow me for much of the distance.

The return is harder than I expected. If I didn't have the stream to follow, Ariadne's thread, it would be easy in the deceptive alternation of moonlight and shadow to take a wrong turn up one of the many side canyons, to spend the rest of the night in bewildered wandering or go to sleep on an empty stomach, covered only with my back. The repeated wading of the stream seems doubly tiring now, especially as the boots become watersoaked and layered with quicksand. I trudge onward, longing for the first sight of Ralph's campfire, hoping that each new bend in the canyon will be the last. The Escalante is no longer the free and friendly place it was during the day but totally different, strange, unknown and unknowable, faintly malevolent.

Endless, too, I'm beginning to feel, before I see at long last the glimmer of coals ahead, the embers of a fire, and in the dimness the outline of the rubber boats, a comforting sight. Ralph is sleeping when I stumble into camp but wakes up easily to show me the mess of catfish he has caught, cleaned and saved for me, wrapped in wet leaves, still cool and fresh.

It's surely after midnight but who wants to sleep? We rebuild the fire and deep-fry the fish in part of the bacon grease which Ralph has wisely been hoarding all along. I pull off my mud-caked boots, twice their original weight, sit close to the fire and eat a tremendous supper, while Newcomb fills the air with huge clouds of fragrant, philosophical pipe smoke. We discuss the day's adventures.

High above our heads the owl hoots under the lost moon. A predawn wind comes sifting and sighing through the cottonwood trees; the sound of their dry, papery leaves is like the murmur of distant water, or like the whispering of ghosts in an ancient, sacrosanct, condemned cathedral.

Late in the morning, close to noon, the sun comes glowering over the wall in a burst of fire and we are driven out of our sacks. Into the green lagoon for a bath and a swim and then Ralph baits a hook with the reliable rotten salami, I build a campfire in the shade and fill the skillet with grease, and once again we dine on channel cat—delicious fish!

After this combined breakfast and dinner we retire to the water again and deeper shade, evading the worst of the midday heat. Naked as savages, we float on our backs in the still water, squat on the cool sand under the sheltering cottonwood and smoke like sachems. We may not have brought enough food but at least we've got plenty of Bull Durham.

"Newcomb," I explain, "we've *got* to go back."

"But why?" he says. "Why?"

"Why do you grow that beard?"

"Why not?"

"Well why?"

"Well why not?"

"Well goddamnit why?"

"Well goddamnit why not?"

"Because," I explain. The role of the Explainer has become a well-established one in recent times. "Because they need us. Because civilization needs us."

"What civilization?" he says.

"You said it. That's why they need us."

"But do we need them?"

"Well," I say, "how long do you think that jar of bacon grease will last?"

That made him think. "Let's go," he says.

Sometime in the middle of the afternoon we shove our fragile boats once more into the water, climb aboard and paddle slowly out of the Escalante's womb, back to the greater world of Glen Canyon and the steady, powerful, unhurried, insouciant Colorado. It is almost like a coming home.

For the rest of the afternoon, keeping to the shady side, we drift down the splendid river, deeper and deeper and deeper into the fantastic. The sandstone walls rise higher than ever before, a thousand, two thousand feet above the water, rounding off on top as half-domes and capitols, golden and glowing in the sunlight, a deep radiant red in the shade.

Beyond those mighty forms we catch occasional glimpses of eroded remnants—tapering spires, balanced rocks on pillars, mushroom rocks, rocks shaped like hamburgers, rocks like piles of melted pies, arches, bridges, potholes, grottoes, all the infinite variety of hill and hole and hollow to which sandstone lends itself, given the necessary conditions and, as Thoreau says, a liberal allowance of time—let us say, about five thousand years? Fifty thousand? Five hundred thousand? Choose whatever sum you like.

We pass beneath *hanging* canyons, the mouths of lateral drainages which terminate above the level of the Colorado; out of these when it storms come roaring falls of thick, muddy water, of logs, trees, cows and thundering boulders, all crashing into the river hundreds of feet below, a gorgeous spectacle which we will not have the good fortune to witness.

Now and then we are offered tantalizing views, far ahead, of the blue dome of Navajo Mountain, another laccolith, a holy place, home of gods, navel of the world in the eyes of the Indians, and the shiplike prow of the high Kaiparowits Plateau.

Not all is rock: we see a redtailed hawk skimming along the cliff, once a golden eagle, and vultures soar in the distance. Closer by we hear though seldom see the wrens, finches and yellow warblers, and a few long-legged water birds.

Heart of the whole and essence of the scene is the river, the flowing river with its thin fringe of green, the vital element in what would be otherwise a glamorous but moon-dead landscape. The living river and the living river alone gives coherence and significance and therefore beauty to the canyon world. "I love all things which flow," said the deepest of Irishmen.

At evening we come to historic Hole in the Rock. Here we float ashore and camp for the night.

What happened here? In the year 1880, eleven years after Powell had passed this way, the Church of Jesus Christ of the Latter-Day Saints commissioned a group of the faithful, living then in south-central Utah, to establish a new settlement in the southeast corner of the state near what is now the village of Bluff.

As obedient as they were courageous, some two hundred and fifty Mormons—men, women and children, with livestock and twenty-six wagons—started east from Panguitch toward the designated place. They followed no road or trail but simply what would have seemed, on a map, to be the shortest line between the two points.

After traversing seventy miles of desert they came to the rim, the jump-off. Two thousand feet below, the Colorado River rolled across their chosen route. Instead of giving up and turning back they hammered and blasted a notch (the Hole in the Rock) down through the rim into the nearest side canyon. From there they carved and constructed a crude wagon road to the edge of the water and descended. In places the wagons had to be lowered on ropes. After fording the river these undaunted people climbed the farther side over terrain almost as difficult and continued on, week after week, through the surreal sandstone wilderness and forests of pinyon and juniper until they reached their goal. The entire expedition required about four months; the trail which they pioneered was never used a second time.

In the morning I decide to climb the old trail, up through the notch to the top of the plateau—haven't seen the outer world for a long time now. While Ralph goes fishing I start off through the willow jungle, around tangles of poison ivy and up enormous sand dunes toward the Hole. A brook trickles down the gulch below the path, a thread of water creeping from pool to pool. At the final opportunity—Last Chance Puddle—I take a hearty drink. I've left my canteen behind at the boats; Hole in the Rock, clearly visible from the river, doesn't seem far away.

The old trail climbs away from the water, switchbacking up the talus slope on the northern side of the canyon. The pitch is steep, the morning sun is blazing on my back, and the heat quickly becomes unpleasant. My sweat dries as fast as it forms—the parched air is sucking at my pores. My belly is full of water, gurgling like a wineskin, but I can almost feel it being drawn away; the knowledge that I've brought no canteen along adds poignancy to my premature thirst. I put a pebble in my mouth and keep climbing.

Above the talus I find the dugway, broad and shallow steps chipped out of the canyon wall by the first and only road-builders here, and the remains of fill and foundation—slabs and blocks of sandstone laid in place, one by one, over eighty years before. The canyon begins to narrow and pucker near the summit and the cleft is jammed with boulders big as boxcars. I squeeze among them, following the tracks of former hikers. Here at least is shade though no water. I sit down to rest, daydreaming of iced limeade, chilled tomato juice, Moorish fountains. The temperature out in the sun must be well over a hundred degrees.

Upward. Under a ledge I find the barest hint of a seep, drops of moisture leaking from the rock and dampening the sand beneath. I am so thirsty by this time that I try digging a waterhole, but the deeper I go the drier the sand. I need water; I put some of the moist sand into my mouth, extracting what refreshment I can from it, and go on.

Up through the notch. I come out on the surface of a rolling plain of cross-bedded sandstone, the petrified dunes of the Navajo formation, and win the view I'd been hoping for. Far in the distance lie the blue ranges under hard-edged, snowy cumulus clouds: the Henry's, Elk Ridge and the Bear's Ears beyond White Canyon, 10,000-foot Navajo Mountain on the other side of the river. On the west, not so far, perhaps ten miles away, rises the Kaiparowits Plateau, also known as Fifty-Mile Mesa, another island in the sky, little-known and uninhabited, cut off on all sides but the north by its sheer, vertical walls.

I walk out onto a point from which I can look down at the river, nearly straight below. I can see the switchbacks of the trail, the fan of greenery at the outlet of the side canyon, but no sign of Newcomb or the boats, deep in the shade of the willows. From up here the sound of the river, until now a permanent part of my auditory background, is no longer perceptible, and the desert silence takes on a deeper dimension. The sound of nothingness? "In the desert," wrote Balzac, somewhere, "there is all and there is nothing. God is there and man is not."

God? Nothing moves but the heat waves, rising from the naked rock. It is somehow comforting to see, nearby, the yuccas growing from the sand and from joints in the stone. They are in full bloom today, clusters of waxy, creamy flowers on tall stalks, supported and nourished by the rosettes of daggerlike leaves that form the base of the plant. God? I think, quibbling with Balzac; in Newcomb's terms, who the hell is *He*? There is nothing here, at the moment, but me and the desert. And that's the truth. Why confuse the issue by dragging in a superfluous entity? Occam's razor. Beyond atheism, nontheism. I am not an atheist but an earthiest. Be true to the earth.

Far off, the muted kettledrums of thunder, *pianissimo* . . . T. S. Eliot and *The Wasteland*. Certain passages in that professorial poem still appeal to me, for they remind me of Moab, Utah. In other words I like the poem for the wrong reasons—and dislike it for the right ones.

Here I am, relaxing into memories of ancient books—a surefire sign of spiritual fatigue. That screen of words, that veil of ideas, issuing from the brain like a sort of mental smog that keeps getting between a man and the world, obscuring vision. Maya. Time to go back down to the river and reality, back to Newcomb and the boats, the smell of frying catfish—there's God for you! I descend.

Evening on the river, a night of moonlight and canyon winds, sleep and the awakening. In a blue dawn under the faintest of stars we break our fast, pack our gear and launch the boats again. Farther still into the visionary world of Glen Canyon, talking somewhat less than before— for what is there to say? I think we've about said it all—we communicate less in words and more in direct denotation, the glance, the pointing hand, the subtle nuances of pipe smoke, the tilt of a wilted hat brim. Configurations are beginning to fade, distinctions shading off into blended amalgams of man and man, men and water, water and rock.

"Who is Ralph Newcomb?" I say. "Who is he?"

"Aye," he says, "and who is who? Which is which?"

"Quite," I agree.

We are merging, molecules getting mixed. Talk about inter-subjectivity—we are both taking on the coloration of river and canyon, our skin as mahogany as the water on the shady side, our clothing coated with silt, our bare feet caked with mud and tough as lizard skin, our whiskers bleached as the sand—even our eyeballs, what little you can see of them between the lids, have taken on a coral-pink, the color of the dunes. And we smell, I suppose, like catfish.

We've forgotten to keep a close track of time, have no clock or calendar, and no longer know for certain exactly how many days and nights we've been on the river.

"Six, I think," he says, my doppelganger.

"No, only five."

"Five? Let's see. . . . No. Yes. Maybe."

"I believe."

"Seven?"

"Four?"

The time passes very slowly but not slowly enough. The canyon world becomes each hour more beautiful, the closer we come to its end. We think we have forgotten but we cannot forget—the knowledge is lodged like strontium in the marrow of our bones—that Glen Canyon has been condemned. We refuse to think about it. We dare not think about it for if we did we'd be eating our hearts, chewing our entrails, consuming ourselves in the fury of helpless rage. Of helpless *out*rage.

We pass the mouth of a large river entering the Colorado from the east—the San Juan. Somewhere not far beyond this confluence, if I recall my Powell rightly, is the opening to what he named Music Temple. We keep watch but see a dozen lovely and mysterious grottoes, all equally beguiling, pass up some, let the current rush us by others, and finally end up by choosing the wrong one. We will not have another opportunity.

"When 'Old Shady' sings us a song at night," wrote Powell in 1869, "we are pleased to find that this hollow in the rock is filled with sweet sounds. It was doubtless made for an academy of music by its storm-loom architect; so we name it Music Temple."

Less than a century later his discovery will be buried under the mud of the reservoir, rendered inaccessible by those who claim they are not only "developing" but also "opening up" the canyon country. What have we lost? Here is Powell's description of the place:

"On entering we find a little grove of box-elder and cottonwood trees, and turning to the right, we find ourselves in a vast chamber carved out of rock. At the upper end there is a clear, deep pool of water, bordered with verdure. Standing by the side of this, we can see the grove at the entrance. The chamber is more than 200 feet high, 500 feet long, and 200 feet wide. Through the ceiling and on through the rock for a thousand feet above, there is a narrow, winding skylight; and this is all carved out by a little stream which runs only during the few showers that fall now and then in this arid country."

Late that evening, after sundown, Ralph and I beach our boats and make camp on a sandy spit near the outlet of a deep, narrow, labyrinthine side canyon, its name, if it has a name, unknown to us. I explore part of its length in the twilight and find another charming stream with pools of remarkable beauty—crystal-clear water in basins of rock and sand, free of weeds or mud, harboring schools of minnows. Darkness sets in before I can go very far. I go back to the campfire.

After a splendid night—clouds like clipperships racing across the starry sky, moon floating along the brink of the crag above us, wind in the tamarisk—we make a quick breakfast and I return to the exploration of the hidden passage, taking the canteens with me to fill with fresh water.

I come to where I had turned back the night before, a deep pool that fills the canyon from wall to wall. Filling the canteens, I cache them nearby, undress and wade into the water. The pool is deep, over my head. I swim across it, following a turn in the narrow canyon, here no more than ten feet wide, and emerge beyond into a curving tunnel of rock with running water on its floor.

This natural tunnel is pure rock, completely devoid of sand, soil and any trace of vegetation. The walls that tower above are so close to one another, overhanging and interlocking, that I cannot see the sky. Through a golden glow of indirect, reflected sunlight I proceed until I come to a very large grotto or chamber, somewhat like the one described by Powell, where a plunge pool and waterfall check any further advance.

Here the canyon walls are a little wider, permitting the sun, for perhaps a couple of hours during the summer day, to shine directly down into this cul-de-sac. A rivulet of clear water pours into the pool; glints and flecks of light reflected from its agitated surface dance over the dark-golden walls of the glen. Lichens are growing there, green, red, orange, and along the seep line are beds of poison ivy, scarlet monkeyflower, maidenhair fern, death camas, helleborine orchid and small pale yellow columbines. There are no trees or shrubs, for the sunlight is too brief.

The sun is gleaming on the pool, on the foam, on the transparent waterfall. I dive in, swim under the fall and take a soapless shower, lie on the rock in a patch of sunshine and gaze up at the small irregular fragment of blue which forms the sky in this place. Then I return through the tunnel to camp and companion.

Has this particular canyon been seen and named by earlier river-runners? No doubt it has, but I find no evidence to dispel the illusion that I may be the first ever to have entered here. And probably the last.

After a lunch of refried pinto beans and dehydrated apricots—a piquant combination—we climb into our double boat and float onward. Since we have missed Music Temple I am more determined than ever that we must not pass Forbidden Canyon and the trail to Rainbow Bridge, climax and culmination of any trip into Glen Canyon.

We stay close to the south and east shore of the river, despite the ferocious afternoon sun, investigating each side canyon that we come to. In one of these I accidentally start a brush fire, and am nearly cooked alive. Sheer carelessness—a gust of wind carries a flaming piece of paper into the dried-out tangle of a willow thicket; the flames spread explosively; in a minute the mouth of the canyon is choked with smoke and fire and there is nothing I can do but get out of there, quick, as the flames rush down through the jungle toward Ralph, waiting for me in the tethered boats.

He is all ready to cast off when I appear, about ten feet in front of the onrushing sheet of fire, running. I push the boats off and roll in; we paddle away as hard as we can from the fiery shore, the final wild flare of heat. With generous tact Ralph does not even ask for an explanation. You can see a photograph of what I did in Eliot Porter's beautiful book on Glen Canyon, *The Place That No One Knew.*

"Hot in there," I say, though Ralph has asked no questions.

"So I noticed."

"Had an accident."

"Is that right?"

Shakily I tamp my pipe and fumble through the pockets of my shirt. All gone.

"Here," he says. "Have a match."

The river carries us past more side canyons, each of which I inspect for signs of a trail, a clue to Rainbow Bridge. But find nothing, so far, though we know we're getting close. We can see in the canyon distance, not far ahead, the southern tip of the Kaiparowits Plateau—the landmark to guide by when seeking the way to Rainbow Bridge.

We bounce over a series of minor ripples and the river picks up speed. There is a corresponding excitement in the sky: the storm that has seemed potential for days is gathering above in definite form—wild gray scuds of vapor, anvil-headed cumuli-nimbi, rumbles of thunder coming closer.

From up ahead comes the familiar freight-train roar of white water again. A new and formidable canyon opens on the left, with a broad delta of pebbled beach, mud banks, rocks and boulders and driftwood issuing fanwise from its mouth. The boulders, carried down from the flanks of Navajo Mountain, cause the rapids which lie before us.

A little wiser now, learning from experience, we do not battle the current but rest until we are close to the rapids, then with a sudden furious effort paddle into the backwash near the shore and have no trouble making a landing in the shallows.

Ralph starts supper. I pull on boots and go exploring. I find a trail but it's a poor one, little more than a deer path, which peters out completely a mile up-canyon. There are ponds of fresh water on the canyon floor; I refill the canteens and return to the boats.

The wind by this time has risen to a magnificent howl, the sky is purple, and jags of lightning strike at Navajo Point, the remote crag two thousand feet above the river on the north side. Cold rain spatters on the hot sand of the beach, raising little puffs of dust and steam. Rock and driftwood and the flashing underside of leaves gleam with a strange, wild, shifting light from the stormy sky.

We rig the tarpaulins into a tent, preparing for rain, and eat our supper of pancakes on which we pour a sauce of stewed raisins, in place of the syrup we haven't got. Very good. Filling, anyhow. Afterwards, tea and tobacco.

We sit outside our tent, enjoying the weather. After a week of clear skies, and the heat and glare of the relentless sun, the cool wind and the sprinkling of hard cold raindrops on our bare heads and bare bodies feel good.

The heavy rain we've been anticipating fails to come. We pile our baggage under the canvas shelter and unroll our sleeping bags in a hollow among the white dunes, under the open sky. Falling asleep, I see a handful of stars blinking through a break in the racing clouds.

A red dawn in the east, cloud banks on fire with the rising sun. I bathe in the cold river, do my laundry, and build a fire for our breakfast: dried pea soup and tea bags. The last box of raisins I have set aside for lunch. Stores seem to be getting low—from now on it'll be catfish or nothing.

Onto the river and through the whirlpools, we glide without mishap into quiet water. Our little boats are holding up well; despite all the rocks we've bounced them off and over, despite the sand and snags we've dragged them over, they have yet to sustain a puncture or spring a single leak. Aye, but the voyage is not over—shouldn't mention these things.

Within a short distance we come to another big tributary canyon on the port side or southerly shore of the river. Navajo Point, the final outcropping of the Kaiparowits Plateau, is directly overhead. This canyon too has tumbled boulders into the river, forming one more stretch of rough water. As before we take advantage of the eddies close to the rapids, swinging briefly upstream and then into the flooded mouth of the side canyon. We tie up on a mud bank and get out to investigate.

At once I spot the unmistakable signs of tourist culture—tin cans and tinfoil dumped in a fireplace, a dirty sock dangling from a bush, a worn-out tennis shoe in the bottom of a clear spring, gum wrappers, cigarette butts, and bottlecaps everywhere. This must be it, the way to Rainbow Bridge; it appears that we may have come too late. *Slobivius americanus* has been here first.

Well, no matter. We had expected this. We know with certainty that we are now only a few hours—by motorboat—from the Glen Canyon dam site. I also happen to know that the natural bridge itself is still six miles up the canyon by foot trail, a distance regarded as semiastronomical by the standard breed of mechanized tourist. His spoor will not be seen much beyond the campground.

We set up a camp of our own well beyond the motorboaters' midden, near the little stream that tumbles down the rocky canyon floor, coming from the great redrock wilderness beyond. The trail to Rainbow Bridge, passing close by, is rough, rocky, primitive. Newcomb, who has brought no boots, decides to go fishing. We divide the box of raisins and the last of the dried apricots. I stuff my share into my shirt pockets and lace up the boots, hang a canteen over my shoulder and march off.

The trail leads beside the clear-running brook and a chain of emerald pools, some of them big enough to go swimming in, with the water so transparent I can see the shadows of the schools of minnows passing over the grains of sand in the bottom of the basins. Along the canyon walls are the seeps and springs that feed the stream, each with the characteristic clinging gardens of mosses, ferns and wildflowers. Above and beyond the rimrock, blue in shadow and amber-gold in light, are alcoves, domes and royal arches, part of the sandstone flanks of Navajo Mountain.

A hot day. Delicate, wind-whipped clouds flow across the burning blue, moving in perfect unison like the fish in the pools below. I stop at one of the largest of these pools, undress and plunge in. Happily I flounder about, terrifying the minnows, and float on my back and spout cheekfuls of water at the sun.

On to the Bridge:

I come to a fork in the canyon, the main branch continuing to the right, a deep dark narrow defile opening to the left. There are no trail markers but even on the naked sandstone I can make out the passage of human feet, boot-shod, leading into the unlikely passage on the left. And so I follow.

Here too a stream is flowing, much smaller than the other, through smoothly sculptured grooves, scoops and potholes in the rock. I go by the dripping little springs that feed it and the stream diminishes to a rill, to a trickle, to a series of stagnant waterholes shrinking under the sun. Frogs and toads will be croaking here, fireflies winking, when I return.

Hot and tired I stop in the shade of an overhanging ledge and take a drink from my canteen. Resting, I listen to the deep dead stillness of the canyon. No wind or breeze, no birds, no running water, no sound of any kind but the stir of my own breathing.

Alone in the silence, I understand for a moment the dread which many feel in the presence of primeval desert, the unconscious fear which compels them to tame, alter or destroy what they cannot understand, to reduce the wild and prehuman to human dimensions. Anything rather than confront directly the antehuman, that *other world* which frightens not through danger or hostility but in something far worse—its implacable indifference.

Out of the shade, into the heat. I tramp on through the winding gorge, through the harsh brittle silence. In this arid atmosphere sounds do not fade, echo or die softly but are extinguished suddenly, sharply, without the slightest hint of reverberation. The clash of rock against rock is like a shot—abrupt, exaggerated, toneless.

I round the next bend in the canyon and all at once, quite unexpectedly, there it is, the bridge of stone.

Quite unexpectedly, I write. Why? Certainly I had faith, I knew the bridge would be here, against all odds. And I knew well enough what it would look like—we've all seen the pictures of it a hundred times. Nor am I disappointed in that vague way we often feel, coming at last upon a long-imagined spectacle. Rainbow Bridge seems neither less nor greater than what I had foreseen.

My second sensation is the feeling of guilt. Newcomb. Why did I not *insist* on his coming? Why did I not grab him by the long strands of his savage beard and haul him up the trail bearing him when necessary like Christopher would across the stream, stumbling from stone to stone, and dump him finally under the bridge, leaving him there to rot or to crawl back to the river if he could? No man could have asked for a lovelier defenestration.

Through God's window into eternity.

Oh well. I climb to the foot of the east buttress and sign for Ralph and myself in the visitors' register. He is the 14,467th and I the next to enter our names in this book since the first white men came to Rainbow Bridge in 1909. Not many, for a period of more than half a century, in the age above all of publicity. But then it's never been an easy journey. Until now.

The new dam, of course, will improve things. If ever filled it will back water to within sight of the Bridge, transforming what was formerly an adventure into a routine motorboat excursion. Those who see it then will not understand that half the beauty of Rainbow Bridge lay in its remoteness, its relative difficulty of access, and in the wilderness surrounding it, of which it was an integral part. When these aspects are removed the Bridge will be no more than an isolated geological oddity, an extension of that museumlike diorama to which industrial tourism tends to reduce the natural world.

All things excellent are as difficult as they are rare, said a wise man. If so, what happens to excellence when we eliminate the difficulty and the rarity? Words, words—the problem makes me thirsty. There is a spring across the canyon, another seep under a ledge below the west footing of the Bridge. I climb down and up the other side and help myself to one of the tins someone has left there, collecting water under the dripping moss.

The heat is stunning. I rest for a while in the shade, dream and sleep through the worst of the midday glare. When the sun passes beyond the rim I get up and start to return to Newcomb and our camp.

But am diverted by a faint pathway which looks as if it might lead up out of the canyon, above Rainbow Bridge. Late afternoon, the canyon filling with shadows—I should not try it. I take it anyway, climbing a talus slope and then traversing a long inclined bench that pinches out in thin air at the base of a higher cliff. Impossible to go on—but a fixed rope dangles there, hanging from some belaying point out of sight above. I test the rope, it seems to be well anchored, and with its help and a few convenient toeholds and fingerholds I work my way to the top of the pitch. From there it's a long but easy scramble to the rim of the canyon.

Now I am in the open again, out of the underworld. From up here Rainbow Bridge, a thousand feet below, is only a curving ridge of sandstone of no undue importance, a tiny object lost in the vastness and intricacy of the canyon systems which radiate from the base of Navajo Mountain. Of more interest is the view to the north, east and west, revealing the general lay of the land through which we have voyaged in our little boats.

The sun, close to the horizon, shines through the clear air beneath the cloud layers, illuminating in soft variations of rose, vermillion, umber, slate-blue, the complex features and details, defined sharply by shadow, of the Glen Canyon landscape. I can see the square-edged mesas beyond the junction of the San Juan and Colorado, the plateau-mountains of south-central Utah, and farthest away, a hundred miles or more by line of sight, the five peaks of the Henry Mountains, including Mount Ellsworth near Hite where our journey began.

Off in the east an isolated storm is boiling over the desert, a mass of lavender clouds bombarding the earth with lightning and trailing curtains of rain. The distance is so great that I cannot hear the thunder. Between here and there and me and the mountains is the canyon wilderness, the hoodoo land of spire and pillar and pinnacle where no man lives, and where the river flows, unseen, through the blue-black trenches in the rock.

Light. Space. Light and space without time, I think, for this is a country with only the slightest traces of human history. In the doctrine of the geologists with their scheme of ages, eons and epochs all is flux, as Heraclitus taught, but from the mortally human point of view the landscape of the Colorado is like a section of eternity—timeless. In all my years in the canyon country I have yet to see a rock fall, of its own volition, so to speak, aside from floods. To convince myself of the reality of change and therefore time I will sometimes push a stone over the edge of a cliff and watch it descend and wait—lighting my pipe— for the report of its impact and disintegration to return. Doing my bit to help, of course, aiding natural processes and verifying the hypotheses of geological morphology. But am not *entirely* convinced.

Men come and go, cities rise and fall, whole civilizations appear and disappear—the earth remains, slightly modified. The earth remains, and the heartbreaking beauty where there are no hearts to break. Turning Plato and Hegel on their heads I sometimes choose to think, no doubt perversely, that man is a dream, thought an illusion, and only rock is real. Rock and sun.

Under the desert sun, in that dogmatic clarity, the fables of theology and the myths of classical philosophy dissolve like mist. The air is clean, the rock cuts cruelly into flesh; shatter the rock and the odor of flint rises to your nostrils, bitter and sharp. Whirlwinds dance across the salt flats, a pillar of dust by day; the thornbush breaks into flame at night.

What does it mean? It means nothing. It is as it is and has no need for meaning. The desert lies beneath and soars beyond any possible human qualification. Therefore, sublime.

The sun is touching the fretted tablelands on the west. It seems to bulge a little, to expand for a moment, and then it drops—abruptly— over the edge. I listen for a long time.

Through twilight and moonlight I climb down to the rope, down to the ledge, down to the canyon floor below Rainbow Bridge. Bats flicker through the air. Fireflies sparkle by the waterseeps and miniature toads with enormous voices clank and grunt and chant at me as I tramp past their ponds down the long trail back to the river, back to campfire and companionship and a midnight supper.

We are close to the end of our journey. In the morning Ralph and I pack our gear, load the boats, and take a last lingering look at the scene which we know we will never again see as we see it now: the great Colorado River, wild and free, surging past the base of the towering cliffs, roaring through the boulders below the mouth of Forbidden Canyon; Navajo Point and the precipice of the Kaiparowits Plateau thousands of feet above, beyond the inner walls of the canyon; and in the east ranks of storm-driven cumulus clouds piled high on one another, gold-trimmed and blazing in the dawn.

Ralph takes a photograph, puts the camera back into the waterproof pouch which he hangs across his chest, and climbs into his boat. We shove off.

This is the seventh day—or is it the ninth?—of our dreamlike voyage. Late in the afternoon, waking from a deep reverie, I observe, as we glide silently by, a pair of ravens roosting on a dead tree near the shore, watching us pass. I wonder where we are. I ask Ralph; he has no idea and cares less, cares only that the journey not yet end.

I light up the last of my tobacco, and watch the blue smoke curl and twist and vanish over the swirling brown water. We are rounding a bend in the river and I see, far ahead on the left-hand shore, something white, rigid, rectangular, out of place. Our boats drift gradually closer and we see the first billboard ever erected in Glen Canyon. Planted in rocks close to the water, the sign bears a message and it is meant for us.

ATTENTION
YOU ARE APPROACHING GLEN CANYON
DAM SITE.   ALL BOATS MUST LEAVE
RIVER AT KANE CREEK LANDING ONE
MILE AHEAD ON RIGHT.   ABSOLUTELY
NO BOATS ALLOWED IN CONSTRUCTION ZONE.
VIOLATORS WILL BE PROSECUTED.
U.S. BUREAU OF RECLAMATION

from Deborah: A Wilderness Narrative
by David Roberts

As Harvard undergraduates, David Roberts and Don Jensen in 1964 attempted an unclimbed ridge on Mount Deborah, a remote and formidable Alaskan peak. Everything was harder than they had imagined: The climbing was extremely difficult and dangerous, the weather was horrible, supplies ran low, their friendship frayed. Thwarted on Deborah, they tried to salvage the trip by crossing a glacier to bag some easier peaks. More difficulties ensued.

We woke comfortably late the next morning and dawdled over breakfast. When we looked out, we saw that a beautiful day had dawned on the Gillam Glacier; it was virtually windless, and a strong sun warmed us and dried the tent and sleeping bags. We were packed up by 12:30 p.m. As soon as we had put on our snowshoes and hefted our packs, we looked over all the glacier, which was blindingly white with sun. The snow looked perfectly smooth, but here and there we could see pale, diagonal hollows that suggested crevasses. Don led off. Only fifty yards from camp he stuck his foot into a crevasse. He yelled back to me, "Give me a belay." I put my axe in the snow and knelt, as he gingerly stepped across. Then we were both moving again.

Perhaps sixty yards farther, Don suddenly plunged into a crevasse and stuck, shoulder-deep. Immediately I thrust my axe into the snow and took in slack. Then I waited for Don to crawl out. I was not terribly worried: I had belayed a few crevasse plunges like this on McKinley, and Don had belayed me in one near the summit of our 11,780-foot peak. I even grew slightly impatient as Don seemed to thrash around helplessly.

But then he yelled, "I'm choking!" I was alarmed; I imagined the pack strap or the edge of the crevasse cutting off Don's wind.

I waited a few more seconds, but it was obvious Don couldn't get out. Perhaps rashly, I took off my pack, untied myself from the rope, tied the rope to my axe, and thrust it in again for an anchor. It didn't seem solid enough, so I quickly took our spare ice axe from my pack and tied the rope to that too. Then I walked quickly up to Don. I could not really see the crevasse at all, but I could see that Don was wedged pretty deeply in it. His hands clawed at the snow, but he said that his snowshoed feet were dangling loose. He was not actually choking, but he was in a cramped situation. The heavy pack seemed to be the obvious problem: its straps were constricting his arms and upper body. I reached out and carefully tried to pull the pack up and back. Don screamed, "Stop! It's the only thing holding me up!" His voice was full of panic. My pulling had made him slip a little farther into the crevasse so that all but his head was below the surface. Don sensed, as his feet waved in space, that the crevasse was huge. He warned me that I was too close to the edge. I backed up about five feet. For a moment I stood there, unable to do anything.

Suddenly Don plunged into the hole. The anchoring axes ripped loose and were dragged across the snow as Don fell within the crevasse. I grabbed the rope, but it was wet and whipped violently through my hands. I heard Don's yell, sharp and loud at first, trail away and fade into the frightening depth. All at once the rope stopped. About sixty feet of it had disappeared into the hole.

An excruciating silence surrounded me. With a kind of dread, I yelled Don's name. There was no answer. I yelled twice more, waiting in the silence, and then I heard a weak, thin shout: "I . . . I'm alive." The words were a great relief, but a scare as well: how badly was he hurt? I yelled, "Are you all right?" After another pause, his voice trickled back: "I think my right thumb is broken! I hit my head and it's bleeding and my right leg is hurt!"

I ran back to reanchor the rope. From my pack I got our snow shovel, dug a pit in the wet snow, tied one of the axes to the rope again, and buried the axe in the pit, stamping down the snow on top. Perhaps in a little while the snow would freeze, making the anchor solid. Through my mind flashed all kinds of thoughts, reminders of warnings before the expedition about the dangers of going with only two men, fears of never getting Don out, the thought of his blood spilling, a curse for the worthless radio.

When the snow had broken around him, Don's first impressions had been of bouncing against ice and of breaking through ice: he was not aware of screaming. He expected to feel the jerk of the rope at any moment, but it had not come. Then suddenly he had been falling fast, free; he somehow supposed that I was falling with him, and he instinctively anticipated death. Once before, in an ice-gully avalanche in New Hampshire, Don had fallen eight hundred feet—but he had been knocked out that time and had remembered only the beginning. This time he stayed conscious throughout the terrible fall.

At last there was a crushing stop, followed by piles of ice and snow falling on top of him in the darkness. Then it was still. The fear of being buried was foremost. He fought his way loose from the ice; some of the blocks were heavy, but he was able to move them and scramble out. He realized that, miraculously, he had landed on his back, wedged between two walls of ice, with the heavy pack under him to break his fall. His hands hurt, his leg felt sharply painful, and his head rang from a blow. He became aware of my shouting, the sound weak and distant, and yelled an answer upwards. As his eyes grew used to the dark, he could see where he was.

The inside of the crevasse was like a huge cavern. The only light came from the small hole, appallingly far above, and from a dim seam in the ceiling that ran in a straight line through the hole: the continuation of the thinly covered crevasse. The bottom was narrow, and the walls pressed in on him, but about thirty feet above him the space bulged to the incredible width of a large room. Above that, the walls narrowed again, arching over him like a gothic roof. Don began to glimpse huge chunks of ice, like the ones that had fallen and shattered with him on the way down, stuck to the ceiling like wasps' nests.

When I had got the anchor buried, I returned to the edge of the crevasse and shouted again to Don. With great presence of mind, he realized how possible it would be for me to fall in too, and shouted, "Dave! Be careful! Don't come near!"

His voice was so urgent that I immediately backed up to a distance of twenty feet from the little hole. But it was much harder to hear each other now. We were shouting at the tops of our lungs; had there been any wind, we could never have heard each other.

Fortunately, Don's bleeding had stopped. Struggling loose from the debris had reassured him that he wasn't seriously hurt; in fact, the thumb seemed only badly sprained instead of broken. Industriously, he got his crampons loose from his pack and put them on in place of his snowshoes. He still had his axe; chopping steps and wedging upward between the walls, he got to a place where he could see better. At once, he discovered the real nature of the subsurface glacier: corridors and chambers, at all depths, shot off in every direction. The whole thing was hideously hollow. At first Don had thought he might climb out; now he realized it would be impossible. But he had a furious desire to get out. He had put on his mittens but was getting cold anyway. Around him, on all sides, water was dripping and trickling: it was impossible to stay dry.

Don became obsessed with warning me away from the edge. If I fell in too, there would be no chance for either of us to get out. I stood still, outside; I could see only the small hole and had little idea in which direction the crevasse ran. Don, on the other hand, could tell which way it ran but had no idea where I was. With a confused series of shouts we managed to orient with respect to each other.

We both realized Don's pack had to come out first. We could not afford to leave it there. He could not wear it on the way out; I would have to haul it up. It would not be safe at all for Don to untie from the rope; I might never be able to feed the end back down to him. But it was the only rope we had. I racked my brain for an alternative. There was some nylon cord in the repair kit, which was in my pack. I ran back and got it out—it was not nearly long enough. Then I remembered our slings and stirrups, nylon loops and ladders we had brought for the technical climbing on Deborah. I dug them out, untied all the knots, found some spare boot laces, and finally tied everything together in one long strand. When it was done, I threw the end into the hole and lowered it. Don yelled that it reached.

He had taken his pack apart. Now he tied his sleeping bag onto the end of the line, and I pulled it up. But as the load neared the top, the line cut into the bad snow at the edge of the crevasse. Just below the top, the load caught under the edge. I jerked and flipped the line, to no avail. Don saw the problem but could think of no solution.

It became obvious that I had somehow to knock loose the rotten snow from the edge. But I didn't dare get near the hole, and Don would be standing beneath all the debris I might knock down. I could imagine only one way to do it.

I checked the rope's buried anchor again: it seemed solidly frozen in. I pulled and jerked on the rope, but it wouldn't budge. With one of the nylon slings I had left, I tied a loop around my waist, then tied a sliding knot to the main rope with it. When I pulled, the knot would hold tight; but when I let up, the knot would slide. Don, meanwhile, had found a relatively shielded place to hide. I inched toward the hole, carrying an axe and the shovel. If the edge broke, I should fall in only a few feet: then I might be able to scramble back out. I got no closer than I had to, but finally I was within two feet of the dangerous edge. The rope was stretched tight behind me. I squatted and reached out with my axe. The stuff broke loose easily and plunged noisily into the crevasse. As the hole enlarged, I slipped the knot tighter and waddled back a foot or so. Some of the snow had to be dug loose; some fell at the blow of the axe. It was awkward work but it was profitable. At last I had dug back to bare, hard ice. The rope would not cut into it. Leaning over, I peered into the awesome cavern. At first I could see only darkness; moments later, I glimpsed the faint outline of Don below, much more distant than I had even imagined.

I retreated from the hole and resumed hauling Don's sleeping bag; this time it came easily. One by one, I fished out the pieces of Don's load. With each, we grew more optimistic. The pack frame itself was hardest—its sharp corners caught on the ice; but at last I shook it loose and jerked it out.

Now there was only Don himself to get out. There was no possibility of hauling him. He would have to use the sliding knots on stirrups, which would support his feet, to climb the rope itself. I dangled some stirrups into the hole for him. He yelled when he got them. Then I retreated to the anchor, added my weight to the solidity of the frozen snow, and waited.

Slowly, painfully, Don ascended the rope. Everything was wet, so he had to tie an extra, tighter loop in the knots. This made them tend to jam, and he had to claw them loose several times. He was shivering now, soaking wet, and tired; in addition, his sprained fingers made handling the knots clumsy and painful. But from time to time he shouted his progress, and each time his voice sounded stronger and closer.

The weather was still perfect, but the sun had traveled far into the western part of the sky. A full four hours had elapsed since Don had fallen in. The peaks, as intriguing as ever, towered out of the smooth, apparently harmless surface of the glacier.

At last Don's head poked out of the hole. I cheered him on, but I was struck by the shaky tiredness I could see in his face. He crawled out of the hole and sat gasping on the edge. I came up to him, full of a strong impulse of loyalty, and put my arm around his shoulders, telling him he had done a good job. We ate a few bites of lunch—the minute the emergency was over, it seemed, our appetites returned.

We decided simply to backtrack the hundred yards to the camp site and pitch the tent again. I gathered the pieces of Don's pack and loaded it up. We staggered back to the fresh platform, very careful as we recrossed the first crevasse. In the subtle light of afternoon, looking back eastward toward the mountains we had been trying to reach, we could see faint blue line after faint blue line intersecting our potential path, parallel marks indicating a dozen farther crevasses like the one Don had fallen into.

I repitched the tent while Don rested. Inside, we looked at his injuries. He was badly bruised, especially on the right thigh; his head was bruised, with a small cut showing through blood-matted hair; half his fingers were sprained, the thumb badly. But it was a blessing there was no injury worse than that. Gradually, Don warmed up as his clothes dried out. We cooked dinner and ate, with a sense of peace and reprieve. Afterward, as it grew dark, we each took a sleeping pill; within a few minutes we were deep in slumber.

In the morning, when we awoke, we found the watch had stopped. We set it arbitrarily and started breakfast. Don was stiff and sore from his injuries, but the sleep had done him good. In my mind there was no question now but that we had to hike out to civilization. I was pretty sure Don would agree; even so, I was reluctant to bring up the matter. Finally I did. To my surprise, Don was set on going on.

We argued for more than an hour. I listed all the reasons for my decision. First, we were down to five days' food (perhaps seven, if we stretched it), and the hike out, we thought, would take about five days. If we went two days farther toward the airdrop basin, we might be forced into a seven-day hike out on only three days' food. And we had encountered only one of the obviously many hideous crevasses on this glacier. I argued that we had been very lucky to get Don out alive and that nothing would keep us from falling into another crevasse. The snow conditions, as we had found, were no better at night. Moreover, part of the hike-out route, to the south down the Susitna Glacier and River, was off our maps, since we hadn't anticipated it: who could say what obstacles we might run into? The radio was worthless, we were constantly hungry, and Don was bruised all over.

Despite all this, Don was determined to push on. He did not want it to be his accident and his injuries that stopped us. We could hike up the glacier on its southern edge, he argued, where the crevasses would be small enough to be safe. He was as eager as ever to climb the peaks ahead, and he was willing to go without food a few days, if need be, so long as we could definitely ascertain whether or not our airdrop was buried.

Don's stand put me in a strange situation. I was torn between admiration for and fear of him: at once he seemed terribly brave and terribly foolish. I remembered his insistence, early on the expedition, on going ahead the night he had been feeling dizzy and losing his balance. I wondered now if he wasn't expressing the same kind of overreaction: if so, it seemed a kind of madness. My inner voice, with its calculation of risks and complications, seemed to be speaking pure common sense, while Don's was fanatic. At the same time I could not help wondering if I was quitting on him, panicking prematurely. After all, before the accident I had been the one who was anxious for the trip to be over. I remembered the urge toward the safe south I had felt that dreary night, a week before, hauling loads across the West Fork Glacier. Perhaps I was "crumping"; perhaps I was not good enough for Don.

Our argument was uncommonly restrained, and for once we seemed objective and frank, as if a residue of respect for each other had settled out of the recent accident. I admitted that I was afraid of the glacier; Don granted that he didn't look forward to getting back to California. But I was possessed with a feeling that Don had gone slightly crazy, or that the crevasse fall had done something to him. I even fancied that the blow on his head had distorted his reason. At one point, as we were arguing about food, he said, "I'd almost rather starve here than go out now." Each symptom of fanaticism, like this one, made me look at Don in a more curious light. Yet I could not bear to attack his motives, as I had before, so soon after his ordeal in the crevasse. Don interpreted my reluctance to force the decision as a cowardice about taking the responsibility for it, which it may partly have been; all the same, I wanted the decision to be both of ours, so that we could not recriminate later.

Gradually, with heavy heart, Don saw that I was firmly set on hiking out. He could not be as staunchly in favor of going ahead—he naturally recoiled at the thought of falling into another crevasse. At last he gave in and agreed with me. I tried not to gloat over the relief I felt, and Don concealed his bitterness. We got dressed and packed up the camp in a marvelous spirit of reconciliation, a spell of grace over our life of antagonism. When we were ready to leave, we called it 2:00 p.m. With wistful glances back at the mountains we would never reach, still holding out their clean arms to us under a warm sun, we started trudging back up the pass to the Susitna Glacier.

My spirits, as always when the doubts and fears that had gnawed inside me were resolved, rose to exuberance. At first Don could not share my feeling, but his disappointment softened. On the climb to the pass we made up four or five verses, to the tune of "The Cowboy's Lament" ("As I walked out in the streets of Laredo"), about the crevasse accident. Instead of funeral roses, we pictured sacrificial piles of our favorite foods all over the glacier. One verse seemed particularly poignant:

It was once with my ice axe I used to go dashing,
Once in my crampons I used to go gay,
First over to Deborah, then down to the Gillam,
But I've broken my thumb, and I'm dying today.

At the top of the pass, we stopped to rest and gathered our last look to the north. Our marks on the snow eloquently told our story. Below us was a flat rectangular patch, where the tent had been pitched. From it a short track led straight east until it abruptly ended in a little hole. There were stray marks around the hole, but the snow lay untouched beyond.

We turned and headed down the Susitna Glacier. For a mile I led, here and there picking out our tracks from two days before, where they still showed under an inch of new snow. At the corner, the tracks turned west toward the pass we had crossed from the West Fork Glacier. We continued straight down the Susitna. We had only about a thousand feet of altitude still to drop before we would reach the nevé line, below which all the snow had melted, leaving bare ice, with the crevasses exposed and safe. But there were still quite a few crevasses to cross. I led for another half mile, through what seemed to be the worst of it. I was nervous about the hidden cracks and stuck my foot through a couple of snow bridges. However, the crevasses didn't look as big as the ones on the Gillam. Still, Don belayed me over any stretch that looked dubious, and we carefully skirted the obvious crevasses. It was slow going. As we seemed to enter a comparatively safe plateau, Don took the lead. The snow was soft and wet, scalloped with confusing sun cups. At about 4:00 p.m. he stopped to ponder an apparent pair of crevasses that nearly touched end to end. At the other end of the rope, I kept the line almost taut between us. Don started to cross what he thought was a little island of snow between the crevasses. Suddenly the island collapsed. I saw Don disappear and plunged the axe in immediately, crouching for the shock. A little pull came but it didn't budge me. I supposed Don had fallen about five feet and waited for him to scramble out. But there was no sign of him. Without getting up, I yelled, "Are you all right?" After a moment I heard his weak, distant voice, tinged with something like hysteria: "I've stopped bleeding, I think!"

With a gust of weariness and fear, I thought, "Not again!" I shouted,

"How far in are you?"

Don's voice came back, "Thirty feet . . . there's blood all over in here. I've got to get out of here quick!" He sounded beaten, as if a vital string in him had broken.

When the island had collapsed, he had fallen slightly backward into the crevasse. The nylon rope had stretched and cut back into the near bank, allowing Don to fall as far as thirty feet. But this time the walls were only three or four feet apart. He had smashed his face brutally on a shelf of ice halfway down.

Outside, I imagined having to go through all the emergency procedure of evacuation again and hurriedly got out our hauling line. But Don, seeing that he could climb out by himself, took off his pack and snowshoes and put on his crampons. This was difficult, wedged as he was between the close walls. The crevasse, at a lower altitude than the one on the Gillam, was dripping and running with water. With the energy of panic, Don forced his way up and out of the crevasse, chimneying between the icy walls. As soon as I realized what he was doing, I pulled the rope in to try to aid him. Within a few minutes he had reached the surface.

I hurried over to help him. He looked scared and exhausted, on the verge of tears. His lower face was covered with blood; I winced at the sight of it. He was in an agony of pain. I made him sit down and got some codeine from the medical kit, which he managed to swallow. We got the bleeding mostly stopped. It was fairly warm, but Don was shivering uncontrollably in his soaked clothes. I helped him take off his shirt and put my own jacket on him. Don apologized for getting blood on it; I told him not to be silly, but I felt suddenly defenseless before his pathetic concern.

I changed to crampons; as Don gave me a nominal belay with one hand, I slithered down into the crevasse to get his pack. The ice on which Don had cut his face was actually sharp to the touch. The wetness was oppressive, and as I got farther into the crevasse, the darkness added to a sense of claustrophobia. I found Don's pack at a place where the walls were not much wider than my body, and tied the rope to it. Don's blood was visible on both walls of the crevasse; I felt an irrational fear of getting it on me. There was a rank smell of stale air and blood in the gloomy, wet cavern. I felt the same panicky urge to get out that Don must have felt. Quickly I chimneyed back to the top of the crevasse; then I sat, wedged feet and back, between the walls of ice, and tried to pull the pack up in one piece. It took an extreme effort, but at last I got the thing up and shoved it over the edge onto the snow. Then I crawled out of the hole myself.

Don was obviously in some kind of shock. The bleeding had essentially stopped, but his chin was a raw, ragged mess, and he could hardly talk. Despite the down jacket, he was shivering miserably. We decided to set up camp on the spot. I pitched the tent and got the stove and food out of our packs. Still, it was 7:30 p.m. before we were settled inside. The codeine had helped numb the pain, but Don was still in great suffering. He had sprained all the fingers on his left hand, so that he could barely use them. The knuckles were scraped raw. At last he could get into his sleeping bag and begin to warm up. I started the stove, which helped warm the tent, and melted snow for hot water with which to bathe Don's cuts. I daubed at the lacerations on his face with some wet cotton, but it only made the blood flow again. With pained words, Don complained of cuts inside his mouth too. I tried to look, and saw gouges on the inside of his lower cheek. Blood was getting all over the tent.

Just when we seemed to be getting the cuts clean, Don closed his mouth, and we heard a soft hissing sound as he breathed. "What's that?" he asked. With alarm, I saw bubbles of air in the blood on his chin. Checking his mouth, I found that the cut went all the way through the cheek below the lip. We both felt nauseated, but I tried to cheer him up by telling him that such things happened all the time. Finally Don settled into his bag, where he could hold a piece of cotton to his mouth to clot the blood. I cooked dinner. When it was ready, Don tried to eat, at my insistence. He found that by cutting the food into small pieces he could feed them into his mouth, chew them delicately, and swallow. This was crucial, even if it took him an hour and a half to finish a meal.

He took another pill for the pain. He seemed numb and sluggish, but he was taking the injury bravely. We divided a sleeping pill between us, Don taking three quarters and I a quarter. We would have taken more, but we felt we had to get up in the early morning, just on the chance that it might be colder and safer then. Ideally, we would have rested there the next day. But we did not have enough food and would have to push on. We had only made about two miles that day, much less than we had planned. We were down to four days' food, and we still had a mile of this treacherous glacier to cross and forty-five miles of wilderness beyond.

As I lay awake in the gathering dark, I heard Don's breathing grow deep and even. It was a blessing that he was able to sleep. Since the moment he had apologized for getting blood on my jacket, I had felt an inarticulate impulse of love for him. He had been so courageous; already he was showing signs of taking this accident, too, in stride. But I could not sleep. I imagined the morning's trek through the last of the crevasses. They were fiendish; there was no way to find them or tell how big they were: the axe could not probe far enough. And there was no way to belay across them safely. Even now, as we camped between a pair of them, I sensed the others crowding around our tent like wolves in the night, waiting for us.

Pearyland

by Barry Lopez

The arctic wilderness is a spooky place in this short story by Barry Lopez (born 1945), whose nonfiction work Arctic Dreams *won a 1986 National Book Award. Lopez knows what to leave out of a story. He refuses to pretend that he knows more than he does; such honesty leaves him open to revelation.*

I apologize for not being able to tell you the whole of this story. It begins at the airport at Søndre Strømfjord in Greenland and it happened to a man named Edward Bowman. He'd just come down from Pearyland, by way of Qânâq and Upernavik, then Nûk. About a hundred of us were waiting around for planes, his out to Copenhagen, with Søndre Strømfjord socked in. He'd been at the airport for six days; I'd been there just a few, with four Inuit friends from Clyde Inlet, on Baffin Island. In those days—1972, just out of law school—I was working with Canadian Eskimos, helping to solidify a political confederation with Eskimos in Greenland.

We were all standing by, long hours at the airport. Some people went into town; but the notion that the weather might suddenly clear for just a few minutes and a plane take off kept most of us around, sleeping in the lounges, eating at the restaurant, using the phones.

Bowman was at work on a master's degree in wildlife biology at Iowa State, though by that time he may have already abandoned the program. His thesis, I remember well, had to do with something very new then—taphonomy. He was looking, specifically, at the way whitetail deer are taken apart by other animals after they die, how they're funneled back into the ecological community—how bone mineral, for example, goes back into the soil. How big animals disappear. Expanding the study a little brought him to Pearyland. He wanted to pursue in northern Greenland some threads of what happens when large animals die.

I should say here that Bowman wasn't eager to talk, that he didn't feel compelled to tell this story. He didn't avoid my questions, but he didn't volunteer much beyond his simple answers. His disinclination to talk was invariably polite, not unlike my Inuit friends', whose patience I must have tried all those years ago with my carefully framed questions and youthful confidence.

Did he go up there just to look at dead animals? I asked him. In a cold place where carcasses decay very slowly? Partly, he said. But when he'd read what little had been written about the place, he said, his interests became more complicated. Pearyland is an arctic oasis, a place where many animals live despite the high latitude—caribou, wolves, arctic hares, weasels, small animals like voles and lemmings, and many birds, including snowy owls. Bowman said he'd tried to get grants to support a summer of study. Of course, he was very curious about the saprophytic food web, the tiny creatures that break down organic matter; but, also, no one understood much about Pearyland. It was remote, with a harsh climate and very difficult and expensive to get to.

No funder was enthusiastic about Bowman's study, or his curiosity. (He told me at one point that part of his trouble in applying for grants was that, after working with the deer carcasses in Iowa, he just had an instinct to go, but no clear, scientific purpose, no definite project, which finally presented the larger institutions with insurmountable problems.) Eventually, he was able to cobble together several small grants and to enlist the support of a foundation in Denmark, which enabled him to buy food and a good tent. For his travel north to Qânâq he was going to depend on hitching rides on available aircraft. With the last of his funds he'd charter a flight out of Qânâq for Brønlund Fjord in early July and then arrange for a pickup in mid-September. All of which he did.

When we met, the only cash he had was his return ticket to

Copenhagen, but he was not worried. Somehow, he said, everything would work out.

Now, here is where it gets difficult for me. I've said Bowman, unlike most white men, seemed to have no strong need or urge to tell his story. And I couldn't force myself to probe very deeply, for reasons you'll see. So there could be—probably are—crucial elements here that were never revealed to me. It's strange to think about with a story like this, but you'll be just as I was—on your own. I can't help it.

What Bowman found at Brønlund Fjord in Pearyland was the land of the dead. The land of dead animals.

When he arrived, Bowman made a camp and started taking long walks, six- or seven-mile loops, east and west along the fjord and north into the flat hills, into the willow draws. The fjord stood to the south— open water at 82° North in July, which surprised him; but that is the nature of arctic oases. Summer comes earlier there than it does farther south, and it lingers a bit longer. In winter it's relatively warmer. Some days, Bowman said, he wore only a T-shirt.

Bowman's treks brought him within sight of many animals in the first few days, but he wasn't able to get near them. And, a little to his wonder, not once on these long walks did he come upon an animal carcass, not even a piece of weathered bone.

The only thing he worried about, he told me, was polar bears. He saw seals regularly in the fjord, so he expected bears would turn up; but he saw no tracks or scat, not even old sign. He wasn't afraid of being attacked so much as of having a bear break into his food. He had no radio, so he ran the risk of starving before the plane came back. For this reason alone, he said, he had agreed to take a gun, which the Danish government insisted he carry. How he learned where he was, that he'd camped in the land of the dead, was that one morning he went for the rifle and it wasn't there.

Of course, no one was around, so its loss made no sense to him. He looked underneath everything in his camp, thinking, absentminded, he might have left it at his defecation pit, or taken it down to the shore of the fjord. Or that in his sleep he'd gotten up and taken the gun somewhere and thrown it away. He said he entertained this last possibility because he was never comfortable with the idea of having the gun; and who could know, he said to me, what the dreaming mind really wanted done?

The day after he missed the gun he saw a few caribou close by, less than a half mile away. He was eating breakfast, sitting on an equipment crate, watching the wind ripple the surface of the fjord and tracing with his eye a pattern in the purple flowers of a clump of saxifrage. The animals' hard stare caused him to turn around. He gazed back at them. Four animals, all motionless. It struck him then that in that first week or so he hadn't seen any caribou or muskoxen grazing or browsing.

He reached for his binoculars, but in that same moment the caribou dropped off behind a hill. He saw no other animals the rest of the day, but the following morning the caribou were back in the same place. This time, he sat very still for a long while. Eventually the caribou walked down to where he was, only about twenty yards away.

"Where is your place?"

Bowman said when he heard these words he thought it was the animals that had made them, but when he turned around he saw, far off near the edge of the water, a man, an Inuk.

"What place are you from?"

It was hard for Bowman to understand that this man's voice was coming to him clearly even though he was standing far away. He didn't know what to answer. He didn't think the man would know about Indiana, so he said he was from very, very far away, to the west and south.

"What do you want here?"

Bowman told me he wished to answer this question in such a way that he would not offend the man because he had a strong feeling he might be hindered in his study here (which, he pointed out again, was nearly aimless). Or possibly harmed.

"I want to listen," he said finally.

"Do you hear the wind? Meltwater trickling down to the fjord? The arctic poppies turning on their stalks in the summer sunshine?"

"Yes. I listen to all this."

"Do you hear the songs of my brothers and sisters?" asked the man by the fjord.

"I'm not sure," answered Bowman. "I don't think I've heard any singing. Perhaps if I listened better."

At that moment, Bowman turned quickly to look at the caribou. They'd come much closer. Swinging still further around, he caught sight of two wolverine, that odd lope of theirs, as they came bounding toward him from the west. Then the Inuk was right next to him, sitting on another crate, looking out over the waters of the fjord. Bowman couldn't make out his face from the side.

"I'm the caretaker here," the man said. Bowman could see now that he was about forty, fifty. "What do you want? What is 'Indiana'?" he asked.

Bowman, startled, described where Indiana was. Then he tried to explain what he did as a biologist, and that he was specifically interested in what happened to animals after they died. After that, he told me, he shouldn't have said anything more, but he went on until he ran out of things to say.

"The dead come here," the man said when Bowman was finished talking. He stood up. Bowman saw he was short, only five feet four inches or so, his short-fingered hands massive, the veins prominent, his forehead receding into a line of close-cropped, raven black hair. "You've come to the right place," he said. Then he walked away. Although he walked slowly, soon he was very far away.

The caribou were gone. The wolverine were still there, watching him, but after a while they, too, disappeared.

Bowman did not see the man again for four or five days, and then he just saw him at a great distance, walking along the low edge of the sky.

One morning Bowman crawled out of his tent and saw an arctic fox resting on its haunches, looking at seals in the fjord. When he made a sound—his sock scraping on tundra gravel—the fox turned around quickly, surprised, and ran away. As he sprinted off, Bowman saw he had no shadow.

Bowman tried to arrange each day according to the same schedule. When he awoke, he took his binoculars and studied the tundra in every direction, writing down whatever he saw—arctic hare, muskoxen, snow geese. He ate, then took a lunch and his pack and went for a long walk. He made lists of all the flowers, the tracks he came upon, the animals he saw; and he fought against a feeling that he was not accomplishing anything. Every day he wrote down the temperature and he estimated the speed and direction of the wind and he made notes about the kind of clouds he saw in the sky. Altostratus. Cumulonimbus.

One day the man came back. "Why aren't you trying to hunt?" he asked. "How come you don't try?"

"When I was a young man I hunted with my father in Indiana. I don't do that now." Bowman told me he wanted to be very careful what he said. "I don't hunt here, in this place, because I brought food with me. Besides, I don't know these animals. I have no relations with them. I wouldn't know how to hunt them."

"No hunting here, anyway."

"I know this is your country," Bowman said cautiously, "but why are you here?"

"Caretaker. Until these animal spirits get bodies and are ready to go back, a human being must be here, to make sure they aren't hungry. If the animals want something—if they want to hear a song, I learn it. I sing it. Whatever they want, I do that. That's my work."

"Have you been here a long time?"

"Yes. Long time. Soon, someone else will come. A long time ago, before Indiana, there was more work. Many caretakers. Now, fewer."

"What do these animals eat?"

"Eating—it's not necessary." After a moment he said, "They are feeding on the sunlight."

"When they are ready, where do they go?"

"All everywhere. They go home. They go back where they're from. But too many, now, they don't come here. They are just killed, you know. No prayer." He made a motion with his fist toward the ground as though he were swinging a hammer. "They can't get back there then. Not that way."

"Which ones come back?"

The man regarded Bowman for a long moment. "Only when that gift is completed. Only when the hunter prays. That's the only way for the animal's spirit to get back here."

"Do they come here to rest?"

The man looked at Bowman strangely, as if Bowman were mocking him with ignorant questions. "They get their bodies here."

"But only if they are able to give their lives away in a certain manner, and if the hunter then says a prayer?"

"Yes."

After a while the man said, "Many religions have no animals. Harder for animals now. They're still trying."

Bowman did not know what to say.

"Very difficult, now," said the man.

"What do you hear in this place?" the Inuk asked abruptly. "Do you hear their songs? Do you hear them crying out?"

"In my sleep," Bowman ventured. "Or perhaps when I am awake but believe I'm sleeping. I hear a sound like a river going over a wall, or wind blowing hard in the crown of a forest. Sometimes I hear heartbeats, many heartbeats overlapping, like caribou hooves."

"The souls of the animals calling out for bodies, bodies calling out for their souls."

"The bodies and the souls, searching."

"Yes. They come together, falling in love again like that. They go back, have children. Then one day someone is hungry, someone who loves his family, who behaves that way. Wolf, human being—the same. That's how everything works."

"Is there another place," asked Bowman, "where the animal souls go if they are just killed?"

The Inuk looked at Bowman as if he weren't there and got up and walked away.

He didn't come back and Bowman didn't see him again.

The animals around Bowman's camp grew less shy. They began to move past him as though he were growing in the ground or part of the sky. The caribou all walked in the same, floating way, some pairs of eyes gleaming, some opaque, looking at the plants and lichens, at the clouds, and staring at rivulets of water moving across the tundra.

Bowman saw his gun one morning, leaning against a crate.

During his last days, he said, he tried to sketch the land. I saw the drawings—all pastels, watercolors, with some small, brilliant patches of red, purple, and yellow: flowers, dwarf willow, bearberry. The land was immense. It seemed to run up against the horizon like a wave. And yet it appeared weightless, as if it could have been canted sideways by air soft as birds breathing.

The pilot came and took him out to Qânâq, nearly five hundred miles. Two days later he began traveling south. Now, with the rest of us, he was waiting for the weather to clear.

Bowman told me this story over three days. He said it only a little at a time, as though he were not certain of it or me. I kept trying to get him to come back to it, but I wasn't insistent, not rude. I had many questions. Did the animals make sounds when their feet touched the ground? Did he see airplanes flying over? Was he afraid ever? What was the Inuk wearing?

The hardest question, for I had no other reason than my own inquisitiveness to pursue him, was asking whether he had an address where I might reach him. He gave me an address in Ames, where the university is, but by the time I wrote he'd moved away; and like so many young people—he was twenty-three, twenty-four—he did not leave a forwarding address.

Sometimes when I am in a library I look up his name. But as far as I know he never wrote anything about this, or anything else.

The last day of September the fog lifted suddenly, as though it had to go elsewhere. Bowman's plane, which had been there on the ground for eight days, left for Copenhagen and an hour later I flew with my friends back to Frobisher Bay, on Baffin Island.

from Young Men & Fire
by Norman Maclean

A River Runs Through It and Other Stories made Norman Maclean (1902–1990) famous at age 74. He died before he could finish his second book, Young Men & Fire. That work is a record of the Mann Gulch fire, which in 1949 killed 13 young smoke jumpers. It also documents Maclean's struggle to come to terms with those men's experience. This passage finds the smoke jumpers running uphill from a wall of flame.

Dodge had come out of the timber ahead of his crew, with the fire just behind. He saw that in front was high dry grass that would burn very fast, saw for the first time the top of the ridge at what he judged to be about two hundred yards above, put two and two together and decided that he and his crew couldn't make the two hundred yards, and almost instantly invented what was to become known as the "escape fire" by lighting a patch of bunch grass with a gofer match. In so doing, he started an argument that would remain hot long after the fire.

At the time it probably made no sense to anyone but Dodge to light a fire right in front of the main fire. It couldn't act as a backfire; there wasn't any time to run a fire-line along its upgulch edge to prevent it from being just an advance arm of the main fire. Uncontrolled, instead of being a backfire it might act as a spot fire on its way upgulch and bring fire from behind that much closer and sooner to the crew.

Dodge was starting to light a second fire with a second match when he looked up and saw that his first fire had already burned one hundred square feet of grass up the slope. "This way," he kept calling to his crew behind. "This way." Many of the crew, as they came in sight of him, must have asked themselves, What's this dumb bastard doing? The smoke lifted twice so that everyone had a good chance to ask the question.

The crew must have been stretched nearly all the way from the edge of the timber to the center of the grassy clearing ahead, where Dodge was lighting his fire. Rumsey and Sallee say that the men did not panic, but by now all began to fear death and were in a race with it. The line had already assumed that erratic spread customary in a race where everything is at stake. When it comes to racing with death, all men are not created equal.

At the edge of the timber the crew for the first time could have seen to the head of the gulch where the fire, having moved up the south side of the gulch, was now circling. From the open clearing they also could see partway toward the bottom of the gulch, where it was presumably rocks that were exploding in smoke. They didn't have to look behind— they could feel the heat going to their lungs straight through their backs. From the edge of the clearing they could also see the top of the ridge for the first time. It wasn't one and a half miles away; to them it seemed only two hundred yards or so away. Why was this son of a bitch stopping to light another fire?

For the first time they could also see a reef twelve to twenty feet high running parallel to the top of the ridge and thirty yards or so below it. This piece of ancient ocean bottom keeps the top of the ridge from eroding, as the rock lid on the top of a butte on the plains keeps the butte from eroding into plains. But no one was thinking of geology or probably even of whether it would be hard to climb over, through, or around. At this moment, its only significance was that it seemed about two hundred yards away.

When the line reached its greatest extension, Rumsey and Sallee were at the head of it—they were the first to reach Dodge and his fire. Diettert was just behind them, and perhaps Hellman, although these two stand there separately forever and ask the same question, What did Rumsey and Sallee do right that we did wrong? For one thing, they stuck together; Diettert and Hellman went their separate ways.

The smoke will never roll away and leave a clear picture of the head of the line reaching Dodge and his burned bunch grass. Dodge later pictured the crew as strung out about 150 feet with at least eight men close enough together and close enough to him so that he could try to explain to them—but without stopping them—that they could not survive unless they got into his grass fire. At the Review, he made very clear that he believed there was not enough time left for them to make it to the top of the hill, and events came close to supporting his belief. In the roar and smoke he kept "hollering" at them—he was sure that at least those closest to him heard him and that those behind understood him from his actions. In smoke that swirled and made sounds, there was a pause, then somebody said, "To hell with that, I'm getting out of here," and a line of them followed the voice.

The line all headed in the same direction, but in the smoke Dodge could not see whether any of them looked back at him. He estimated that the main fire would hit them in thirty seconds.

In the smoke and roar Rumsey and Sallee saw a considerably different arrangement of characters and events from Dodge's. Indeed, even the roommates differ from each other. Both agree with Dodge, however, that the line was stretched out, with a group at the head close to Dodge, then a gap, and then the rest scattered over a distance that neither could estimate exactly but guessed to be nearly a hundred yards. In fact, when in the summer of 1978 Rumsey, Sallee, Laird Robinson, and I spent a day together in Mann Gulch, the two survivors told Laird and me they were now sure some of the crew had fallen so far behind that they were never close enough to Dodge to hear whatever he was saying. The implication of Dodge's account is that they all passed him by, but Rumsey and Sallee believed that some of them hadn't. As to the head of the column, Sallee limits it to three—himself and Rumsey plus Diettert, who was also a pal and had been working on the same project with Rumsey before the two of them were called to the fire. To these three, Rumsey adds Hellman, the second-in-command, and indeed suggests, with Dodge agreeing, that it was Hellman who said, "To hell with that, I'm getting out of here," and so furnishes the basis for the charge that Hellman was doubly guilty of insubordination by being near the head of the line after Dodge had ordered him to the rear and by encouraging the crew to ignore Dodge's order to remain with him and enter his fire. Rumsey's testimony, however, will never settle Hellman's place in the line and hence his role in the tragedy, for Sallee was positive and still is that Hellman was at the head of the line when Dodge ordered the men to drop their tools but that he then returned to the tail of it, repeating Dodge's order and remaining there to enforce it. So direct testimony leaves us with opposite opinions of Hellman's closing acts as second-in-command of Smokejumpers on their most tragic mission. Either he countermanded his superior and contributed to the tragedy or, according to Sallee, being the ideal second-in-command, he returned to the rear to see that all the crew carried out the foreman's orders and to keep their line intact.

An outline of the events that were immediately to come probably would not agree exactly with the testimony of any one of the survivors or make a composite of their testimony, as might be expected, but would be more like what follows, and even what follows will leave some of the most tragic events in mystery and litigation.

Rumsey, Sallee, and Diettert left Dodge as one group and took the same route to the reef; two of them survived. Some of the crew never got as high up the slope as Dodge's fire. Hellman reached the top of the ridge by another route and did not survive. The rest scattered over the hillside upgulch from the route taken by the first three, and none of those who scattered reached the top. As Sallee said the summer we were together in Mann Gulch, "No one could live who left Dodge even seconds after we did."

In fact, the testimony makes clear that Diettert, Rumsey, and Sallee scarcely stopped to listen to Dodge. As Rumsey says, "I was thinking only of my hide." He and Diettert turned and made for the top of the ridge. Sallee paused for only a moment, because he soon caught up with Diettert and Rumsey, and actually was the first to work his way through the opening in the reef above. When asked at the Review whether others of the crew were piling up behind while he stood watching Dodge light his fire, Sallee said, "I didn't notice, but I don't believe there were. Rumsey and Diettert went ahead—went on—I just hesitated for a minute and went on too."

In the roar of the main fire that was now only thirty seconds behind them they may not even have heard Dodge, and, if they did hear words, they couldn't have made out their meaning. Rumsey says, "I did not hear him say anything. There was a terrible roar from the main fire. Couldn't hear much."

It probably wasn't just the roar from without that precluded hearing. It was also the voice from inside Mount Sinai: "I kept thinking the ridge—if I can make it. On the ridge I will be safe. I went up the right-hand side of Dodge's fire."

Although Sallee stopped a moment for clarification, he also misunderstood Dodge's actions. "I understood that he wanted us to follow his fire up alongside and maybe that his fire would slow the other fire down." Like Rumsey, Sallee interpreted Dodge's fire as a buffer fire, set to burn straight up for the top and be a barrier between them and the main fire. And like Rumsey, Sallee followed the right edge of Dodge's fire to keep it between them and the fire that was coming up the gulch.

The question of how Hellman reached the top of the ridge after leaving Dodge at his fire cannot be answered with certainty. What is known is that he made his way from where Dodge lit his fire to the top of the ridge alone, that he was badly burned, that he joined up with Rumsey and Sallee after the main fire had passed, that he told Rumsey he had been burned at the top of the ridge, and that he died the next day in a hospital in Helena. The most convincing guess about how he reached the top of the ridge is Sallee's. When he and I stood on the ridge in the summer of 1978, I asked him about Hellman's route to the top and he said that naturally he had thought about it many times and was convinced there was only one explanation: while he, Rumsey, and Diettert followed the upgulch (right) side of Dodge's fire and so for important seconds at least used it as a buffer protecting them from the main fire coming upgulch, Hellman must have followed the opposite, or downgulch, side of Dodge's fire and so had no protection from the main fire, which caught him just before he could get over the ridge.

Sallee talks so often about everything happening in a matter of seconds after he and Rumsey left Dodge's fire that at first it seems just a manner of speaking. But if you combine the known facts with your imagination and are a mountain climber and try to accompany Rumsey and Sallee to the top, you will know that to have lived you had to be young and tough and lucky.

And young and tough they were. In all weather Sallee had walked four country miles each way to school, and a lot of those eight miles he ran. He and Rumsey had been on tough projects all summer. They gave it everything they had, and everything was more, they said, than ever before or after.

As they approached the reef, its significance changed for the worse. They saw that the top of the ridge was beyond the reef, and unless they could find an opening in it, it would be the barrier keeping them from reaching the top. They might die in its detritus. The smoke lifted only twice, but they saw a crevice and steered by it even after it disappeared again. "There was an opening between large rocks, and I had my eye on that and I did not look either way," Sallee says.

Halfway up, the heat on Rumsey's back was so intense he forgot about Dodge's buffer fire, if that is what it was, and, having spotted the opening, headed straight for it. It was not only upslope but slightly upgulch and to the right. In the smoke nothing was important but this opening, which was like magnetic north—they could steer toward it when they couldn't see it. Rumsey was in the center. Sallee was even with him on his left; Diettert was just a few steps behind on his right.

The world compressed to a slit in the rocks. Rumsey and Sallee saw neither right nor left. When asked at the Review whether they saw pincers of fire closing in on them from the sides, they said no; they saw only straight ahead. Ahead they saw; behind they felt; they shut out the sides.

To them the reef was another one of those things—perhaps the final one—that kept coming out of smoke to leave no place to run from death. They can remember feeling sorry for themselves because they were so young. They also tried not to think of anything they had done wrong for fear it might appear in the flames. They thought God might have made the opening and might take it away again. Besides, the opening might be a trap for the sins of youth to venture into.

Beyond the opening and between it and the top of the ridge they could see no flames but there was dense smoke. Beyond the opening in the smoke there could be fire—beyond, there could be more reefs, reefs without openings. It could be that beyond the opening was the end of God and the end of youth. Maybe that's what Diettert thought.

Rumsey and Sallee felt they were about to jump through a door in a plane and so had to steady themselves and believe something was out there that would hold them up. It was as if there were a tap on the leg. Sallee was in the lead and was first through the crevice. It was cooler, and he believed his faith had been confirmed. He stopped to lower the temperature in his back and lungs. Rumsey was through next. As a Methodist, he believed most deeply in what he had been first taught. Early he had been taught that in a time of crisis the top of a hill is safest. It was still some distance to the top, and he never stopped till he got there.

Diettert stopped just short of the opening. On his birthday, not long after his birthday dinner and just short of the top of the hill, he silently rejected the opening in the reef, turned, and went upgulch parallel to the base of the reef, where for some distance there is no other opening. No one with him, neither Rumsey nor Sallee, saw him do this—it is known by where his body was found. Diettert, the studious one, had seen something in the opening he did not like, had rejected it, and had gone looking for something he did not find. It is sometimes hard to understand fine students. Be sure, though, he had a theory, as fine students nearly always have.

While Sallee was cooling his lungs, he looked down and back at Dodge and the crew and for the first time realized why Dodge had lit his fire.

> I saw Dodge jump over the burning edge of the fire he had set and saw him waving his arms and motioning for the other boys to follow him. At that instant I could see what I believe was all the balance of the crew. They were within twenty to fifty feet of Dodge and just outside the burning edge of the fire Dodge had set. The last I recall seeing the group of boys, they were angling up the slope in the unburned grass and fairly close to the burning edge of the fire Dodge had set. . . .
>
> When Dodge first set the fire I did not understand that he wanted us boys to wait a few seconds and then get inside the burned-out grass area for protection from the main fire.

Dodge's description of his fire is mostly from inside it.

> After walking around to the north side of the fire I started as
> an avenue of escape, I heard someone comment with these
> words, "To hell with that, I'm getting out of here!" and for all
> my hollering, I could not direct anyone into the burned area.
> I then walked through the flames toward the head of the fire
> into the inside and continued to holler at everyone who went
> by, but all failed to heed my instructions; and within seconds
> after the last man had passed, the main fire hit the area I was
> in.

When asked at the Review if any of the crew had looked his way as they
went by, he said no, "They didn't seem to pay any attention. That is the
part I didn't understand. They seemed to have something on their
minds—all headed in one direction."

He wet his handkerchief from his canteen, put it over his mouth, and
lay face down on the ground. Whether he knew it or not, there is
usually some oxygen within fifteen inches of the ground, but even if he
knew it, he needed a lot of luck besides oxygen to have lived, although
Rumsey and Sallee were to say later that the whole crew would probably
have survived if they had understood and followed Dodge's
instructions.

It is doubtful, though, that the crew had the training and composure
to interpret Dodge's instructions even if some of his words reached
them over the roar. The close questioning Rumsey and Sallee received
later at the Review revealed that their training in how to meet fire
emergencies consisted of a small handful of instructions, four to be
exact and only one of which had any bearing on their present
emergency. The first was to backfire if they had time and the right
situation, but they had neither. The second was to get to the top of the
ridge where the fuel is usually thinner, where there are usually stretches
of rock and shale, and where the winds usually meet and fluctuate. This
is the one they tried, and it worked with only seconds to spare. The
third instruction was designed to govern an emergency in which neither
time nor situation permits backfiring or reaching a bare ridgetop. When

it's that tough, the best you can do is turn into the fire and try to work through it, hoping to piece together burned-out stretches. The fourth and final warning was to remember that, whatever you do, you must not allow the fire to pick the spot where it hits you. The chances are it will hit you where it is burning fiercest and fastest. According to Dodge's later testimony, the fire about to hit them had a solid front 250 to 300 feet deep—no one works through that deep a front and lives.

Even if the crew's training had included a section on Dodge's escape fire, it is not certain that the crew would have listened to Dodge, would have entered the fire and buried their faces in the ashes. When asked at the Review if he would have gone into Dodge's fire had he received previous instruction about it, Rumsey replied, "I think that if I had seen it on a blackboard and seen it done and had it explained so that I understood it I think I surely would have gone in—but of course you never can tell for sure."

Dodge survived, and Rumsey and Sallee survived. Their means of survival differed. Rumsey and Sallee went for the top and relied on the soul and a fixation from basic training. The soul in a situation like this is mostly being young, in tune with time, and having good legs, an inflexible destination, and no paralyzing questions about what lies beyond the opening. When asked whether he had "ever been instructed in setting an escape fire," Dodge replied, "Not that I know of. It just seemed the logical thing to do." Being logical meant building one fire in front of another, lying down in its ashes, and breathing close to the ground on a slight elevation. He relied on logic of a kind and the others on time reduced to seconds. But no matter where you put your trust, at a time like this you have to be lucky.

The accounts that come down to us of the flight of the crew up the hillside nearly all conclude at this point, creating with detail only the happenings of those who survived, if only for a day, as Hellman did, or, like Diettert, at least reached the reef. Counting these two, only five are usually present in the story that goes on up the ridge. Only a sentence or two is given to those who, when last seen by Dodge, were all going in one direction and when seen finally by Sallee were angling through openings in the smoke below him as he looked down from the top of the ridge. Although they are the missing persons in this story, they are also its tragic victims. There is a simple aspect of historiography, of course, to explain why, after last seen by the living, they pass silently out of the story and their own tragedy until their tragedy is over and they are found as bodies: no one who lived saw their sufferings. The historian, for a variety of reasons, can limit his account to firsthand witnesses, although a shortage of firsthand witnesses probably does not explain completely why contemporary accounts of the Mann Gulch fire avert their eyes from the tragedy. If a storyteller thinks enough of storytelling to regard it as a calling, unlike a historian he cannot turn from the sufferings of his characters. A storyteller, unlike a historian, must follow compassion wherever it leads him. He must be able to accompany his characters, even into smoke and fire, and bear witness to what they thought and felt even when they themselves no longer knew. This story of the Mann Gulch fire will not end until it feels able to walk the final distance to the crosses with those who for the time being are blotted out by smoke. They were young and did not leave much behind them and need someone to remember them.

The foreman, Dodge, also must be remembered, as well as his crew, and it is again the storyteller's special obligation to see that he is. History will determine the direction or directions in which the storyteller must look for his enduring memories, and history says Dodge must live or die in his escape fire. Ordinary history says he lived by lying in the ashes of his escape fire until the main fire swept over him and cooled enough to let him stand up and brush himself off. The controversial history that was soon to follow and has lasted ever since charges that Dodge's escape fire, set in front of the main fire, was the fire that actually burned some of the crew and cut off others from escaping. Historical questions the storyteller must face, although in a place of his own choosing, but his most immediate question as he faces new material is always, Will anything strange or wonderful happen here? The rights and wrongs come later and likewise the scientific know-how.

The most strange and wonderful thing on the hillside as the escape fire swept up it, shutting it out of sight in smoke and heat, is that a spot of it remained cool. The one cool spot was inside Dodge. It was the "characteristic in him" that Rumsey had referred to when Dodge returned from the head of the fire with Harrison and muttered something about a death trap. It was the "characteristic" he was best known by, the part of him that always kept cool and aloof and believed on principle in thinking to itself and keeping its thoughts to itself because thinking out loud only got him into trouble. It was this characteristic in him that had started him to lead the crew downgulch to safety, then didn't like what it saw ahead and turned the crew back upgulch trying to outrun the fire without his ever explaining his thoughts to the crew. His running but not his thinking stopped when he saw the top of the ridge, for he immediately thought his crew could not make the top and so he immediately set his escape fire. When he tried to explain it, it was too late—no one understood him; except for himself, they passed it by. Except to him, whom it saved, his escape fire has only one kind of value—the value of a thought of a fire foreman in time of emergency judged purely as thought. The immediate answer to the storyteller's question about the escape fire is yes, it was strange and wonderful that, in this moment of time when only a moment was left, Dodge's head worked.

To see how Dodge's life as a woodsman shaped his thoughts in an emergency and to follow his thoughts closely, one more tick must be added to the tock of his makeup. In an emergency he thought with his hands. He had an unusual mechanical skill that helped him think, that at least structured his thoughts. It was a woodsman's mechanical skill— he liked to work with rifles, fix equipment, build lean-to's or log cabins. He wasn't fancy, he was handy. And in fact that spring he had been excused from training with the Smokejumpers so that he could be maintenance man for the whole Smokejumper base—no doubt part of the cause of the tragedy he was about to face with a crew only three of whom he knew. The foreman, then, was facing this tragic emergency alone, withdrawn as he often was into his own thoughts, which were the thoughts men and women have who are wired together in such a way that their brains can't start moving without their hands moving at the same time.

The present question, then, in its purest form is, How many brains, how much guts, did it take in those fiery seconds to conceive of starting another fire and lying down in it? In its maximum form, the question would be, Did Dodge actually make an invention when 250 or 300 feet of solid flames were about to catch up to him?

Two of the Forest Service's greatest fire experts, W. R. ("Bud") Moore and Edward G. Heilman, Moore's successor as director of fire control and aviation management for the Forest Service's Region One, have told me they never heard of this kind of escape fire before Dodge's use of it, and their experience corresponds to my own, which, though limited to summers when I was young, goes back to 1918. Rumsey and Sallee say under oath that in 1949 nothing like it had been mentioned in their training course, and, as Rumsey adds, even if it had been explained to him and he had seen it work, it seemed crazy enough so that he wasn't sure he would have stepped into it if it had been for real.

A lot of questions about the woods can't be answered by staying all the time in the woods, and it also works the other way—a lot of deep inner questions get no answer unless you go for a walk in the woods. My colleague at the University of Chicago Robert Ferguson pointed out to me that James Fenimore Cooper had something like Dodge's fire burning in his favorite of his own novels, *The Prairie*, first published in 1827. Cooper's eastern readers are held in suspense throughout most of chapter 13 by the approach of a great prairie fire from which the old trapper rescues his party at the last moment by lighting a fire in advance of the main one and having it ready for human occupancy by the time the sheet of flames arrives. He stepped his party into the burned-off grass and moved them from side to side as the main fire struck.

Cooper's readers clearly were not expected to know of this device or there would be no justification for the prolonged suspense which the chapter is supposed to create, but the escape fire on the prairie is no literary invention.

Mavis Loscheider of the Department of Anthropology at the University of Missouri, an outstanding authority on the life of the Plains Indians, sent me evidence showing that something like this kind of fire was traditionally set by Plains Indians to escape from grass fires and that pioneers on the plains picked up the invention from the Indians.

In his second volume of *The American Fur Trade of the Far West*, Hiram

M. Chittenden describes how the prairie escape fire worked in the early 1800s:

> The usual method of avoiding the danger of these [prairie] fires was to start one in the immediate vicinity of the person or company in peril. This fire, at first small and harmless, would soon burn over an area large enough to form a safe asylum and when the sweeping cohorts of flame came bearing down upon the apparently doomed company, the mighty line would part as if by prearrangement and pass harmlessly by on either side.

• • •

There are still good grounds, however, to believe Dodge "invented" his escape fire. Why doubt his word before the Board of Review that he had never heard of such a thing before? Even if it was known to mountain men, it could not have been much used in timbered country, if for no other reason than that it would seldom work there. The heat of a timber fire is too intense, and the fire is too slow and prolonged and consumes too much oxygen to permit walking around in it. Chances are Dodge's fire wouldn't have worked (wouldn't even have been thought of) if Dodge had been caught on the other, timbered side of Mann Gulch where the fire started. Moreover, Dodge's escape fire differs in important ways from the escape fires used by Indians and pioneers. Dodge's fire was started so close to the main fire that it had no chance to burn a large "asylum" in which the refugee could duck and dodge the main fire. Not being able to duck and dodge and remain alive, Dodge lay down in the ashes, where the heat was least intense and where he was close enough to the ground to find some oxygen.

Of course, Dodge had a Smokejumper's knowledge that if you can't reach the top of the hill you should turn and try to work back through burned-out areas in the front of a fire. But with the flames of the fire front solid and a hundred yards deep he had to invent the notion that he could burn a hole in the fire. Perhaps, though, his biggest invention was not to burn a hole in the fire but to lie down in it. Perhaps all he could patent about his invention was the courage to lie down in his fire. Like a lot of inventions, it could be crazy and consume the inventor. His invention, taking as much guts as logic, suffered the immediate fate of many other inventions—it was thought to be crazy by those who first saw it. Somebody said, "To hell with that," and they kept going, most of them to their deaths.

Dodge later told Earl Cooley that, when the fire went over him, he was lifted off the ground two or three times.

"This lasted approximately five minutes," he concludes in his testimony, and you and I are left to guess what the "this" was like. His watch said 6:10 when he sat up. By that time, death had come to Mann Gulch.

Dodge himself was allowed to live a little over five years more, what then was thought to be about the maximum time one who had Hodgkin's disease could live. However, he would never jump again. His wife knew when he entered the hospital for the last time that he knew it was for the last time. Like many woodsmen, he always carried a jackknife with him in his pants pocket, always. She told me that when he entered the hospital for the last time he left his jackknife home on his bedroom table, so he and she knew.

When Rumsey and Sallee reached the crevice, the main fire had reached the bottom of Dodge's escape fire. They were ahead of the flames, or at least thought they were, but couldn't be sure because of the rolling and unrevealing smoke. Rumsey fell into what he thought was a juniper bush and would not have bothered to get up if Sallee hadn't stopped and coldly looked at him. In the summer of 1978, when Rumsey and I were where he thought the juniper bush must have been, he said to me, "I guess I would be dead if he hadn't stopped. Funny thing, though, he never said a word to me. He just stood there until I said it to myself, but I don't think he said anything. He made me say it." They ran upgulch on the top of the ridge for a hundred yards or so and staggered down the slope on the other side of the ridge. There they stumbled onto a rock slide "several hundred feet long and perhaps seventy-five feet wide." The dimensions hardly seem large enough, but there weren't any other rock slides around. Within five minutes, the fire, coming down from the top of the ridge, had reached them.

Although Rumsey says they were both "half hysterical," they were objective enough to see that the fire as it approached them was following the patterns of a fire coming over a ridge and starting down the other side. At the top of the ridge it burned slowly, veering back and forth in the way fires do as winds from opposite sides of a ridge meet each other. It flapped, sometimes it turned downhill toward them, and once it turned sideways and jumped a draw with a spot fire and, well started there, it jumped back again. Once below the fluctuations at the top of the ridge it settled down and burned straight toward them. It burned with such intensity that it created an updraft, sucking in its center so that it was now a front with two pincers. It hit the rock slide on two sides. Rumsey and Sallee, like the early prairie pioneers, tried to duck and dodge in their asylum, but there wasn't much room for running. Rumsey says the fuel was thinner near the top of the ridge. "The flames were only eight to ten feet high."

A form like a solidification of smoke stumbled out of the smoke ahead and died in the rocks. It was a four-point buck burned hairless except for the eyelashes.

After the fire passed the rock slide "it really started rolling" downhill, replacing trees with torches.

Soon they heard someone calling from far off, but it turned out to be "only thirty yards away." It was Bill Hellman. His shoes and pants were burned off, and his flesh hung in patches. When asked at the Review, "Did Hellman at that time seem to be suffering tremendously?" Sallee answered, "Yes." To the next question, "Did he make any statement to you?" Sallee's reply was, "He just said to tell his wife something, but I can't remember what it was."

They laid him on a long, flat rock to keep his burns out of the ashes. As Rumsey says, "There wasn't much else we could do," having thrown away all their first-aid supplies on their flight from the fire.

Suddenly, there was a shout and a form in the smoke. It was Dodge answering the shouting that had gone on between them and Hellman. He "didn't appear excited," but he "looked kind of—well, you might say, dumbfounded or shocked." His eyes were red from smoke and his clothes black with ashes. He obviously was not his fastidious self, but he still had a characteristic about him.

They didn't say much about anything, least of all about whether the missing were alive. Dodge, in coming over the hill, had seen one alive and couldn't remember his name except that it began with "S" (Joe Sylvia). When Dodge sat up in his own fire he heard someone "holler" faintly to the east and, after a long time, found him only 150 to 200 feet upgulch and, oddly, below him, perhaps 100 feet. He was badly burned and euphorically happy. Dodge moved him to the shelter of a big rock and cut the shoes off his swollen feet, but there was no use in Dodge leaving his only worldly gift with him, his can of Irish white potatoes, since Sylvia could not feed himself with the charred and useless remains of his hands. In the hours to come, he would be without water because he could not lift his canteen.

Evidently Dodge hadn't seen any others as he came up the hill or crossed to the other side, and, as he said at the Review, by the time he reached Rumsey, Sallee, and Hellman he "didn't think any of [the others] were still alive."

Rumsey and Sallee had come to a more hopeful conclusion once the fire passed them by in the rock slide—after all, they had made it, and, besides, once they understood the intention of Dodge's fire, they believed it would work and assumed at least some of the crew behind them had understood Dodge's fire and crowded into it. But Dodge's arrival eliminated that possibility, so there was very little they dared to talk about. After a while Dodge and Sallee left Hellman in Rumsey's care and started back uphill through the ashes without saying just why. Since none had been saved with Dodge, the assumption now was that any survivors would have made it over the hill, as Rumsey and Sallee had, so their search was a short one. Besides, the heat was still so intense it soon drove them back. They didn't have to explain why they didn't have anything to say when they returned.

It was getting dark. Hellman already had drunk most of their water, even though it made him sick. He could see the glare of the Missouri a mile and a half below, and it inflamed his thirst, but he was not allowed to think of walking. He did revive enough to become talkative. It was here that he told Rumsey he had been burned at the top of the ridge, and it was partly on the basis of this remark that Sallee formed his assumption that Hellman had reached the top of the ridge by following the downgulch side of Dodge's fire and so had had no buffer between him and the main fire raging upgulch. Once burned, though, like a wounded deer, he had started downhill for water but had collapsed after a few hundred yards. He was told to lie still on the rock and keep talking to forget the pain. Rumsey stayed with him, and at dusk Dodge and Sallee started for the river, Dodge leaving with them his canteen of water and his can of Irish white potatoes.

Dodge and Sallee had a tough time getting down to the river. They had to go half a mile or more before they could find a weak spot in the fire front through which to work their way. They had no map or compass, and when they reached the river they went the wrong way.

For the next few hours, the Smokejumpers who had landed in Mann Gulch passed from human remembrance perhaps as completely as they ever will. There were only five known to be alive at that moment, two of these soon to die, one with a name that began with "S."

Although Hellman had made it over the top of the ridge, he was despairing and smelling of burned flesh and was praying with Rumsey, who had been left to take care of him. They both had let their church attendance lapse and could not remember their prayers, so in embarrassment they prayed silently. From their position near the top of the ridge they could see, when the smoke opened, reflections of the fire in the Missouri River below, and Hellman had to be told again and again that he could not run to the river and immerse himself.

Dodge had left his can of white potatoes with Hellman because Rumsey would be there to feed him, but instead of eating the potatoes Hellman drank the salt water in the can and further inflamed his thirst.

For Dodge and Sallee on their way to the river, it was a never-never land in the night and the smoke, and without a map or compass. Both were near exhaustion and shock when they reached the river, and going downstream, which was easier for the water, also seemed easier for them. A boat passed that did not see them, then turned and went back upstream, and on this slight evidence they turned around too. They didn't know much about the world anymore, not even whether it was up or down.

Among other things, there were eleven of the crew they didn't know anything about. The missing were probably in a world one hundred by three hundred yards—the world between the boy with a canteen of water and no hands to lift it and Hellman on the other side of the ridge, who was looking for forgotten prayers.

• • •

The two top men in the Helena National Forest, supervisor Moir and assistant supervisor Eaton, had left Meriwether in haste for the fire at York because they and Jansson had agreed it was probably more important than the Mann Gulch fire. They had left in special haste because they could not reestablish radio contact with the crew on the York fire to determine its extent and the psychological stability of the crew that was fighting it. Matters got no more composed after they left when Jansson found out that the receiver of the radio at York had been dropped and broken by a hysterical volunteer sobbing for help. Both men and equipment were breaking.

Dodge and Sallee had been going downriver to nowhere. At the same time, coming downriver from above were hordes of picnickers. Full of beer and the desire to be mistaken for firefighters, they landed at the Meriwether picnic grounds and crowded into the guard station to hear whatever they could get near enough to hear. Soon it became impossible for Jansson to tell the picnickers from his volunteer barflies, so he tried by radio to stop all except official boating on the river, but the radio operator at Canyon Ferry was off somewhere.

Jansson forever held himself guilty for not being concerned about the jumpers at this time, although it is hard to see the justice of his continual prosecution of himself. As everyone did who did not think of them, he assumed the jumpers were too good to be caught in a fire—they either had joined up with Hersey's crew on the Meriwether ridge or had escaped over the head of the gulch into Willow Creek or perhaps hadn't liked the looks of things from the very first and had not jumped at all.

Once Jansson did try to radio Missoula about the jumpers, but another frequency kept cutting him off. Then he went back to the job of trying to get some coherence in his camp. As he knew, there is no better way to do this than to start a training school—he tried to make a fire foreman out of one of the three men who had been on a fire before, and he tried to make a radio operator out of another volunteer, but his best luck was with two picnickers pretending to be firefighters whom he trained to be camp cooks for a crew that had now grown to thirty-five. A mystery of the universe is how it has managed to survive with so much volunteer help.

Jansson was also keeping an eye on the fire near the top of Meriwether ridge where he had sent alternate ranger Hersey and his crew of nineteen men with two hold-at-all-cost orders: (1) hold the trail from the east open so that the jumpers could come down the ridge and join them, and (2) above all, hold the perpendicular trail behind them open so that, if they had to, they could escape back to the camp and, if they had to, from there into the river. The fire now was definitely moving down the Meriwether slope.

As it darkened, Jansson began to see flames making movies of themselves on the faces of the cliffs fifteen hundred feet straight above him.

Hersey says that when some of the crew saw the cliffs reenact the fire they tried to jump off them.

In the wide world, Hersey was probably the only man in whose mind the Smokejumpers were constantly present. Their absence was heightened by the fact that Hersey had followed Harrison's tracks on the trail to the top of the ridge and the front of the fire—his tracks were easy to follow because he had been using his Pulaski as a walking stick, and going up that stepladder trail he had relied on it as if he and his Pulaski were a cripple and a crutch. What worried Hersey most was that at the top of the ridge Harrison's tracks headed into some second growth that the fire was already burning. Hersey spent most of his time organizing his crew into a fire-line and giving them another speech about how to face danger. He gave them a speech about facing danger every time he walked around the head of the fire and every time the fire ran a reel of itself on a cliff. It would be interesting to know what he told them, because it seems to have worked fairly well. Anyway, his crew stayed on the line even after the trail up the ridge to the east had disappeared in flames. His crew, though, were drinking gallons of water more than seasoned firefighters would have, so he had to send one of them all the way down to Meriwether Station with a canvas sack for another load.

When Jansson saw the waterbuck in camp, he became alarmed. Because the Smokejumpers had become nonexistent in Jansson's mind, it was his own men fifteen hundred feet above his head who, he thought, were in danger. The returned waterbuck was a sure sign that Hersey intended to stay on the ridge and fight, and Jansson did not want him fighting fire after dark on the edge of fifteen-hundred-foot pinnacles with a bunch of drunks. Now, for the first time, he also became alarmed about the jumpers, who, the waterbuck was telling him, had not shown up on the Meriwether ridge. If they weren't with Hersey's crew, there were few places in the world that they could reach where they would be safe.

Jansson immediately ordered the radio at Canyon Ferry to get the radio at Missoula to use all frequencies to locate the whereabouts of the jumpers. When he was advised by Missoula that it was unable to establish contact with the jumpers on any frequency, he then asked for the exact location of their jumping area. "While they were giving me the exact spot," he says, "foreman Dodge and jumper Sallee walked into the guard cabin at Meriwether and Dodge reported that he had two injured men. This was at approximately 8:50 p.m."

The volunteers and the picnickers and the drunks crowded into the cabin. Jansson had to take Dodge outside and up the canyon to get any coherent information from him, but what did Dodge know that was coherent? He knew that back in what earlier in the day had been Mann Gulch were two badly burned men, one with a name Dodge did not remember, and one unburned man, Rumsey, watching the burned man with a name, Hellman. What else was in the amphitheater for sure was fear and the smell of overcooked flesh.

Jansson immediately ordered through the Canyon Ferry radio one doctor, two litters, blankets, and blood plasma. At ten o'clock Hersey came in with his terrified postdrunks, having kept them on the fire until they had been several times trapped by it. He told Jansson about Harrison's tracks, and, even more alarming, he told Jansson he had seen no jumpers or their tracks.

"We decided," Jansson says, "to consider the rescue work the No. 1 job and the fire the No. 2 job. I asked Hersey to look after the fire job while I went for the jumpers."

It is like that in the woods and even in the wide world generally—the rescue of men and women, alive or dead, comes first. Of course, some step on the gas and leave them lying on the pavement where they landed and some sneak off, like Egyptian bas-relief, with their profiles looking one way and their bodies going the other way. But most people think they can be of help, and some even seem born to rescue others, as poets think they are. The best of them goof, especially at first, because only a few have the opportunity to keep in practice. Then as they catch on again they become beautiful in performance if one can step back for a moment to look. Almost as beautiful as when, having completed their job of deposing death, they fade into complete anonymity. It was very hard, for instance, to rescue the names of those Jansson picked for his rescue team. Even though he must have regarded them as his best, they all made mistakes, especially at first. But they also support the statement that one of the finest things men and women do is rescue men and women, even when they know they are rescuing the dead. This statement takes into account the Egyptian bas-relief, the drunks, and the sobbing radios.

At 10:30, while the rescuers were still waiting at Meriwether for the doctor and medical supplies to arrive, rumors and uncertainties were spreading through the camp. They spread in waves and, like waves, spent themselves draining into the sand, but one kept resurfacing—the rumor that there were injured men downriver waiting to be picked up. Jansson left in a speedboat hoping to bring back the eleven missing men, but the report turned out to be about Dodge and Sallee who had been seen walking upriver by several boatloads of picnickers. This is a common enough way to start off a rescue operation—running after a rumor that turns out to be a misinterpretation of something already known.

For a while Jansson patrolled the lower river, signaling with a flashlight and occasionally cutting off his motor and yelling. Finally a speedboat arrived with two doctors in it, T. L. Hawkins of Helena and his guest, R. E. Haines of Phoenix, Arizona, and Jansson transferred to their boat and landed at the mouth of Mann Gulch. Soon the big excursion boat with the rescue party in it arrived, only to discover they all were at the mouth of the wrong gulch—Dodge and Sallee had come down a gulch below Mann Gulch. When they arrived at this lower one that came to be called Rescue Gulch, they discovered that the litters had been left six miles back at Hilger Landing. Almost as soon as the speedboat started back to get them, rumors and tension mounted among the crew. One of the worst things a rescue crew does is wait—they wanted to start uphill immediately to find the injured men and let the litter crew come when the litters arrived. Jansson knew he had only one man who could lead them back through night and fire and rolling rocks and exploding trees—Sallee, who alone knew that he was just seventeen years old. Acting again on the assumption that the one sure way to quiet a crew is to get them to do something, Jansson lined them up and conducted roll call, only to discover he had six or seven men too many. They were picnickers who had smuggled themselves into the big excursion boat in the hope they could join the rescue crew. He had to cut them out and send them back. That left him with a crew of twelve, counting himself, the doctors, and Sallee, all tough men who had worked all day and now would work all night and probably the coming day in the agonizing valley.

It was 11:30 before Jansson and his crew started up Rescue Gulch. They had two litters but only one blanket, which, as it turned out, was all that was sent back to them when they had sent out for blankets. By now the insanity of the fire had passed on, and it lay twitching around its edges, like something dead but still with nerve ends. Its self-inflicted injuries had been great and had turned black. It lay in burned grass and split rocks with its passion spent. The crew crossed through the weakened fire-line into the world that might be dead.

About two-thirds of the way to the top they heard a shout, which turned out to be Rumsey coming down the hill to refill the canteen for Hellman, who had been drinking water, getting sick at the stomach, then drinking more water until he drank it all. Rumsey told Jansson that he thought his guard Harrison was dead, because when last seen Harrison had been sitting with his pack on his back not able to take it off. Rumsey didn't know if the others had survived.

Later at the Review, when Jansson was asked if Rumsey had made any detailed comment to him at this time about himself, Jansson replied, "He made the following comment, 'The Lord was good to me—he put wings on my feet and I ran like hell.'" This was one good Methodist talking to another.

Nearly half a mile away the crew could hear Hellman shouting for water. In the valley of ashes there was another sound—the occasional explosion of a dead tree that would blow to pieces when its resin became so hot it passed the point of ignition. There was little left alive to be frightened by the explosions. The rattlesnakes were dead or swimming the Missouri. The deer were also dead or swimming or euphoric. Mice and moles came out of their holes and, forgetting where their holes were, ran into the fire. Following the explosion that sent the moles and ashes running, a tree burst into flames that almost immediately died. Then the ashes settled down again to rest until they rose in clouds when the crew passed by.

Jansson, Rumsey, and Sallee pushed ahead of the main party to get water to Hellman. Jansson was the leader of the rescue crew, and he should tell it: "Hellman's face, arms, legs, and back were severely burned with loose flesh hanging in patches. He complained of the cold and was very thirsty. We let him rinse out his mouth and take on a little water. Water upset his stomach at first."

In ten or fifteen minutes the two doctors arrived. They gave Hellman a hypo and one quart of plasma, applied salve, transferred him to a litter, and then covered him with the one blanket. According to Jansson, "Bill's burned flesh had a terrific odor. He was in severe pain but took his experience magnificently. Bill's courage made men weep."

Jansson had seen men weep and had wept himself, but as soon as he saw that the problem was medical and the medical men were there, he was on the move again. He picked two of the rescue crew to accompany him across the ridge and into Mann Gulch to explore ahead for the doctors and be ready to point out where the living and the dead lay hidden. He must have picked out the two he trusted most—one was Don Roos, assistant ranger from the Lincoln District, and the other the seventeen-year-old boy he had met only a few hours before who by now was on his way to prove his own secret belief that he was the best man on the crew.

It was 1:20 a.m. when the three crossed the ridge and started down the other side, where they soon ran into what Jansson describes as a "twelve-foot rim rock breaking off on the Mann Gulch side." Jansson says they had trouble finding a gap in it; others before them had, too.

It would not be exact to say that the three in descending at night into the remnants of Mann Gulch were descending into the valley of the shadow of death, because there was practically nothing left standing to cast a shadow. Since dead trees occasionally exploded and then subsided weakly into dying flames, perhaps it would be more exact to say they were descending into the valley of the candles of death. Rumsey speaks of the night as a "pincushion of fire."

At about 1:50 they heard a cry below and to the right. As they continued to descend, "the updrafts brought a very suspicious smell," but Jansson says that, because the wind was tricky, it was difficult to determine "whether there was a series of bodies ahead or whether we were just smelling Sylvia."

It took them another ten minutes to find Sylvia, probably because Sylvia had been slipping in and out of consciousness during that time.

When Jansson, Roos, and Sallee reached him, Sylvia was standing on a rock slanting heavily downhill. Hunched over and wobbling to keep his balance, he couldn't stop talking. "Please don't come around and look at my face; it's awful." Then he said, "Say, it didn't take you fellows long to get here." He thought it was 5:00 in the morning. Jansson pulled out his watch and said, "It's 2:00 a.m. on the nose." Then in his report, Jansson speaks to us. "Since his hands were burned to charred clubs, I peeled an orange and fed it to him section by section."

Sylvia said, "Say, fellows, I don't think I'll be able to walk out of here." Jansson told him his walking days were over for the time being and he was "going to get a free ride out." He tried to make this a joke, although it is hard to make jokes at night on a hillside that smells of burned flesh.

Sylvia was worried about his shoes, which Dodge had taken off and placed behind a rock, so Jansson combed the slope with a flashlight until he found them. The knowledge that his shoes had been discovered comforted Sylvia, probably because he could not retain knowledge and had slipped back to thinking he would have to walk to the river.

About 2:20 the doctors and most of the rescue crew arrived and treated Sylvia as they had Hellman. Dr. Hawkins agreed with Jansson that it would be dangerous to attempt to move Sylvia and Hellman before daybreak, although the crew was ready to start stumbling in darkness through rocks and reefs to the river.

Sylvia complained of the cold, as Hellman had, but Hellman was wrapped in the only blanket the crew had brought back on its return trip from Hilger Landing. Since most of the men were not wearing jackets, "some of them stripped off their shirts and undershirts to wrap around Joe to keep him warm." As he was still cold, half-naked they huddled close to him.

When he got warm, he got happy again. Several years ago Dr. Hawkins, who treated both Hellman and Sylvia on the ridge and then in the hospital, told me that, if I were burned and wanted to be as happy as Joe Sylvia had been, I should get terribly burned. "Then," he said, "your sensory apparatus dumps into your bloodstream." He added, "Usually it takes until the next day to clog your kidneys. In the meantime, it is possible to have spells when you think you are happy."

Since only two could cuddle close to Sylvia at a time, others of the rescue crew spread out across the hillside looking for eleven missing men by flashlight and candlelight. It was like high mass until dawn—lights walked about all night in darkness.

Sylvia encouraged those who remained with him by telling them that before they had arrived he had heard voices of men calling from above. They were the voices of men working and he had shouted back at them. Perhaps, then, it would be more exact to call Mann Gulch on this night the valley of candles and voices of dead men working.

Daylight came a little after four o'clock, and Jansson walked only a few yards before running into Harrison's body. He identified it by the Catholic medallion around its neck and the snake-bite kit which he had given Harrison when Harrison became recreation guard at Meriwether. His body lay face down pointing uphill and looking as if, instead of being a Catholic, he were a Moslem fallen in prayer. Jansson describes the earth as it looked at daybreak.

The ground appearance was that a terrific draft of superheated air of tremendous velocity had swept up the hill exploding all inflammable material, causing a wall of flame (which I had observed from below at 5:30 p.m. the previous evening) six hundred feet high to roll over the ridge and down the other side and continue over ridges and down gulches until the fuels were so light that the wall could not maintain heat enough to continue. This wall covered three thousand acres in ten minutes or less. Anything caught in the direct path of the heat blast perished.

Three thousand acres is close to four and three-quarters square miles.

At about 4:40 a.m. they started to carry Sylvia down Mann Gulch to the river. The crew that left with him was only six men and the doctors, so Sallee had to take his turn carrying the litter. It was also up to him to help identify the bodies—they tagged three while carrying Sylvia down the hillside. Jansson, who was noted for being a hard man on himself and his men, was sorry for Sallee. What a great compliment for a seventeen-year-old.

While they continued downhill, Jansson continued to be puzzled about why Harrison's body had been found so close to Sylvia. He had heard from both Sallee and Rumsey that Harrison had given out from exhaustion, so Jansson had expected to find his body much lower on the hillside and farther back than any of the others. That he got up and climbed to where he did is as much a monument to his courage as the cross they put there afterwards.

Jansson is the only one to have left an account at all inclusive of the discovery, identification, and removal of the bodies. Near each body he left a note under a pile of rocks identifying the body and summarizing the evidence on which the identification had been made. He may have intended to expand these notes into a more complete account, but he never did. If he had tried to say more, it would have been too much, for him and for us.

Lower down the hillside than they thought any of the crew would be found, they came upon Stanley J. Reba's body; but when they examined it, they found he had broken a leg and then no doubt had rolled down the slope into the fire. He had literally burned to death. Most of the others, in all likelihood, had died of suffocation and were burned afterwards.

Sylvia was carried to the mouth of Mann Gulch by Jansson and his crew of six, arriving there only a short time before Hellman reached the river by way of Rescue Gulch, carried by Rumsey and other members of the rescue crew. Neither Sylvia nor Hellman was suffering, because, as Dr. Hawkins adds, "their burns were so deep and hard their nerve ends were destroyed."

Each man was soon picked up by a speedboat, and each man's spirits rose. Sylvia arrived at the hospital in Helena about 10:00 a.m. and Hellman about half an hour later. Dr. Hawkins told me that 10:00 was about time for the kidneys to fail. He immediately ordered an examination, and the report was as expected, "no urine found." There soon came an end to euphoria; both Sylvia and Hellman were dead by noon.

By 1:00, Jansson, who had been in charge of moving Sylvia to the hospital in Helena, was back in Mann Gulch to renew the search with a fresh crew, including Dodge, and a helicopter to fly the bodies to Helena. According to his plans, he should have been there at least three hours earlier, but the "eggbeater," which had been ordered from Missoula, picked him up at 12:30 instead of 9:00. It's hard for the woods and machines to run on the same schedule, and almost never is it the woods that are late.

Jansson had been the first one to be taken in on the helicopter shuttle, and he immediately started uphill tagging bodies. He started where they had found the three at daybreak and then, as he says, worked up the ridge "by contours." He says that he did not have much time to gather up the personal effects scattered around the bodies: "The terrific blast of heat burned all clothing off, releasing non-inflammable effects, which, if not pinned down by the body, were carried as high as one hundred feet farther up the hill." He found watches or the remains of wallets only by rolling a body over.

Late in the afternoon he looked downhill and saw a "charred stump of a man." He already had found the ninth body, "so I didn't count him and didn't go close enough to determine if it was really a remains." He was through for the day, a long day that had begun early the day before. Not until the next morning, the morning of the seventh, were all the remains found.

Only when all the Smokejumpers in his crew had been accounted for did Dodge fly back to Missoula. It is not hard to visualize him, eyes bloody and clothes dirty, as Sallee found him near the top of the ridge after the fire had passed over him, but it takes a moment of thinking to see him as his wife saw him when he stepped down from the plane in Missoula, fastidious as ever except for the tobacco stains at the corners of his mouth. He had five more years to construct a life out of the ashes of this fire.

Jansson had longer to live than Dodge, but those who knew him say he also had great problems rescuing himself. Asked by the Board of Review at what point he had given up being in charge of the rescue, he replied he just couldn't remember. He couldn't remember because he never gave up the charge. For instance, the year of the fire he twice returned to Mann Gulch to check his original observations of the blowup. Afterwards he wrote "Jansson's Ground Check Statement." Having twice walked and rerun his route with a stopwatch in hand, he concluded that his present report "is within two minutes of the time I have shown in previous statements."

In the end, he had to rescue himself from Mann Gulch by asking to be transferred to another ranger district. It had got so that he could not sleep at night, remembering the smell of it, and his dog would no longer come in but cried all night outside, knowing that something had gone wrong with him.

from Arabian Sands

by Sir Wilfred Thesiger

Sir Wilfred Thesiger (born 1910) went to Arabia ". . . just in time" he writes of his 1947 sojourn. "Others will go there . . . but they will never know the spirit of the land or the greatness of the Arabs." Thesiger convinced four Bedu to undertake with him the difficult crossing the vast and barren Empty Quarter. He could have wished for no better companions.

T he Rashid took the lead, their faded brown clothes harmonizing with the sands: al Auf, a lean, neat figure, very upright; bin Kabina, more loosely built, striding beside him. The two Bait Kathir followed close behind, with the spare camel tied to Musallim's saddle. Their clothes, which had once been white, had become neutral-coloured from long usage. Mabkhaut was the same build as al Auf, whom he resembled in many ways, though he was a less forceful character. In the distance he was distinguishable from him only by the colour of his shirt. Musallim, compactly built, slightly bow-legged, and physically tough, was of a different, coarser breed. The least likeable of my companions, his personality had suffered from too frequent sojourns in Salala and he tended to be ingratiating.

After a short distance al Auf suggested that, as he did not know what we should find to the north, it would be wise to halt near by, with the Bait Imani, to allow our camels a further day's grazing. The Arabs, he added, would give us milk so that we need not touch our food and water. I answered that he was our guide and that from now on such decisions must rest with him.

Two hours later we saw a small boy, dressed in the remnants of a loin-cloth and with long hair falling down his back, herding camels. He led us to the Bait Imani camp, where three men sat round the embers of a fire. They rose as we approached. 'Salam Alaikum, Alaikum as Salam', and then, after we had exchanged the news, they handed us a bowl of milk, its surface crusted with blown sand. These Bait Imani belonged to the same section of the Rashid as al Auf and bin Kabina and were from three different families. Only one of them, a grizzled elderly man called Khuatim, wore a shirt over his loin-cloth, and all were bareheaded. They had no tent; their only possessions were saddles, ropes, bowls, empty goatskins, and their rifles and daggers. The camping ground was churned and furrowed where the camels slept, and littered with camel droppings, hard and clean on the sand like dried dates. These men were cheerful and full of talk. The grazing was good; their camels, several in milk, would soon be fat. Life by their standards would be easy this year, but I thought of other years when the exhausted scouts rode back to the wells to speak through blackened, bleeding lips of desolation in the Sands, of emptiness such as I myself had seen on the way here from Ghanim; when the last withered plants were gone and walking skeletons of men and beasts sank down to die. Even tonight, when they considered themselves well off, these men would sleep naked on the freezing sand, covered only with their flimsy loin cloths. I thought, too, of the bitter wells in the furnace heat of summer, when, hour by reeling hour, they watered thirsty, thrusting camels, until at last the wells ran dry and importunate camels moaned for water which was not there. I thought how desperately hard were the lives of the Bedu in this weary land, and how gallant and how enduring was their spirit. Now, listening to their talk and watching the little acts of courtesy which they instinctively performed, I knew by comparison how sadly I must fail, how selfish I must prove.

The Bait Imani talked of Mahsin and of the accident which had befallen him, asking endless questions. Then Khuatim shouted to the small herdsboy, his son, to fetch the yellow four-year-old and the old grey which was still in milk. When the boy had brought them, Khuatim told him to couch them and loosed the hobbles from our bull's forelegs. Already the bull was excited, threshing itself with its tail, grinding its teeth, or blowing a large pink air sac from its mouth and sucking it back with a slobbering sound. Clumsily it straddled the yellow camel, a comic figure of ill-directed lust, while Khuatim, kneeling beside it, tried to assist. Bin Kabina observed to me, 'Camels would never manage to mate without human help. They would never get it in the right place.' I was thankful that there were no more than these two camels to be served; there might have been a dozen to exhaust our bull.

The boy brought in the rest of the herd, thirty-five of them, at sunset. Khuatim washed his hands beneath a staling camel and scrubbed out the bowls with sand, for Bedu believe that a camel will go dry if milked with dirty hands or into a bowl which was soiled with food, especially meat or butter. He stroked a camel's udder, talking to her and encouraging her to let down her milk, and then standing on one leg, with his right foot resting on his left knee, he milked her into a bowl which he balanced on his right thigh. She gave about two quarts; several of the others, however, gave less than a quart. There were nine of these camels in milk. Al Auf milked Qamaiqam, bin Kabina's camel. She had given us a quart twice a day at Mughshin, but now from hard work and lack of food she only gave about a pint.

After milking, the Bait Imani couched their camels for the night, tying their knees to prevent them from rising. Al Auf told us to leave ours out to graze, adding that he would keep an eye on them. Our hosts brought us milk. We blew the froth aside and drank deep; they urged us to drink more, saying, 'You will find no milk in the sands ahead of you. Drink—drink. You are our guests. God brought you here—drink.' I drank again, knowing even as I did so that they would go hungry and thirsty that night, for they had nothing else, no other food and no water. Then while we crouched over the fire bin Kabina made coffee. The chill wind whispered among the shadowy dunes, and fingered us through our clothes and through the blankets which we wrapped about us. They talked till long after the moon had set, of camels and grazing, of journeys across the Sands, of raids and blood feuds and of the strange places and people they had seen when they had visited the Hadhramaut and Oman.

In the morning bin Kabina went with one of the Bait Imani to collect our camels, and when he came back I noticed he was no longer wearing a loin-cloth under his shirt. I asked him where it was and he said that he had given it away. I protested that he could not travel without one through the inhabited country beyond the Sands and in Oman, and that I had no other to give him. I said he must recover it and gave him some money for the man instead. He argued that he could not do this. 'What use will money be to him in the Sands. He wants a loin-cloth', he grumbled, but at length he went off to do as I had told him.

Meanwhile the other Bait Imani had brought us bowls of milk which al Auf poured into a small goatskin. He said we could mix a little every day with our drinking water and that this would improve its taste, a custom which enables Arabs who live in the Sands to drink from wells which would otherwise be undrinkable. They call this mixture of sour milk and water *shanin*. When we had finished this milk a week later we found in the bottom of the skin a lump of butter, the size of a walnut and colourless as lard. Al Auf also poured a little milk into another skin which was sweating, explaining that this would make it waterproof.

Then, wishing our hosts the safe keeping of God, we turned away across the Sands. As he walked along, al Auf held out his hands palms upwards, and recited verses from the Koran. The sand was still very cold beneath our feet. Usually, when they are in the Sands during the winter or summer, Arabs wear socks knitted from coarse black hair. None of us owned these socks and our heels were already cracking from the cold. Later these cracks became deeper and very painful. We walked for a couple of hours, and then rode till nearly sunset; encouraging our camels to snatch mouthfuls from any plants they passed. They would hasten towards each one with their lower lips flapping wildly.

At first the dunes were brick-red in colour, separate mountains of sand, rising above ash-white gypsum flats ringed with vivid green salt-bushes; those we passed in the afternoon were even higher—500 to 550 feet in height and honey-coloured. There was little vegetation here.

Musallim rode the black bull and led his own camel, which carried the two largest water-skins. Going down a steep slope the female hesitated. The head-rope attached to the back of Musallim' saddle tightened and slowly pulled her over on to her side. I was some way behind and could see what was going to happen but there was no time to do anything. I shouted frantically at Musallim but he could not halt his mount on the slope. I prayed that the rope would break, and as I watched the camel collapse on top of the water-skins I thought, 'Now we will never get across the Sands.' Al Auf was already on the ground slashing at the taut rope with his dagger. As I jumped from my saddle I wondered if we should have even enough water left to get back to Ghanim. The fallen camel kicked out, and as the rope parted heaved herself to her knees. The water-skins which had fallen from her back still seemed to be full. Hardly daring to hope I bent over them, as al Auf said 'Praise be to God. They are all right', and the others reiterated 'The praise be to God, the praise be to God!' We reloaded them on to the bull, which, bred in the sands, was accustomed to these slithering descents.

Later we came on some grazing and stopped for the night. We chose a hollow sheltered from the wind, unloaded the water-skins and saddle-bags, hobbled the camels, loosened the saddles on their backs and drove them off to graze.

At sunset al Auf doled out a pint of water mixed with milk to each person, our first drink of the day. As always, I had watched the sun getting lower, thinking 'Only one more hour till I can drink', while I tried to find a little saliva to moisten a mouth that felt like leather. Now I took my share of water without the milk and made it into tea, adding crushed cinnamon, cardamom, ginger, and cloves to the brew to disguise the taste.

Firewood could always be found, for there was no place in the Sands where rain had not fallen in the past, even if it was twenty or thirty years before. We could always uncover the long trailing roots of some dead shrub. These Arabs will not burn tribulus if they can find any other fuel, for *zahra*, 'the flower' as they call it, is venerated as the best of all food for their camels and has almost the sanctity of the date palm. I remember how I once threw a date-stone into the fire and old Tamtaim leant forward and picked it out.

Bin Kabina brewed coffee. He had stripped off his shirt and headcloth, and I said, 'You couldn't take your shirt off if I had not rescued your loin-cloth for you.' He grinned, and said, 'What could I do? He asked for it', and went over to help Musallim scoop flour out of a goatskin: four level mugfuls measured in a pint mug. This, about three pounds of flour, was our ration for the day and I reflected that there must be very few calories or vitamins in our diet. Yet no scratch festered or turned septic during the years I lived in the desert. Nor did I ever take precautions before drinking what water we found. Indeed, I have drunk unboiled water from wells, ditches, and drains all over the Middle East for twenty-five years without ill effect. Given a chance, the human body—mine at any rate—seems to create its own resistance to infection.

When Musallim had made bread, he called to al Auf and Mabkhaut, who were herding the camels. It was getting dark. Though a faint memory of the vanished day still lingered in the west, the stars were showing, and the moon cast shadows on the colourless sand. We sat in a circle round a small dish, muttered 'In the name of God', and in turn dipped fragments of bread into the melted butter. When we had fed, bin Kabina took the small brass coffee-pot from the fire and served us with coffee, a few drops each. Then we crouched round the fire and talked.

I was happy in the company of these men who had chosen to come with me. I felt affection for them personally, and sympathy with their way of life. But though the easy equality of our relationship satisfied me, I did not delude myself that I could be one of them. They were Bedu and I was not; they were Muslims and I was a Christian. Nevertheless, I was their companion and an inviolable bond united us, as sacred as the bond between host and guest, transcending tribal and family loyalties. Because I was their companion on the road, they would fight in my defence even against their brothers and they would expect me to do the same.

But I knew that for me the hardest test would be to live with them in harmony and not to let my impatience master me; neither to withdraw into myself, nor to become critical of standards and ways of life different from my own. I knew from experience that the conditions under which we lived would slowly wear me down, mentally if not physically, and that I should be often provoked and irritated by my companions. I also knew with equal certainty that when this happened the fault would be mine, not theirs.

During the night a fox barked somewhere on the slopes above us. At dawn al Auf untied the camels, which he had brought in for the night, and turned them loose to graze. There would be no food till sunset, but bin Kabina heated what was left of the coffee. After we had travelled for an hour we came upon a patch of grazing freshened by a recent shower. Faced with the choice of pushing on or of feeding the camels al Auf decided to stop, and as we unloaded them he told us to collect bundles of tribulus to carry with us. I watched him scoop a hole in the sand to find out how deeply the rain had penetrated, in this case about three feet; he invariably did this wherever rain had fallen—if no plants had yet come up on which to graze the camels while we waited, we went on, leaving him behind to carry out his investigations. It was difficult to see what practical use this information about future grazing in the heart of the Empty Quarter could possibly be to him or to anyone else, and yet I realized that it was this sort of knowledge which made him such an exceptional guide. Later I lay on the sand and watched an eagle circling overhead. It was hot. I took the temperature in the shade of my body and found it was 84 degrees. It was difficult to believe that it had been down to 43 degrees at dawn. Already the sun had warmed the sand so that it burnt the soft skin round the sides of my feet.

At midday we went on, passing high, pale-coloured dunes, and others that were golden, and in the evening we wasted an hour skirting a great mountain of red sand, probably 650 feet in height. Beyond it we travelled along a salt-flat, which formed a corridor through the Sands. Looking back I fancied the great, red dune was a door which was slowly, silently closing behind us. I watched the narrowing gap between it and the dune on the other side of the corridor, and imagined that once it was shut we could never go back, whatever happened. The gap vanished and now I could see only a wall of sand. I turned back to the others and they were discussing the price of a coloured loin-cloth which Mabkhaut had bought in Salala before we started. Suddenly al Auf pointed to a camel's track and said, 'Those were made by my camel when I came this way on my way to Ghanim.'

Later Musallim and al Auf argued how far it was from Mughshin to Bai, where Tamtaim and the others were to wait for us. I asked al Auf if he had ever ridden from the Wadi al Amairi to Bai. He answered, 'Yes, six years ago.'

'How many days did it take?'

'I will tell you. We watered at al Ghaba in the Amairi. There were four of us, myself, Salim, Janazil of the Awamir, and Alaiwi of the Afar; it was in the middle of summer. We had been to Ibri to settle the feud between the Rashid and the Mahamid, started by the killing of Fahad's son.'

Musallim interrupted, 'That must have been before the Riqaishi was Governor of Ibri. I had been there myself the year before. Sahail was with me and we went there from. . . .'

But al Auf went on, 'I was riding the three-year-old I had bought from bin Duailan.'

'The one the Manahil raided from the Yam?' Bin Kabina asked.

'Yes. I exchanged it later for the yellow six-year-old I got from bin Ham. Janazil rode a Batina camel. Do you remember her? She was the daughter of the famous grey which belonged to Harahaish of the Wahiba.'

Mabkhaut said, 'Yes, I saw her last year when he was in Salala, a tall animal; she was old when I saw her, past her prime but even then a real beauty.'

Al Auf went on, 'We spent the night with Rai of the Afar.'

Bin Kabina chimed in, 'I met him last year when he came to Habarut; he carried a rifle, 'a father often shots', which he had taken from the Mahra he had killed in the Ghudun. Bin Mautlauq offered him the grey yearling, the daughter of Farha, and fifty *riyals* for this rifle, but he refused.'

Al Auf continued, 'Rai killed a goat for our dinner and told us . . .', but I interrupted: 'Yes, but how many days did it take you to get to Bai.' He looked at me in surprise and said, 'Am I not telling you?'

We stopped at sunset for the evening meal, and fed to our camels the tribulus we had brought with us. All the skins were sweating and we were worried about our water. There had been a regular and ominous drip from them throughout the day, a drop falling on to the sand every few yards as we rode along, like blood dripping from a wound that could not be staunched. There was nothing to do but to press on, and yet to push the camels too hard would be to founder them. They were already showing signs of thirst. Al Auf had decided to go on again after we had fed, and while Musallim and bin Kabina baked bread I asked him about his former journeys through these Sands. 'I have crossed them twice', he said. 'The last time I came this way was two years ago. I was coming from Abu Dhabi.' I asked, 'Who was with you?' and he answered, 'I was alone.' Thinking that I must have misunderstood him, I repeated, 'Who were your companions?' 'God was my companion.' To have ridden alone through this appalling desolation was an incredible achievement. We were travelling through it now, but we carried our own world with us: a small world of five people, which yet provided each of us with companionship, with talk and laughter and the knowledge that others were there to share the hardship and the danger. I knew that if I travelled here alone the weight of this vast solitude would crush me utterly.

I also knew that al Auf had used no figure of speech when he said that God was his companion. To these Bedu, God is a reality, and the conviction of his presence gives them the courage to endure. For them to doubt his existence would be as inconceivable as for them to blaspheme. Most of them pray regularly, and many keep the fast of Ramadhan, which lasts for a whole month, during which time a man may not eat or drink from dawn till sunset. When this fast falls in summer—and the Arab months being lunar it is eleven days earlier each year—they make use of the exemption which allows travellers to observe the fast when they have finished their journey, and keep it in the winter. Several of the Arabs whom we had left at Mughshin were fasting to compensate for not having done so earlier in the year. I have heard townsmen and villagers in the Hadhramaut and the Hajaz disparage the Bedu, as being without religion. When I have protested, they have said, 'Even if they pray, their prayers are not acceptable to God, since they do not first perform the proper ablutions.'

These Bedu are not fanatical. Once I was travelling with a large party of Rashid, one of whom said to me, 'Why don't you become a Muslim and then you would really be one of us?' I answered, 'God protect me from the Devil!' They laughed. This invocation is one which Arabs invariably use in rejecting something shameful or indecent. I would not have dared to make it if other Arabs had asked me this question, but the man who had spoken would certainly have used it if I had suggested that he should become a Christian.

After the meal we rode for two hours along a salt-flat. The dunes on either side, colourless in the moonlight, seemed higher by night than by day. The lighted slopes looked very smooth, the shadows in their folds inky black. Soon I was shivering uncontrollably from the cold. The others roared out their songs into a silence, broken otherwise only by the crunch of salt beneath the camels' feet. The words were the words of the south, but the rhythm and intonation were the same as in the songs which I had heard other Bedu singing in the Syrian desert. At first sight the Bedu of southern Arabia had appeared to be very different from those of the north, but I now realized that this difference was largely superficial and due to the clothes which they wore. My companions would not have felt out of place in an encampment of the Rualla, whereas a townsman from Aden or Muscat would be conspicuous in Damascus.

Eventually we halted and I dismounted numbly. I would have given much for a hot drink but I knew that I must wait eighteen hours for that. We lit a small fire and warmed ourselves before we slept, though I slept little. I was tired; for days I had ridden long hours on a rough camel, my body racked by its uneven gait. I suppose I was weak from hunger, for the food which we ate was a starvation ration, even by Bedu standards. But my thirst troubled me most; it was not bad enough really to distress me but I was always conscious of it. Even when I was asleep I dreamt of racing streams of ice-cold water, but it was difficult to get to sleep. Now I lay there trying to estimate the distance we had covered and the distance that still lay ahead. When I had asked al Auf how far it was to the well, he had answered, 'It is not the distance but the great dunes of the Uruq al Shaiba that may destroy us.' I worried about the water which I had watched dripping away on to the sand, and about the state of our camels. They were there, close beside me in the dark. I sat up and looked at them. Mabkhaut stirred and called out, 'What is it, Umbarak?' I mumbled an answer and lay down again. Then I worried whether we had tied the mouth of the skin properly when we had last drawn water and wondered what would happen if one of us was sick or had an accident. It was easy to banish these thoughts in daylight, less easy in the lonely darkness. Then I thought of al Auf travelling here alone and felt ashamed.

The others were awake at the first light, anxious to push on while it was still cold. The camels sniffed at the withered tribulus but were too thirsty to eat it. In a few minutes we were ready. We plodded along in silence. My eyes watered with the cold; the jagged salt-crusts cut and stung my feet. The world was grey and dreary. Then gradually the peaks ahead of us stood out against a paling sky; almost imperceptibly they began to glow, borrowing the colours of the sunrise which touched their crests.

A high unbroken dune-chain stretched across our front. It was not of uniform height, but, like a mountain range, consisted of peaks and connecting passes. Several of the summits appeared to be seven hundred feet above the salt-flat on which we stood. The southern face confronting us was very steep, which meant that this was the lee side to the prevailing winds. I wished we had to climb it from the opposite direction, for it is easy to take a camel down these precipices of sand but always difficult to find a way up them.

Al Auf told us to wait while he went to reconnoitre. I watched him walking away across the glistening salt-flat, his rifle on his shoulder and his head thrown back as he scanned the slopes above. He looked superbly confident, but as I viewed this wall of sand I despaired that we would ever get the camels up it. Mabkhaut evidently thought the same, for he said to Musallim, 'We will have to find a way round. No camel will ever climb that.' Musallim answered, 'It is al Auf's doing. He brought us here. We should have gone much farther to the west, nearer to Dakaka.' He had caught a cold and was snuffling, and his rather high-pitched voice was hoarse and edged with grievance. I knew that he was jealous of al Auf and always ready to disparage him, so unwisely I gibed, 'We should have got a long way if you had been our guide!' He swung round and answered angrily, 'You don't like the Bait Kathir. I know that you only like the Rashid. I defied my tribe to bring you here and you never recognize what I have done for you.'

For the past few days he had taken every opportunity of reminding me that I could not have come on from Ramlat al Ghafa without him. It was done in the hope of currying favour and of increasing his reward, but it only irritated me. Now I was tempted to seek relief in angry words, to welcome the silly, bitter squabble which would result. I kept silent with an effort and moved apart on the excuse of taking a photograph. I knew how easily, under conditions such as these, I could take a violent dislike to one member of the party and use him as my private scapegoat. I thought, 'I must not let myself dislike him. After all, I do owe him a great deal; but I wish to God he would not go on reminding me of it.'

I went over to a bank and sat down to wait for al Auf's return. The ground was still cold, although the sun was now well up, throwing a hard, clear light on the barrier of sand ahead of us. It seemed fantastic that this great rampart which shut out half the sky could be made of wind-blown sand. Now I could see al Auf, about half a mile away, moving along the salt-flat at the bottom of the dune. While I watched him he started to climb a ridge, like a mountaineer struggling upward through soft snow towards a pass over a high mountain. I even saw the tracks which he left behind him. He was the only moving thing in all that empty, silent landscape.

What were we going to do if we could not get the camels over it? I knew that we could not go any farther to the east, for al Auf had told me that the quicksands of Umm al Samim were in that direction. To the west the easier sands of Dakaka, where Thomas had crossed, were more than two hundred miles away. We had no margin, and could not afford to lengthen our journey. Our water was already dangerously short, and even more urgent than our own needs were those of the camels, which would collapse unless they were watered soon. We *must* get them over this monstrous dune, if necessary by unloading them and carrying the loads to the top. But what was on the other side? How many more of these dunes were there ahead of us? If we turned back now we might reach Mughshin, but I knew that once we crossed this dune the camels would be too tired and thirsty to get back even to Ghanim. Then I thought of Sultan and the others who had deserted us, and of their triumph if we gave up and returned defeated. Looking again at the dune ahead I noticed that al Auf was coming back. A shadow fell across the sand beside me. I glanced up and bin Kabina stood there. He smiled, said 'Salam Alaikum', and sat down. Urgently I turned to him and asked, 'Will we ever get the camels over that?' He pushed the hair back from his forehead, looked thoughtfully at the slopes above us, and answered, 'It is very steep but al Auf will find a way. He is a Rashid; he is not like these Bait Kathir.' Unconcernedly he then took the bolt out of his rifle and began to clean it with the hem of his shirt, while he asked me if all the English used the same kind of rifle.

When al Auf approached we went over to the others. Mabkhaut's camel had lain down; the rest of them stood where we had left them, which was a bad sign. Ordinarily they would have roamed off at once to look for food. Al Auf smiled at me as he came up but said nothing, and no one questioned him. Noticing that my camel's load was unbalanced he heaved up the saddle-bag from one side, and then picking up with his toes the camel-stick which he had dropped, he went over to his own camel, caught hold of its head-rope, said 'Come on', and led us forward.

It was now that he really showed his skill. He picked his way unerringly, choosing the inclines up which the camels could climb. Here on the lee side of this range a succession of great faces flowed down in unruffled sheets of sand, from the top to the very bottom of the dune. They were unscalable, for the sand was poised always on the verge of avalanching, but they were flanked by ridges where the sand was firmer and the inclines easier. It was possible to force a circuitous way up these slopes, but not all were practicable for camels, and from below it was difficult to judge their steepness. Very slowly, a foot at a time, we coaxed the unwilling beasts upward. Each time we stopped I looked up at the crests where the rising wind was blowing streamers of sand into the void, and wondered how we should ever reach the top. Suddenly we were there. Before slumping down on the sand I looked anxiously ahead of us. To my relief I saw that we were on the edge of rolling downs, where the going would be easy among shallow valleys and low, rounded hills. 'We have made it. We are on top of Uruq al Shaiba', I thought triumphantly. The fear of this great obstacle had lain like a shadow on my mind ever since al Auf had first warned me of it, the night we spoke together in the sands of Ghanim. Now the shadow had lifted and I was confident of success.

We rested for a while on the sand, not troubling to talk, until al Auf rose to his feet and said 'Come on'. Some small dunes built up by cross-winds ran in curves parallel with the main face across the back of these downs. Their steep faces were to the north and the camels slithered down them without difficulty. These downs were brick-red, splashed with deeper shades of colour; the underlying sand, exposed where it had been churned up by our feet, showing red of a paler shade. But the most curious feature was a number of deep craters resembling giant hoof-prints. These were unlike normal crescent-dunes, since they did not rise above their surroundings, but formed hollows in the floor of hard undulating sand. The salt-flats far below us looked very white.

We mounted our camels. My companions had muffled their faces in their head-cloths and rode in silence, swaying to the camels' stride. The shadows on the sand were very blue, of the same tone as the sky; two ravens flew northward, croaking as they passed. I struggled to keep awake. The only sound was made by the slap of the camels' feet, like wavelets lapping on a beach.

To rest the camels we stopped for four hours in the late afternoon on a long gentle slope which stretched down to another salt-flat. There was no vegetation on it and no salt-bushes bordered the plain below us. Al Auf announced that we would go on again at sunset. While we were feeding I said to him cheerfully, 'Anyway, the worst should be over now that we are across the Uruq al Shaiba.' He looked at me for a moment and then answered, 'If we go well tonight we should reach them tomorrow.' I said, 'Reach what?' and he replied, 'The Uruq al Shaiba', adding, 'Did you think what we crossed today was the Uruq al Shaiba? That was only a dune. You will see them tomorrow.' For a moment, I thought he was joking, and then I realized that he was serious, that the worst of the journey which I had thought was behind us was still ahead.

It was midnight when at last al Auf said, 'Let's stop here. We will get some sleep and give the camels a rest. The Uruq al Shaiba are not far away now.' In my dreams that night they towered above us higher than the Himalayas.

Al Auf woke us again while it was still dark. As usual bin Kabina made coffee, and the sharp-tasting drops which he poured out stimulated but did not warm. The morning star had risen above the dunes. Formless things regained their shape in the first dim light of dawn. The grunting camels heaved themselves erect. We lingered for a moment more beside the fire; then al Auf said 'Come', and we moved forward. Beneath my feet the gritty sand was cold as frozen snow.

We were faced by a range as high as, perhaps even higher than, the range we had crossed the day before, but here the peaks were steeper and more pronounced, rising in many cases to great pinnacles, down which the flowing ridges swept like draperies. These sands, paler coloured than those we had crossed, were very soft, cascading round our feet as the camels struggled up the slopes. Remembering how little warning of imminent collapse the dying camels had given me twelve years before in the Danakil country, I wondered how much more these camels would stand, for they were trembling violently whenever they halted. When one refused to go on we heaved on her head-rope, pushed her from behind, and lifted the loads on either side as we manhandled the roaring animal upward. Sometimes one of them lay down and refused to rise, and then we had to unload her, and carry the water-skins and the saddle-bags ourselves. Not that the loads were heavy. We had only a few gallons of water left and some handfuls of flour.

We led the trembling, hesitating animals upward along great sweeping ridges where the knife-edged crests crumbled beneath our feet. Although it was killing work, my companions were always gentle and infinitely patient. The sun was scorching hot and I felt empty, sick, and dizzy. As I struggled up the slope, knee-deep in shifting sand, my heart thumped wildly and my thirst grew worse. I found it difficult to swallow; even my ears felt blocked, and yet I knew that it would be many intolerable hours before I could drink. I would stop to rest, dropping down on the scorching sand, and immediately it seemed I would hear the others shouting, 'Umbarak, Umbarak'; their voices sounded strained and hoarse.

It took us three hours to cross this range.

On the summit were no gently undulating downs such as we had met the day before. Instead, three smaller dune-chains rode upon its back, and beyond them the sand fell away to a salt-flat in another great empty trough between the mountains. The range on the far side seemed even higher than the one on which we stood, and behind it were others. I looked round, seeking instinctively for some escape. There was no limit to my vision. Somewhere in the ultimate distance the sands merged into the sky, but in that infinity of space I could see no living thing, not even a withered plant to give me hope. 'There is nowhere to go', I thought. 'We cannot go back and our camels will never get up another of these awful dunes. We really are finished.' The silence flowed over me, drowning the voices of my companions and the fidgeting of their camels.

We went down into the valley, and somehow—and I shall never know how the camels did it—we got up the other side. There, utterly exhausted, we collapsed. Al Auf gave us each a little water, enough to wet our mouths. He said, 'We need this if we are to go on.' The midday sun had drained the colour from the sands. Scattered banks of cumulus cloud threw shadows across the dunes and salt-flats, and added an illusion that we were high among Alpine peaks, with frozen lakes of blue and green in the valley, far below. Half asleep, I turned over, but the sand burnt through my shirt and woke me from my dreams.

Two hours later al Auf roused us. As he helped me load my camel, he said, 'Cheer up, Umbarak. This time we really are across the Uruq al Shaiba', and when I pointed to the ranges ahead of us, he answered, 'I can find a way through those; we need not cross them.' We went on till sunset, but we were going with the grain of the country, following the valleys and no longer trying to climb the dunes. We should not have been able to cross another. There was a little fresh *qassis* on the slope where we halted. I hoped that this lucky find would give us an excuse to stop here for the night, but, after we had fed, al Auf went to fetch the camels, saying, 'We must go on again while it is cool if we are ever to reach Dhafara.'

We stopped long after midnight and started again at dawn, still exhausted from the strain and long hours of yesterday, but al Auf encouraged us by saying that the worst was over. The dunes were certainly lower than they had been, more uniform in height and more rounded, with fewer peaks. Four hours after we had started we came to rolling uplands of gold and silver sand, but still there was nothing for the camels to eat.

A hare jumped out from under a bush, and al Auf knocked it over with his stick. The others shouted 'God has given us meat.' For days we had talked of food; every conversation seemed to lead back to it. Since we had left Ghanim I had been always conscious of the dull ache of hunger, yet in the evenings my throat was dry even after my drink, so that I found it difficult to swallow the dry bread Musallim set before us.

All day we thought and talked about that hare, and by three o'clock in the afternoon could no longer resist stopping to cook it. Mabkhaut suggested, 'Let's roast it in its skin in the embers of a fire. That will save our water—we haven't got much left.' Bin Kabina led the chorus of protest. 'No, by God! Don't even suggest such a thing'; and turning to me he said, 'We don't want Mabkhaut's charred meat. Soup. We want soup and extra bread. We will feed well today even if we go hungry and thirsty later. By God, I am hungry!' We agreed to make soup. We were across the Uruq al Shaiba and intended to celebrate our achievement with this gift from God. Unless our camels foundered we were safe; even if our water ran out we should live to reach a well.

Musallim made nearly double our usual quantity of bread while bin Kabina cooked the hare. He looked across at me and said, 'The smell of this meat makes me faint.' When it was ready he divided it into five portions. They were very small, for an Arabian hare is no larger than an English rabbit, and this one was not even fully grown. Al Auf named the lots and Mabkhaut drew them. Each of us took the small pile of meat which had fallen to him. Then bin Kabina said, 'God! I have forgotten to divide the liver', and the others said, 'Give it to Umbarak.' I protested, saying that they should divide it, but they swore by God that they would not eat it and that I was to have it. Eventually I took it, knowing that I ought not, but too greedy for this extra scrap of meat to care.

Our water was nearly finished and there was only enough flour for about another week. The starving camels were so thirsty that they had refused to eat some half-dried herbage which we had passed. We must water them in the next day or two or they would collapse. Al Auf said that it would take us three more days to reach Khaba well in Dhafara, but that there was a very brackish well not far away. He thought that the camels might drink its water.

That night after we had ridden for a little over an hour it grew suddenly dark. Thinking that a cloud must be covering the full moon, I looked over my shoulder and saw that there was an eclipse and that half the moon was already obscured. Bin Kabina noticed it at the same moment and broke into a chant which the others took up.

• • •

God endures for ever.
The life of man is short.
The Pleiades are overhead.
The moon's among the stars.

Otherwise they paid no attention to the eclipse (which was total), but looked round for a place to camp.

We started very early the next morning and rode without a stop for seven hours across easy rolling downs. The colour of these sands was vivid, varied, and unexpected: in places the colour of ground coffee, elsewhere brick-red, or purple, or a curious golden-green. There were small white gypsum-flats, fringed with *shanan*, a grey-green salt-bush, lying in hollows in the downs. We rested for two hours on sands the colour of dried blood and then led our camels on again.

Suddenly we were challenged by an Arab lying behind a bush on the crest of a dune. Our rifles were on our camels, for we had not expected to meet anyone here. Musallim was hidden behind mine. I watched him draw his rifle clear. But al Auf said, 'It is the voice of a Rashid', and walked forward. He spoke to the concealed Arab, who rose and came to meet him. They embraced and stood talking until we joined them. We greeted the man, and al Auf said, 'This is Hamad bin Hanna, a sheikh of the Rashid.' He was a heavily-built, bearded man of middle age. His eyes were set close together and he had a long nose with a blunt end. He fetched his camel from behind the dune while we unloaded.

We made coffee for him and listened to his news. He told us that he had been looking for a stray camel when he crossed our tracks and had taken us for a raiding party from the south. Ibn Saud's tax-collectors were in Dhafara and the Rabadh, collecting tribute from the tribes; and there were Rashid, Awamir, Murra, and some Manahil to the north of us.

We had to avoid all contact with Arabs other than the Rashid, and if possible even with them, so that news of my presence would not get about among the tribes, for I had no desire to be arrested by Ibn Saud's tax-collectors and taken off to explain my presence here to Ibn Jalawi, the formidable Governor of the Hasa. Karab from the Hadhramaut had raided these sands the year before, so there was also a serious risk of our being mistaken for raiders, since the tracks of our camels would show that we had come from the southern steppes. This risk would be increased if it appeared that we were avoiding the Arabs, for honest travellers never pass an encampment without seeking news and food. It was going to be very difficult to escape detection. First we must water our camels and draw water for ourselves. Then we must lie up as close as possible to Liwa and send a party to the villages to buy us enough food for at least another month. Hamad told me that Liwa belonged to the Al bu Falah of Abu Dhabi. He said that they were still fighting Said bin Maktum of Dibai, and that, as there was a lot of raiding going on, the Arabs would be very much on the alert.

We started again in the late afternoon and travelled till sunset. Hamad came with us and said he would stay with us until we had got food from Liwa. Knowing where the Arabs were encamped he could help us to avoid them. Next day, after seven hours' travelling, we reached Khaur Sabakha on the edge of the Dhafara sands. We cleaned out the well and found brackish water at seven feet, so bitter that even the camels only drank a little before refusing it. They sniffed thirstily at the water with which al Auf tried to coax them from a leather bucket, but only dipped their lips into it. We covered their noses but still they would not drink. Yet al Auf said that Arabs themselves drank this water mixed with milk, and when I expressed my disbelief he added that if an Arab was really thirsty he would even kill a camel and drink the liquid in its stomach, or ram a stick down its throat and drink the vomit. We went on again till nearly sunset.

The next day when we halted in the afternoon al Auf told us we had reached Dhafara and that Khaba well was close. He said that he would fetch water in the morning. We finished what little was left in one of our skins. Next day we remained where we were. Hamad said that he would go for news and return the following day. Al Auf, who went with him, came back in the afternoon with two skins full of water which, although slightly brackish, was delicious after the filthy evil-smelling dregs we had drunk the night before.

It was December 12th, fourteen days since we had left Khaur bin Atarit in Ghanim.

In the evening, now that we needed no longer measure out each cup of water, bin Kabina made extra coffee, while Musallim increased our rations of flour by a mugful. This was wild extravagance, but we felt that the occasion called for celebration. Even so, the loaves he handed us were woefully inadequate to stay our hunger, now that our thirst was gone.

The moon was high above us when I lay down to sleep. The others still talked round the fire, but I closed my mind to the meaning of their words, content to hear only the murmur of their voices, to watch their outlines sharp against the sky, happily conscious that they were there and beyond them the camels to which we owed our lives.

For years the Empty Quarter had represented to me the final, unattainable challenge which the desert offered. Suddenly it had come within my reach. I remembered my excitement when Lean had casually offered me the chance to go there, the immediate determination to cross it, and then the doubts and fears, the frustrations, and the moments of despair. Now I had crossed it. To others my journey would have little importance. It would produce nothing except a rather inaccurate map which no one was ever likely to use. It was a personal experience, and the reward had been a drink of clean, nearly tasteless water. I was content with that.

Looking back on the journey I realized that there had been no high moment of achievement such as a mountaineer must feel when he stands upon his chosen summit. Over the past days new strains and anxieties had built up as others eased, for, after all, this crossing of the Empty Quarter was set in the framework of a longer journey, and already my mind was busy with the new problems which our return journey presented.

from The Sea and the Jungle
by H. M. Tomlinson

Journalist and family man H. M. Tomlinson (1873–1958) in 1909 threw over his job at the London Morning Leader *to take a berth on a freighter bound for the Amazon's upper reaches. Near the end of his trip, he and a companion took a shortcut through the jungle's interior, where even local inhabitants wouldn't venture. Reading Tomlinson's account, it's hard to blame them: His jungle is a place of phantoms, of eerily slow-motion violence—a place to lose one's self in every sense of the phrase.*

W hen in the neighbourhood of the Girau Falls we returned to a camp known as 22, which was merely a couple of huts, the station of two English surveyors, who had with them a small party of Bolivians. The Bolivian frontier was then but a little distance to the south-west. We rested for a day there, and planned to make a journey of ten miles across country, to the falls of the Caldeirão do Inferno. By doing so we should save the wearying return ride along the track to the Rio Jaci-Parana, for at the Caldeirão a launch was kept, and in that we could shoot the rapids and reach the camp on the Jaci two days earlier. Some haste was necessary now, for my steamer must be nearing her sailing time. And again, I agreed the more readily to the plan of making a traverse of the forest because it would give me the opportunity of seeing the interior of the virgin jungle away from any track. Though I had been so long in a land which all was forest I had not been within the universal growth except for little journeys on used trails. A journey across country in the Amazon country is never made by the Brazilians. The only roads are the rivers. It is a rare traveller who goes through those forests, guided only by a compass and his lore of the wilderness. That for months I had never been out of sight of the jungle, and yet had rarely ventured to turn aside from a path for more than a few paces, is some indication of its character. At the camp where we were staying I was told that once a man had gone merely within the screen of leaves, and then no doubt had lost, for a few moments, his sense of direction of the camp, for he was never seen again.

The equatorial forest is popularly pictured as a place of bright and varied colours, with extravagant flowers, an abundance of fruits, and huge trees hung with creepers where lurk many venomous but beautiful snakes with gem-like eyes, and a multitude of birds as bright as the flowers; paradise indeed, though haunted by a peril. Those details are right, but the picture is wrong. It is true that some of the birds are decorated in a way which makes the most beautiful of our temperate birds seem dull; but the toucans and macaws of the Madeira forest, though common, are not often seen, and when they are seen they are likely to be but obscure atoms drifting high in a white light. About the villages and in the clearings there are usually many superb butterflies and moths, and a varied wealth of vegetation not to be matched outside the tropics, and there will be the fireflies and odours in evening pathways. But the virgin forest itself soon becomes but a green monotony which, through extent and mystery, dominates and compels to awe and some dread. You will see it daily, but will not often approach it. It has no splendid blossoms; none, that is, which you will see, except by chance, as by luck one day I saw from the steamer's bridge some trees in blossom, domes of lilac surmounting the forest levels. Trees are always in blossom there, for it is a land of continuous high summer, and there are orchids always in flower, and palms and vines that fill acres of forest with fragrance, palms and other trees which give wine and delicious fruits, and somewhere hidden there are the birds of the tropical picture, and dappled jaguars perfect in colouring and form, and brown men and women who have strange gods. But they are lost in the ocean of leaves as are the pearls and wonders in the deep. You will remember the equatorial forest but as a gloom of foliage in which all else that showed was rare and momentary, was foundered and lost to sight instantly, as an unusual ray of coloured light in one mid-ocean wave gleams, and at once goes, and your surprise at its apparition fades too, and again there is but the empty desolation which is for ever but vastness sombrely bright.

One morning, wondering greatly what we should see in the place where we should be the first men to go, Hill and I left camp 22 and returned a little along the track. It was a hot still morning. A vanilla vine was in fragrant flower somewhere, unseen, but unescapable. My little unknown friend in the woods, who calls me at odd times—but I think chiefly when I am near a stream—by whistling thrice, let me know he was about. Hill said he thinks he has seen him, and that my little friend looks like a blackbird. On the track in many places were objects which appeared to be long cups inverted, of unglazed ware. Picking up one I found it was the cap to a mine of ants, the inside of the clay cup being hollowed in a perfect circle, and remarkably smooth. A paca dived into the scrub near us. It was early morning, scented with vanilla, and the intricacy of leaves was radiant. Nowhere in the screen could I see a place through which it was possible to crawl to whatever was behind it. The front of leaves was unbroken. Hill presently bent double and disappeared, and I followed in the break he made. So we went for about ten minutes, my leader cutting obstructions with his machete, and mostly we had to go almost on hands and knees. The undergrowth was green, but in the etiolated way of plants which have little light, though that may have been my fancy. One plant was very common, making light-green feathery barriers. I think it was a climbing bamboo. Its stem was vapid and of no diameter, and its grasslike leaves grew in whorls at the joints. It extended to incredible distances. We got out of that margin of undergrowth, which springs up quickly when light is let into the woods, as it was there through the cutting of the track, and found ourselves on a bare floor where the trunks of arborescent laurels grew so thickly together that our view ahead was restricted to a few yards. We were in the forest. There was a pale tinge of day, but its origin was uncertain, for overhead no foliage could be seen, but only deep shadows from which long ropes were hanging without life. In that obscurity were points of light, as if a high roof had lost some tiles. Hill set a course almost due south, and we went on, presently descending to a deep clear stream over which a tree had fallen. Shafts of daylight came down to us there, making the sandy bottom of the stream luminous, as by a lantern, and betraying crowds of small fishes. As we climbed the tree, to cross upon it, we disturbed several morphos. We had difficulties beyond in a hollow, where the bottom of the forest was lumbered with fallen trees, dry rubbish, and thorns, and once, stepping on what looked timber solid enough, its treacherous shell collapsed, and I went down into a cloud of dust and ants. In clearing this wreckage, which was usually as high as our faces, and doubly confused by the darkness, the involutions of dead thorny creepers, and clouds of dried foliage, Hill got at fault with our direction, but reassured himself, though I don't know how—but I think with the certain knowledge that if we went south long enough we should strike the Madeira somewhere—and on we went. For hours we continued among the trees, seldom knowing what was ahead of us for any distance, surviving points of noise intruding again after long in the dusk of limbo. So still and nocturnal was the forest that it was real only when its forms were close. All else was phantom and of the shades. There was not a green sign of life, and not a sound. Resting once under a tree I began to think there was a conspiracy implied in that murk and awful stillness, and that we should never come out again into the day and see a living earth. Hill sat looking out, and said, as if in answer to an unspoken thought of mine which had been heard because there was less than no sound there, that men who were lost in those woods soon went mad.

Then he led on again. This forest was nothing like the paradise a tropical wild is supposed to be. It was as uniformly dingy as the old stones of a London street on a November evening. We did not see a movement, except when the morphos started from the uprooted tree. Once I heard the whistle call us from the depths of the forest, urgent and startling; and now when in a London by-way I hear a boy call his mate in a shrill whistle, it puts about me again the spectral aisles, and that unexpectant quiet of the sepulchre which is more than mere absence of sound, for the dead who should have no voice. This central forest was really the vault of the long-forgotten, dank, mouldering, dark, abandoned to the accumulations of eld and decay. The tall pillars rose, upholding night, and they might have been bastions of weathered limestone and basalt, for they were as grim as ancient and ruinous masonry. There was no undergrowth. The ground was hidden in a ruin of perished stuff, uprooted trees, parchments of leaves, broken boughs, and mummied husks, the iron globes of nuts, and pods. There was no day, but some breaks in the roof were points of remote starlight. The crowded columns mounted straight and far, almost branchless, fading into indistinction. Out of that overhead obscurity hung a wreckage of distorted cables, binding the trees, and often reaching the ground. The trees were seldom of great girth, though occasionally there was a dominant basaltic pillar, its roots meandering over the floor like streams of old lava. The smooth ridges of such a fantastic complexity of roots were sometimes breast high. The walls ran up the trunk, projecting from it as flat buttresses, for great heights. We would crawl round such an occupying structure, diminished groundlings, as one would move about the base of a foreboding, plutonic building whose limits and meaning were ominous and baffling. There were other great trees with compound boles, built literally of bundles of round stems, intricate gothic pillars, some of the props having fused in places. Every tree was the support of a parasitic community, lianas swathing it and binding it. One vine moulded itself to its host, a flat and wide compress, as though it were plastic. We might have been witnessing what had been a riot of manifold and insurgent life. It had been turned to stone when in the extreme pose of striving violence. It was all dead now.

But what if these combatants had only paused as we appeared? It was a thought which came to me. The pause might be but an appearance for our deception. Indeed, they were all fighting as we passed through, those still and fantastic shapes, a war ruthless but slow, in which the battle day was ages long. They seemed but still. We were deceived. If time had been accelerated, if the movements in that war of phantoms had been speeded, we should have seen what really was there, the greater trees running upwards to starve the weak of light and food, and heard the continuous collapse of the failures, and have seen the lianas writhing and constricting, manifestly like serpents, throttling and eating their hosts. We did see the dead everywhere, shells with the worms at them. Yet it was not easy to be sure that we saw anything at all, for these were not trees, but shapes in a region below the day, a world sunk abysmally from the land of living things, to which light but thinly percolated down to two travellers moving over its floor, trying to get out to their own place.

Late in the afternoon we were surprised by a steep hill in our way, where the forest was more open. Palms became conspicuous on the slopes, and the interior of the sombre woods was lighted with bright and graceful foliage. The wild banana was frequent, its long rippling pennants showing everywhere. The hill rose sharply, perhaps for six hundred feet, and over its surface were scattered large stones, and stones are rare indeed in this land of vegetable humus. They were often six inches in diameter, and I should have said they were waterworn but that I had seen them *in situ* at one camp, where they occurred but little below the surface in a friable sandstone, the largest of them easily broken in the hand, for they were but ferrous concretions of quartz grains. After exposure to the air they so hardened that they could be fractured only with difficulty. We kept along the ridge of the hill, finding breaks in the forest through which, as through unexpected windows, we could see, for a wonder, over the roof of the forest, looking out of our prison to a wide world where the sun was declining. In the south-west we caught the gleam of the Madeira, and beyond it saw a continuation of the range of hills on which we stood.

In the low ground between the hill range and the river the forest was lower, and was so tangled a mass that I doubted whether we could make a way through it. We happened upon a deserted Caripuna village, three large sheds, without sides, each but a ragged thatch propped on four legs. The clearing was just large enough to hold them. I could find no relics of the forest folk about. Damp leaves were thick on the floor of each shelter. But it was lucky we found the huts, for thence a trail led us to the river. We emerged suddenly from the forest, just as one goes through a little door into the open street. We were on the bank of the Madeira by the upper falls of the Caldeirao. It was still a great river, with the wall of the forest opposite, just above which the sunset was flaming, so far away that its tree trunks were but vertical lines of silver in dark cliffs. A track used by the Bolivian rubber boatmen led us down stream to the camp by the lower falls.

It was night when we got to the three huts of the camp, and the river could not be seen, but it was heard, a continuous low thundering.

Sometimes a greater shock of deep waters falling, an orgasm of the flood pouring unseen, more violent than the rest, made the earth tremulous. Men held up lanterns to our faces, and led us to a hut. It was but the usual roof of leaves. We rested in hammocks slung between the posts, and I ached in every limb. But here we were at last; and there is no more luxurious bed than a hammock, yielding and resilient, as though you were cradled on air; and there is no pipe like that smoked in a hammock at night in the tropics after a day of toil and anxiety in a dissolving heat, for the heat makes a pipe bitter and impossible; but if a tropic night is cool and cloudless it comes like a benediction, and the silence is a peace that is below you and around, and as high as the stars towards which your face is turned. The ropes of the hammock creaked. Sometimes a man spoke quietly, as though he were at a great distance. The sound of the water receded, was heard only as in a sleep, and it might have been the loud murmur of the spinning globe, heard because we had left this world and had leisure for trifles in a securer world apart.

In the morning, while they prepared the little steam launch for its journey down the rapids, I had time to climb about the smooth granite boulders of the foreshore below the hut. A rock is so unusual in this country that it is a luxury when found. The granite was bare, but in its crevices grew cacti and other plants with fleshy leaves and swollen stems. Shadowing the hut was a tree bearing trumpet-shaped flowers, and before the blossoms humming-birds were hovering, glowing and evanescent morsels, remaining miraculously suspended when inserting their long bills into the flowers, their little wings beating so rapidly that the air seemed visible and radiant about them. Another tree here interested me, for it was Bates' assacu, the only one I saw. It was a large tree, with palmate leaves having seven fingers. Ugly spines studded even its brown trunk.

I looked out on the river dubiously. A rocky island was just off shore, crowned with trees. Between us and the island, and beyond, the waters heaved and circled, evidently of great depth, and fearfully disturbed and swift. It looked all its name, the Caldeirão do Inferno—hell's cauldron. There was not much white and broken water. But its surface was always changing, whirlpools forming and revolving, then disappearing in long wrenched strands of water. Sometimes a big tree would leap out of the water, as though it had travelled upwards from the bottom, and then would vanish again.

We set out upon it, with an engineman and two half-breeds, and went off obliquely for mid-stream. The engineman and navigator was a fair-haired German. If the river had been sane and usual I should have had my eyes on the forest which stood along each shore, for few white men had ever looked upon it. But the river took our minds, and never in bad weather in the western ocean have I seen water so full of menace. Yet below the falls it was silent and unbroken. It was its smooth swiftness, its strange checks and mysterious and deep convulsions, as though the river bed itself was insecure, the startling whirlpools which appeared without warning, circling depressions on the surface in which our launch would have been but a straw which shocked the mind. It was stealthy and noiseless. The water was but an inch or two below our gunwale. We saw trees afloat, greater and heavier than our midget of a craft, shooting down the gently inclined shining expanse just as we were, and express; and then, as if an awful hand had grasped them from below, they were pulled under, and we saw them no more; or, again, and near to us and ahead, a tree bole would shoot from below like an arrow, though no tree had been drifting there. The shores were far away.

The water ahead grew worse. The German crouched by his little throbbing engine, looking anxiously—I could see his fixed stare—over the bows. We were travelling indeed now. The boat, in a rapid tremor, and oscillating violently, was clutched at the keel by something which coiled strongly about us, gripped us, and held us; and the boat, mad and terrified, in an effort to escape, made a circuit, the water lipping at her gunwale and coming over the bows. The river seemed poised a foot above the bows, ready to pour in and swamp us. The German tried to get her head down stream. Hill began tearing at his ammunition belt, and I stooped and tugged at my boot laces. . . .

The boat jumped, as if released. The German turned round on us grinning. "It ees all right," he said. He began to roll a cigarette nervously. "We pull it off all right, " said the German, wetting his cigarette paper. The boat was free, dancing lightly along. The little engine was singing quickly and freely.

The Madeira here was as wide as in its lower reaches, with many islands. There were hosts of waterfowl. We landed once at a rubber hunter's sitio on the right bank. Its owner, a Bolivian, and his pretty Indian wife, who had tattoo marks on her forehead, made much of us, and gave us coffee. They had an orchard of guavas, and there, for it was long since I had tasted fruit, I was an immoderate thief, in spite of a pet curassow which followed me through the garden with distracting pecks. The Rio Jaci-Parana, a black-water stream, opened up soon after we left the sitio. The boundary between the clay-coloured flood of the Madeira and the dark water of the tributary was straight and distinct. From a distance the black water seemed like ink, but we found it quite clear and bright. The Jaci is not an important branch river, but it was, at this period of the rains, wider than the Thames at Richmond, and without doubt very much deeper. The appearance of the forest on the Jaci was quite different from the palisades of the parent stream. On the Madeira there is commonly a narrow shelf of bank, above which the jungle rises as would a sheer cliff. The Jaci had no banks. The forest was deeply submerged on either side, and whenever an opening showed in the woods we could see the waters within, but could not see their extent because of the interior gloom. The outer foliage was awash, and mounted, not straight, but in rounded clouds. For the first time I saw many vines and trees in flower, presumably because we were nearer the roof of the woods. One tree was loaded with the pendent pear-shaped nests of those birds called "hang nests," and scores of the beauties in their black and gold plumage were busy about their homes, which resembled monstrous fruits. Another tree was weighted with large racemes of orange-coloured blossoms, but as the launch passed close to it we discovered the blooms were really bundles of caterpillars. The Jaci appeared to be a haunt of the alligators, but all we saw of them was their snouts, which moved over the surface of the water out of our way like rubber balls afloat and mysteriously propelled. I had a sight, too, of that most regal of the eagles, the harpy, for one, well within view, lifted from a tree ahead, and sailed finely over the river and away.

That night I slept again in my old hut at the Jaci camp, and with Hill and another official set off early next morning for the construction camp on Rio Caracoles, which we hoped to reach before the commissary train left for Pôrto Velho. At Pôrto Velho the *Capella* was, and I wished, perhaps as much as I have ever wished for anything, that I should not be left behind when she departed. I knew she must be on the point of sailing.

My two companions had reasons of their own for thinking the catching of that train was urgently necessary. In our minds we were already settled and safe in a waggon, comfortable among the empty boxes, going back to the place where the crowd was. But still we had some way to ride; and, I must tell you, I was now possessed of all I desired of the tropical forest, and had but one fixed idea in my dark mind, but one bright star shining there; I had turned about, and was going home, and now must follow hard and unswervingly that star in the east of my mind. The rhythmic movements of the mule under me— only my legs knew he was there—formed in my darkened mind a refrain: get out of it, get out of it.

And at last there were the huts and tents of the Caracoles, still and quiet under the vertical sun. No train was there, nor did it look a place for trains. My steamer was sixty miles away, beyond a track along which further riding was impossible, and where walking, for more than two miles, could not be even considered. The train, the boys told us blithely, went back half an hour before. The audience of trees regarded my consternation with the indifference which I had begun to hate with some passion. The boys naturally expected that we should take it in the right way for hot climates, without fuss, and that now they had some new gossip for the night. But they should have understood Hill better. My tall gaunt leader waved them aside, for he was a man who could do things, when there seemed nothing that one could do. "The terminus or bust!" he cried. "Where's the boss?" He demanded a handcart and a crew. I thought he spoke in jest. A handcart is a contrivance propelled along railway metals by pumping at a handle. The handle connects with the wheels by a crank and cogs through a slot in the centre of the platform, and you get five miles an hour out of it, while the crew continues. For sixty miles, in that heat, it was impossible. Yet Hill persisted; the cart was put on the metals, five half-breeds manned the pump handle, three facing the track ahead, two with their backs to it.

We three passengers sat on the sides and front of the trolley. Away we went.

The boys cheered and laughed, calling out to us the probabilities of our journey. We trundled round a corner, and already I had to change my cramped position; fifty-eight miles to go. We sat with our legs held up out of the way of the vines and rocks by the track, and careful to remember that our craniums must be kept clear of the pump handle. The crew went up and down, with fixed looks. The sun was the eye of the last judgment, and my lips were cracked. The trees made no sign. The natives went up and down; and the forest went by, tree by tree.

My tired and thoughtless legs dropped, and a thorn fastened its teeth instantly in my boots, and nearly had me down. The trees went by, one by one. There was a large black and yellow butterfly on a stone near us. I was surprised when no sound came as it made a grand movement upwards. Then, in the heart of nowhere, the trolley slackened, and came to a stand. We had lost a pin. Half a mile back we could hardly credit we really had found that pin, but there it was; and the men began to go up and down again. Hill got a touch of fever, and the natives had changed to the colour of impure tallow, and flung their perspiration on my face and hands as they swung mechanically. The poor wretches! We were done. The sun weighed untold tons.

But the sun declined, some monkeys began to howl, and the sunset tempest sprang down on us its assault, shaking the high screens on either hand, and the rain beat with the roll of kettle-drums. Then we got on an up grade, and two of the spent natives collapsed, their chests heaving. So I and the other chap stood up in the night, looked to the stars, from which no help could be got, took hold of the pump handle like gallant gentlemen, and tried to forget there were twenty miles to go. Away we went, jog, jog, uphill. I thought that gradient would not end till my heart and head had burst; but it did, just in time.

We gathered speed on a down grade. We flew. Presently the man with the fever yelled, "The brake, the brake! " But the brake was broken. The trolley was not running, but leaping in the dark. Every time it came down it found the metals. A light was coming towards us on the line; and the others prepared to jump. I could not even see that light, for my back was turned to our direction, and I could not let go the flying handle, else would all control have gone, and also I should have been smashed. I shut my eyes, pumped swiftly and involuntarily, and waited for doom to hit me in the back. The blow was a long time coming. Then Hill's gentle voice remarked, "All right, boys, it's a firefly."

. . . I became only a piece of machinery, and pumped, and pumped, with no more feeling than a bolster. Shadows undulated by us everlastingly. I think my tongue was hanging out . . .

Lights were really seen at last. Kind hands lifted us from the engine of torture; and I heard the remembered voice of the Skipper, "Is he there? I thought it was a case."

That night of my return a full moon and a placid river showed me the *Capella* doubled, as in a mirror, and admiring the steamer's deep inverted shape I saw a heartening portent—I saw steam escaping from the funnel which was upside down. A great joy filled me at that, and I turned to the Skipper, as we strode over the ties of the jetty. "Yes. We go home to-morrow," he said. The bunk was super-heated again by the engine room, but knowing the glad reason, I endured it with pleasure. Tomorrow we turned about.

Yet on the morrow there was still the persistence of the spacious idleness which encompassed us impregnably, beyond which we could not go. The little that was left of the fuel in the holds went out of us with dismal unhaste. The Skipper and the mates fumed, and the Doctor took me round to see the *Capella*'s pets, so that we might fill up time. A monkey, an entirely secular creature once with us, had died while I was away. It was well. He had no name; Vice was his name. There were no tears at his death, and Tinker the terrier began to get back some of his full and lively form again after that day when, in a sudden righteous revolution, he slew, and barbarously mangled, the insolent tyrant of the ship. The monkey had feared none but Mack, our red, blue and yellow macaw, a monstrous and resplendent fowl in whose iron bill even Brazil nuts were soft.

But we all respected Mack. He was the wisest thing on the ship. If an idle man felt high-spirited and approached Mack to demonstrate his humour, that great bird gave an inquiring turn to its head, and its deliberate and unwinking eyes hid the rapid play of its prescient mind. The man stopped, and would speak but playfully. Nobody ever dared.

When Mack first boarded the ship, a group of us, gloved, smothered him with a heavy blanket and fastened a chain to his leg. He knew he was overpowered, and did not struggle, but inside the blanket we heard some horrible chuckles. We took off the blanket and stood back expectantly from that dishevelled and puzzling giant of a parrot. He shook his feathers flat again, quite self-contained, looked at us sardonically and murmured "Gur-r-r" very distinctly; then glanced at his foot. There was a little surprise in his eye when he saw the chain there. He lifted up the chain to examine it, tried it, and then quietly and easily bit it through. "Gur-r-r! " he said again, straightening his vest, still regarding us solemnly. Then he moved off to a davit, and climbed the mizzen shrouds to the topmast.

When he saw us at food he came down with nonchalance, and overlooked our table from the cross beam of an awning. Apparently satisfied, he came directly to the mess table, sitting beside me, and took his share with all the assurance of a member, allowing me to idle with his beautiful wings and his tail. He was a beauty. He took my finger in his awful bill and rolled it round like a cigarette. I wondered what he would do to it before he let it go; but he merely let it go. He was a great character, magnanimously minded. I never knew a tamer creature than Mack. That evening he rejoined a flock of his wild brothers in the distant tree-tops. But he was back next morning, and put everlasting fear into the terrier, who was at breakfast, by suddenly appearing before him with wings outspread on the deck, looking like a disrupted and angry rainbow, and making raucous threats. The dog gave one yell and fell over backwards.

We had added a bull-frog to our pets, and he must have weighed at least three pounds. He had neither vice nor virtue, but was merely a squab in a shady corner. Whenever the dog approached him he would rise on his legs, however, and inflate himself till he was globular. This was incomprehensible to Tinker, who was contemptuous, but being a little uncertain, would make a circuit of the frog. Sitting one day in the shadow of the box which enclosed the rudder chain was the frog, and we were near, and up came Tinker a-trot all unthinking, his nose to the deck. The frog hurriedly furnished his pneumatic act when Tinker, who did not know froggie was there, was close beside him, and Tinker snapped sideways in a panic. Poor punctured froggie dwindled instantly, and died.

I could add to the list of our creatures the anaconda which was found coming aboard by the gangway but that a stoker saw him first, became hysterical, and slew the reptile with a shovel; there were the coral snakes which came inboard over the cables and through the hawse pipes, and the vampire bats which frequented the forecastle. But they are insignificant beside our peccary. I forgot to tell you the Skipper never made a tame creature of her. She refused us. We brought her up from the bunkers where first she was placed, because the stokers flatly refused her society in the dark. She was brought up on deck in bonds, snapping her tushes in a direful way, and when released did most indomitably charge all our ship's company, bristles up, and her automatic teeth louder and more rapid than ever. How we fled! When I turned on my vantage, the manner of my getting there all unknown, to see who was my neighbour, it was my abashed and elderly captain, who can look upon sea weather at its worst with an easy eye, but who then was striving desperately to get his legs (which were in pyjamas) ten feet above the deck, in case the very wild pig below had wings.

After the peccary was released we could not call the ship ours. We crept about as thieves. It was fortunate that she always gave warning of her proximity by making the noise of castanets with her tusks, so that we had time to get elevated before she arrived. But I never really knew how fast she could move till I saw her chase the dog, whom she despised and ignored. One morning his valiant barking at her, from a distance he judged to be adequate, annoyed her, and she shot at him like a projectile. Her slender limbs and diminutive hooves were those of a deer, and they became merely a haze beneath her body, which was a flying passion. The terrified dog had no chance, but just as she closed with him her feet slipped, and so Tinker's life was saved.

Her end was pitiful. One day she got into the saloon. The Doctor and I were there, and saw her trot in at one door, and we trotted out at another door. Now, the saloon was the pride of the Skipper; and when the old man tried to bribe her out of it—he talked to her from the open skylight above—and she insulted him with her mouth, he sent for his men. From behind a shut door of the saloon alley way we heard a fusilade of tusks in the saloon, shrieks from the maddened dog, uproar from the parrots, and the hoarse shouts of the crew. The pig was charging ten ways at once. Stealing a look from the cabin we saw the boatswain appear with a bunch of cotton waste, soaked in kerosene, blazing at the end of a bamboo, and the mate with a knife lashed to another pole. The peccary charged the lot. There broke out the cries of Tophet, and through chaos champed insistently the high note of the tusks. She was noosed and caged; but nothing could be done with the little fury, and when I peeped in at her a few days later she was full length, and dying. She opened one glazing eye at me, and snapped her teeth slowly, game to the end.

March 6.—It was reported at breakfast that we sail to-morrow. The bread was sour, the butter was oil, the sugar was black with flies, the sausages were tinned and very white and dead, and the bacon was all fat. And even the awning could not keep the sun away.

March 7.—We got the hatches on number four hold. It is reported we sail to-morrow.

March 8.—The ship was crowded this night with the boys, for a last jollification. We fired rockets, and swore enduring friendships with anybody, and many sang different songs together. It is reported that we sail to-morrow.

March 9.—It is reported that we sail to-morrow.

March 10.—The *Capella* has come to life. The master is on the bridge, the first mate is on the forecastle head, the second mate is on the poop, and the engineers are below. There are stern and minatory cries, and men who run. At the first slow clanking of the cable we raised wild cheers. The ship's body began to tremble, and there was thunder under her counter. We actually came away from the jetty, where long we had seemed a fixture. We got into mid-stream—stopped; slowly turned tail on Pôrto Velho. There was old man Jim, diminished on the distant jetty, waving his hat. Pôrto Velho looked strange again. Away we went. We

reached the bend of the river, and turned the corner. There was the last
we shall ever see of Pôrto Velho. Gone!

The forest unfolding in reverse order seemed brighter, and all would
have been quite well, but the fourth engineer came up from his duty,
and fell insensible. He was very yellow, and the Doctor had work to do.
Here was the first of our company to succumb to the country.

There were but six more days of forest; for the old *Capella*, empty and
light as a balloon, the collisions with the floating timber causing
muffled thunder in her hollow body, came down the swift floods of the
Madeira and the Amazon rivers "like a Cunarder, at sixteen knots," as
the Skipper said. And there on the sixth day was Pará again, and the sea
near. Our spirits mounted, released from the dead weight of heat and
silence. But I was to lose the Doctor at Pará, for he was then to return
to Pôrto Velho, having discharged his duty to the *Capella*'s company.
The Skipper took his wallet, and we went ashore with him, he to his
day-long task of clearing his vessel, and we for a final sad excursion.
Much later in the day, suspecting an unnameable evil was gathering to
my undoing, I called at the agent's office, and found the Skipper had
returned to the ship, that she was sailing that night, and, the regulations
of Pará being what they were, it being after six in the evening I could not
leave the city till next morning. My haggard and dismayed array of
thoughts broke in confusion and left me gibbering, with not one idea
for use. Without saying even good-bye to my old comrade I took to my
heels, and left him; and that was the last I saw of the Doctor. (Aha! my
staunch support in the long, hot and empty time at the back of things,
where were but trees, bad food, and a jest to brace our souls, if ever you
should see this—How!—and know, dear lad, I carried the damnable
regulations and a whole row of officials, the Union Jack at the main,
firing every gun as I bore down on them. I broke through. Only death
could have barred me from my ship and the way home.)

Next morning we were at sea. We dropped the pilot early and
changed our course to the north, bound for Barbados. Though on the
line, the difference in the air at sea, after our long enclosure in the rivers
of the forest, was keenly felt. And the ship too had been so level and
quiet; but here she was lively again, full of movements and noises. The

bows were at their old difference with the skyline, and the steady wind of the outer was driving over us. Before noon, when I went in to the Chief, my crony was flat and moribund with a temperature at 105°, and he had no interest in this life whatever. I had added the apothecary's duties to those of the Purser, and here found my first job. (Doctor, I gave him lots of grains of quinine, and lots more afterwards; and plenty of calomel when he was at 98 again. Was that all right?)

The sight of the big and hearty Chief, when he was about once more, yellow, insecure, and somewhat shrunken, made us dubious. Yet now were we rolling home. She was breasting down into a creaming smother, the seas were blue, and the world was fresh and wide all the way back. There was one fine night, as we were climbing slowly up the slope of the globe, when we lifted the whole constellation of the Great Bear, the last star of the tail just dipping below the seas, straight over the *Capella*'s bows, as she pitched. Then were we assured affairs were rightly ordered, and slept well and contented.

from A Walk in the Woods
by Bill Bryson

The Appalachian Trail hardly qualifies as wilderness, but it's nonetheless wild. Bill Bryson (born 1951) and his overweight, ex-con partner Stephen Katz found that walking the A.T. is dangerous; they helped make it so—for themselves, anyway. We join the pair early in their absurdly ambitious attempt to hike the 2,100-mile trail from start to finish. Already, they are desperate for diner food and porcelain toilets; now things get really bad.

O n the fourth evening, we made a friend. We were sitting in a nice little clearing beside the trail, our tents pitched, eating our noodles, savoring the exquisite pleasure of just sitting, when a plumpish, bespectacled young woman in a red jacket and the customary outsized pack came along. She regarded us with the crinkled squint of someone who is either chronically confused or can't see very well. We exchanged hellos and the usual banalities about the weather and where we were. Then she squinted at the gathering gloom and announced she would camp with us.

Her name was Mary Ellen. She was from Florida, and she was, as Katz forever after termed her in a special tone of awe, a piece of work. She talked nonstop, except when she was clearing out her eustachian tubes (which she did frequently) by pinching her nose and blowing out with a series of violent and alarming snorts of a sort that would make a dog leave the sofa and get under a table in the next room. I have long known that it is part of God's plan for me to spend a little time with each of the most stupid people on earth, and Mary Ellen was proof that even in the Appalachian woods I would not be spared.

It became evident from the first moment that she was a rarity.

"So what are you guys eating?" she said, plonking herself down on a spare log and lifting her head to peer into our bowls. "Noodles? Big mistake. Noodles have got like no energy. I mean like zero." She unblocked her ears. "Is that a Starship tent?"

I looked at my tent. "I don't know."

"Big mistake. They must have seen you coming at the camping store. What did you pay for it?"

"I don't know."

"Too much, that's how much. You should have got a three-season tent."

"It is a three-season tent."

"Pardon me saying so, but it is like seriously dumb to come out here in March without a three-season tent." She unblocked her ears.

"It is a three-season tent."

"You're lucky you haven't froze yet. You should go back and like punch out the guy that sold it to you because he's been like, you know, negligible selling you that."

"Believe me, it is a three-season tent."

She unblocked her ears and shook her head impatiently. "*That's* a three-season tent." She indicated Katz's tent.

"That's exactly the same tent."

She glanced at it again. "Whatever. How many miles did you do today? "

"About ten." Actually we had done eight point four, but this had included several formidable escarpments, including a notable wall of hell called Preaching Rock, the highest eminence since Springer Mountain, for which we had awarded ourselves bonus miles, for purposes of morale.

"Ten miles? Is that all? You guys must be like *really* out of shape. I did fourteen-two."

"How many have your lips done?" said Katz, looking up from his noodles.

She fixed him with one of her more severe squints. "Same as the rest of me, of course." She gave me a private look as if to say, "Is your friend like seriously weird or something?" She cleared her ears. "I started at Gooch Gap."

"So did we. That's only eight point four miles."

She shook her head sharply, as if shooing a particularly tenacious fly. "Fourteen-two."

"No, really, it's only eight point four."

"Excuse me, but I just *walked* it. I think I ought to know." And then suddenly: "God, are those Timberland boots? *Mega* mistake. How much did you pay for them?"

And so it went. Eventually I went off to swill out the bowls and hang the food bag. When I came back, she was fixing her own dinner but still talking away at Katz.

"You know what your problem is?" she was saying. "Pardon my French, but you're too fat."

Katz looked at her in quiet wonder. "Excuse me?"

"You're too fat. You should have lost weight before you came out here. Shoulda done some training, 'cause you could have like a serious, you know, heart thing out here."

"Heart thing?"

"You know, when your heart stops and you like, you know, die."

"Do you mean a heart attack?"

"That's it."

Mary Ellen, it should be noted, was not short on flesh herself, and unwisely at that moment she leaned over to get something from her pack, displaying an expanse of backside on which you could have projected motion pictures for, let us say, an army base. It was an interesting test of Katz's forbearance. He said nothing but rose to go for a pee, and out of the side of his mouth as he passed me he rendered a certain convenient expletive as three low, dismayed syllables, like the call of a freight train in the night.

The next day, as always, we rose chilled and feeling wretched, and set about the business of attending to our small tasks, but this time with the additional strain of having our every move examined and rated. While we ate raisins and drank coffee with flecks of toilet paper in it, Mary Ellen gorged on a multicourse breakfast of oatmeal, Pop Tarts, trail mix, and a dozen small squares of chocolate, which she lined up in a row on the log beside her. We watched like orphaned refugees while she plumped her jowls with food and enlightened us as to our shortcomings with regard to diet, equipment, and general manliness.

And then, now a trio, we set off into the woods. Mary Ellen walked sometimes with me and sometimes with Katz, but always with one of us. It was apparent that for all her bluster she was majestically inexperienced and untrailworthy (she hadn't the faintest idea how to read a map, for one thing) and ill at ease on her own in the wilderness. I couldn't help feeling a little sorry for her. Besides, I began to find her strangely entertaining. She had the most extraordinarily redundant turn of phrase. She would say things like "There's a stream of water over there" and "It's nearly ten o'clock a.m." Once, in reference to winters in central Florida, she solemnly informed me, "We usually get frosts once or twice a winter, but this year we had 'em a couple of times." Katz for his part clearly dreaded her company and winced beneath her tireless urgings to smarten his pace.

For once, the weather was kindly—more autumnal than springlike in feel, but gratifyingly mild. By ten o'clock, the temperature was comfortably in the sixties. For the first time since Amicalola I took off my jacket and realized with mild perplexity that I had absolutely no place to put it. I tied it to my pack with a strap and trudged on.

We labored four miles up and over Blood Mountain—at 4,461 feet the highest and toughest eminence on the trail in Georgia—then began a steep and exciting two-mile descent towards Neels Gap. Exciting because there was a shop at Neels Gap, at a place called the Walasi-Yi Inn, where you could buy sandwiches and ice cream. At about half past one, we heard a novel sound—motor traffic—and a few minutes later we emerged from the woods onto U.S. Highway 19 and 129, which despite having two numbers was really just a back road through a high pass between wooded nowheres. Directly across the road was the Walasi-Yi Inn, a splendid stone building constructed by the Civilian Conservation Corps (a kind of army of the unemployed) during the Great Depression and now a combination hiking outfitters, grocery, bookshop, and youth hostel. We hastened across the road—positively scurried across—and went inside.

Now it may seem to stretch credibility to suggest that things like a paved highway, the whoosh of passing cars, and a proper building could seem exciting and unfamiliar after a scant five days in the woods, but in fact it was so. Just passing through a door, being inside, surrounded by walls and a ceiling, was novel. And the Walasi-Yi's stuff was, well, I can't begin to describe how wonderful it was. There was a single modest-sized refrigerator filled with fresh sandwiches, soft drinks, cartons of juice, and perishables like cheese, and Katz and I stared into it for ages, dumbly captivated. I was beginning to appreciate that the central feature of life on the Appalachian Trail is deprivation, that the whole point of the experience is to remove yourself so thoroughly from the conveniences of everyday life that the most ordinary things—processed cheese, a can of pop gorgeously beaded with condensation—fill you with wonder and gratitude. It is an intoxicating experience to taste Coca-Cola as if for the first time and to be conveyed to the very brink of orgasm by white bread. Makes all the discomfort worthwhile, if you ask me.

Katz and I bought two egg salad sandwiches each, some potato chips, chocolate bars, and soft drinks and went to a picnic table in back, where we ate with greedy smackings and expressions of rapture, then returned to the refrigerator to stare in wonder some more. The Walasi-Yi, we discovered, provided other services to bona fide hikers for a small fee— laundry center, showers, towel rental—and we greedily availed ourselves of all those. The shower was a dribbly, antiquated affair, but the water was hot and I have never, and I mean never, enjoyed a grooming experience more. I watched with the profoundest satisfaction as five days of grime ran down my legs and out the drainhole, and noticed with astonished gratitude that my body had taken on a noticeably svelter profile. We did two loads of laundry, washed out our cups and food bowls and pots and pans, bought and sent postcards, phoned home, and stocked up liberally on fresh and packaged foods in the shop.

The Walasi-Yi was run by an Englishman named Justin and his American wife, Peggy, and we fell into a running conversation with them as we drifted in and out through the afternoon. Peggy told me that already they had had a thousand hikers through since January 1, with the real start of the hiking season still to come. They were a kindly couple, and I got the sense that Peggy in particular spends a lot of her time talking people into not quitting. Only the day before, a young man from Surrey had asked them to call him a cab to take him to Atlanta. Peggy had almost persuaded him to persevere, to try for just another week, but in the end he had broken down and wept quietly and asked from the heart to be let go home.

My own feeling was that for the first time I really wanted to keep going. The sun was shining. I was clean and refreshed. There was ample food in our packs. I had spoken to my wife by phone and knew that all was well. Above all, I was starting to feel fit. I was sure I had lost nearly ten pounds already. I was ready to go. Katz, too, was aglow with cleanness and looking chipper. We packed our purchases on the porch and realized, together in the same instant, with joy and amazement, that Mary Ellen was no longer part of our retinue. I put my head in the door and asked if they had seen her.

"Oh, I think she left about an hour ago," Peggy said.

Things were getting better and better.

It was after four o'clock by the time we set off again. Justin had said there was a natural meadow ideal for camping about an hour's walk farther on. The trail was warmly inviting in late afternoon sunlight— there were long shadows from the trees and expansive views across a river valley to stout, charcoal-colored mountains—and the meadow was indeed a perfect place to camp. We pitched our tents and had the sandwiches, chips, and soft drinks we had bought for dinner.

Then, with as much pride as if I had baked them myself, I brought out a little surprise—two packets of Hostess cupcakes.

Katz's face lit up like the birthday boy in a Norman Rockwell painting.

"Oh, wow!"

"They didn't have any Little Debbies," I apologized.

"Hey," he said. "Hey." He was lost for greater eloquence. Katz loved cakes.

We ate three of the cupcakes between us and left the last one on the log, where we could admire it, for later. We were lying there, propped against logs, burping, smoking, feeling rested and content, talking for once—in short, acting much as I had envisioned it in my more optimistic moments back home—when Katz let out a low groan. I followed his gaze to find Mary Ellen striding briskly down the trail towards us from the wrong direction.

"I *wondered* where you guys had got to," she scolded. "You know, you are like *really* slow. We could've done another four miles by now easy. I can see I'm going to have to keep my eyes on you from now—say, is that a Hostess cupcake?" Before I could speak or Katz could seize a log with which to smite her dead, she said, "Well, I don't mind if I do," and ate it in two bites. It would be some days before Katz smiled again.

"So what's your star sign?" said Mary Ellen.

"Cunnilingus," Katz answered and looked profoundly unhappy.

She looked at him. "I don't know that one." She made an I'll-be-darned frown and said, "I thought I knew them all. Mine's Libra." She turned to me. "What's yours?"

"I don't know." I tried to think of something. "Necrophilia."

"I don't know that one either. Say, are you guys putting me on?"

"Yeah."

It was two nights later. We were camped at a lofty spot called Indian Grave Gap, between two brooding summits—the one tiring to recollect, the other dispiriting to behold. We had hiked twenty-two miles in two days—a highly respectable distance for us—but a distinct listlessness and sense of anticlimax, a kind of midmountain lassitude, had set in. We spent our days doing precisely what we had done on previous days and would continue to do on future days, over the same sorts of hills, along the same wandering track, through the same endless woods. The trees were so thick that we hardly ever got views, and when we did get views it was of infinite hills covered in more trees. I was discouraged to note that I was grubby again already and barking for white bread. And then of course there was the constant, prattling, awesomely brainless presence of Mary Ellen.

"When's your birthday?" she said to me.

"December 8."

"That's Virgo."

"No, actually it's Sagittarius."

"Whatever." And then abruptly: "Jeez, you guys stink."

"Well, uh, we've been walking."

"Me, I don't sweat. Never have. Don't dream either."

"Everybody dreams," Katz said.

"Well, I don't."

"Except people of extremely low intelligence. It's a scientific fact."

Mary Ellen regarded him expressionlessly for a moment, then said abruptly, to neither of us in particular: "Do you ever have that dream where you're like at school and you look down and like you haven't got any clothes on?" She shuddered. "I hate that one."

"I thought you didn't dream," said Katz.

She stared at him for a very long moment, as if trying to remember where she had encountered him before. "And falling," she went on, unperturbed. "I hate that one, too. Like when you fall into a hole and just fall and fall." She gave a brief shiver and then noisily unblocked her ears.

Katz watched her with idle interest. "I know a guy who did that once," he said, "and one of his eyes popped out."

She looked at him doubtfully.

"It rolled right across the living room floor and his dog ate it. Isn't that right, Bryson?"

I nodded.

"You're making that up."

"I'm not. It rolled right across the floor and before anybody could do anything, the dog gobbled it down in one bite."

I confirmed it for her with another nod.

She considered this for a minute. "So what'd your friend do about his eye hole? Did he have to get a glass eye or something?"

"Well, he wanted to, but his family was kind of poor, you know, so what he did was he got a Ping-Pong ball and painted an eye on it and he used that."

"Ugh," said Mary Ellen softly.

"So I wouldn't go blowing out your ear holes any more."

She considered again. "Yeah, maybe you're right," she said at length, and blew out her ear holes.

In our few private moments, when Mary Ellen went off to tinkle in distant shrubs, Katz and I had formed a secret pact that we would hike fourteen miles on the morrow to a place called Dicks Creek Gap, where there was a highway to the town of Hiawassee, eleven miles to the north. We would hike to the gap if it killed us, and then try to hitchhike into Hiawassee for dinner and a night in a motel. Plan B was that we would kill Mary Ellen and take her Pop Tarts.

And so the next day we hiked, really hiked, startling Mary Ellen with our thrusting strides. There was a motel in Hiawassee—clean sheets! shower! color TV!—and a reputed choice of restaurants. We needed no more incentive than that to perk our step. Katz flagged in the first hour, and I felt tired too by afternoon, but we pushed determinedly on. Mary Ellen fell farther and farther off the pace, until she was behind even Katz. It was a kind of miracle in the hills.

At about four o'clock, tired and overheated and streaked about the face with rivulets of gritty sweat, I stepped from the woods onto the broad shoulder of U.S. Highway 76, an asphalt river through the woods, pleased to note that the road was wide and reasonably important looking. A half mile down the road there was a clearing in the trees and a drive—a hint of civilization—before the road curved away invitingly. Several cars passed as I stood there.

Katz tumbled from the woods a few minutes later, looking wild of hair and eye, and I hustled him across the road against his voluble protests that he needed to sit down *immediately*. I wanted to try to get a lift before Mary Ellen came along and screwed things up. I couldn't think how she might, but I knew she would.

"Have you seen her?" I asked anxiously.

"Miles back, sitting on a rock with her boots off rubbing her feet. She looked real tired."

"Good."

Katz sagged onto his pack, grubby and spent, and I stood beside him on the shoulder with my thumb out, trying to project an image of wholesomeness and respectability, making private irked tutting noises at every car and pickup that passed. I had not hitchhiked in twenty-five years, and it was a vaguely humbling experience. Cars shot past very fast—unbelievably fast to us who now resided in Foot World—and gave us scarcely a glance. A very few approached more slowly, always occupied by elderly people—little white heads, just above the window line—who stared at us without sympathy or expression, as they would at a field of cows. It seemed unlikely that anyone would stop for us. I wouldn't have stopped for us.

"We're never going to get picked up," Katz announced despondently after cars had forsaken us for fifteen minutes.

He was right, of course, but it always exasperated me how easily he gave up on things. "Can't you try to be a little more positive?" I said.

"OK, I'm positive we're never going to get picked up. I mean, look at us." He smelled his armpits with disgust. "Jesus. I smell like Jeffrey Dahmer's refrigerator."

There is a phenomenon called Trail Magic, known and spoken of with reverence by everyone who hikes the trail, which holds that often when things look darkest some little piece of serendipity comes along to put you back on a heavenly plane. Ours was a baby blue Pontiac Trans Am, which flew past, then screeched to a stop on the shoulder a hundred yards or so down the road, in a cloud of gravelly dust. It was so far beyond where we stood that we didn't think it could possibly be for us, but then it jerked into reverse and came at us, half on the shoulder and half off, moving very fast and a little wildly. I stood transfixed. The day before, we had been told by a pair of seasoned hikers that sometimes in the South drivers will swerve at A.T. hitchhikers, or run over their packs, for purposes of hilarity, and I supposed this was one of those moments. I was about to fly for cover, and even Katz was halfway to his feet, when it stopped just before us, with a rock and another cloud of dust, and a youthful female head popped out the passenger side window.

"Yew boys wunna rod?" she called.

"Yes, ma'am, we sure do," we said, putting on our best behavior.

We hastened to the car with our packs and bowed down at the window to find a very handsome, very happy, very drunk young couple, who didn't look to be more than eighteen or nineteen years old. The woman was carefully topping up two plastic cups from a three-quarters empty bottle of Wild Turkey. "Hi!" she said. "Hop in."

We hesitated. The car was packed nearly solid with stuff—suitcases, boxes, assorted black plastic bags, hangerloads of clothes. It was a small car to begin with and there was barely room for them.

"Darren, why'nt you make some room for these gentlemen," the young woman ordered and then added for us: "This yere's Darren."

Darren got out, grinned a hello, opened the trunk, and stared blankly at it while the perception slowly spread through his brain that it was also packed solid. He was so drunk that I thought for a moment he might fall asleep on his feet, but he snapped to and found some rope and quite deftly tied our packs on the roof. Then, ignoring the vigorous advice and instructions of his partner, he tossed stuff around in the back until he had somehow created a small cavity into which Katz and I climbed, puffing out apologies and expressions of the sincerest gratitude.

Her name was Donna, and they were on their way to some desperate-sounding community—Turkey Balls Falls or Coon Slick or someplace—another fifty miles up the road, but they were pleased to drop us in Hiawassee, if they didn't kill us all first. Darren drove at 127 miles an hour with one finger on the wheel, his head bouncing to the rhythm of some internal song, while Donna twirled in her seat to talk to us. She was stunningly pretty, entrancingly pretty.

"Y'all have to excuse us. We're celebrating." She held up her plastic cup as if in toast.

"What're you celebrating?" asked Katz.

"We're gittin married tomorrah," she announced proudly.

"No kidding," said Katz. "Congratulations."

"Yup. Darren yere's gonna make a honest woman outta me." She tousled his hair, then impulsively lunged over and gave the side of his head a kiss, which became lingering, then probing, then frankly lascivious, and concluded, as a kind of bonus, by shooting her hand into a surprising place—or at least so we surmised because Darren abruptly banged his head on the ceiling and took us on a brief but exciting detour into a lane of oncoming traffic. Then she turned to us with a dreamy, unabashed leer, as if to say, "Who's next?" It looked, we reflected later, as if Darren might have his hands full, though we additionally concluded that it would probably be worth it.

"Hey, have a drink," she offered suddenly, seizing round the neck and looking for spare cups on the floor.

"Oh, no thanks," Katz said, but looked tempted.

"*G'won*," she encouraged.

Katz held up a palm. "I'm reformed."

"Yew *are*? Well, good for you. Have a drink then."

"No really."

"How 'bout yew?" she said to me.

"Oh, no thanks." I couldn't have freed my pinned arms even if I had wanted a drink. They dangled before me like tyrannosaur limbs.

"*Yer* not reformed, are ya?"

"Well, kind of." I had decided, for purposes of solidarity, to forswear alcohol for the duration.

She looked at us. "You guys like Mormons or something?"

"No, just hikers."

She nodded thoughtfully, satisfied with that, and had a drink. Then she made Darren jump again.

They dropped us at Mull's Motel in Hiawassee, an old-fashioned, nondescript, patently nonchain establishment on a bend in the road near the center of town. We thanked them profusely, went through a little song-and-dance of trying to give them gas money, which they stoutly refused, and watched as Darren returned to the busy road as if fired from a rocket launcher. I believe I saw him bang his head again as they disappeared over a small rise.

And then we were alone with our packs in an empty motel parking lot in a dusty, forgotten, queer-looking little town in northern Georgia. The word that clings to every hiker's thoughts in north Georgia is *Deliverance*, the 1970 novel by James Dickey that was made into a Hollywood movie. It concerns, as you may recall, four middle-aged men from Atlanta who go on a weekend canoeing trip down the fictional Cahulawasee River (but based on the real, nearby Chattooga) and find themselves severely out of their element. "Every family I've ever met up here has at least one relative in the penitentiary," a character in the book remarks forebodingly as they drive up. "Some of them are in for making liquor or running it, but most of them are in for murder. They don't think a whole lot about killing people up here." And so of course it proves, as our urban foursome find themselves variously buggered, murdered, and hunted by a brace of demented backwoodsmen.

Early in the book Dickey has his characters stop for directions in some "sleepy and hookwormy and ugly" town, which for all I know could have been Hiawassee. What is certainly true is that the book was set in this part of the state, and the movie was filmed in the area. The famous banjo-plucking albino who played "Dueling Banjos" in the movie still apparently lives in Clayton, just down the road.

Dickey's book, as you might expect, attracted heated criticism in the state when it was published (one observer called it "the most demeaning characterization of southern highlanders in modern literature," which, if anything, was an understatement), but in fact it must be said that people have been appalled by northern Georgians for 150 years. One nineteenth-century chronicler described the region's inhabitants as "tall, thin, cadaverous-looking animals, as melancholy and lazy as boiled cod-fish," and others freely employed words like "depraved," "rude," "uncivilized," and "backward" to describe the reclusive, underbred folk of Georgia's deep, dark woods and desperate townships. Dickey, who was himself a Georgian and knew the area well, swore that his book was a faithful description.

Perhaps it was the lingering influence of the book, perhaps simply the time of day, or maybe nothing more than the unaccustomedness of being in a town, but Hiawassee did feel palpably weird and unsettling—the kind of place where it wouldn't altogether surprise you to find your gasoline being pumped by a cyclops. We went into the motel reception area, which was more like a small, untidy living room than a place of business, and found an aged woman with lively white hair and a bright cotton dress sitting on a sofa by the door. She looked happy to see us.

"Hi," I said. "We're looking for a room."

The woman grinned and nodded.

"Actually, two rooms if you've got them."

The woman grinned and nodded again. I waited for her to get up, but she didn't move.

"For tonight," I said encouragingly. "You do have rooms?" Her grin became a kind of beam and she grasped my hand, and held on tight; her fingers felt cold and bony. She just looked at me intently and eagerly, as if she thought—hoped—that I would throw a stick for her to fetch.

"Tell her we come from Reality Land," Katz whispered in my ear.

At that moment, a door swung open and a gray-haired woman swept in, wiping her hands on an apron.

"Oh, ain't no good talking to her," she said in a friendly manner. "She don't know nothing, don't say nothing. Mother, let go the man's hand." Her mother beamed at her. "Mother, let *go* the man's hand."

My hand was released and we booked into two rooms. We went off with our keys and agreed to meet in half an hour. My room was basic and battered—there were cigarette burns on every possible surface, including the toilet seat and door lintels, and the walls and ceiling were covered in big stains that suggested a strange fight to the death involving lots of hot coffee—but it was heaven to me. I called Katz, for the novelty of using a telephone, and learned that his room was even worse. We were very happy.

We showered, put on such clean clothes as we could muster, and eagerly repaired to a popular nearby bistro called the Georgia Mountain Restaurant. The parking lot was crowded with pickup trucks, and inside it was busy with meaty people in baseball caps. I had a feeling that if I'd said, "Phone call for you, Bubba," every man in the room would have risen. I won't say the Georgia Mountain had food I would travel for, even within Hiawassee, but it was certainly reasonably priced. For $5.50 each, we got "meat and three," a trip to the salad bar, and dessert. I ordered fried chicken, black-eyed peas, roast potatoes, and "ruterbeggars," as the menu had it—I had never had them before, and can't say I will again. We ate noisily and with gusto, and ordered many refills of iced tea.

Dessert was of course the highlight. Everyone on the trail dreams of something, usually sweet and gooey, and my sustaining vision had been an outsized slab of pie. It had occupied my thoughts for days, and when the waitress came to take our order I asked her, with beseeching eyes and a hand on her forearm, to bring me the largest piece she could slice without losing her job. She brought me a vast, viscous, canary-yellow wedge of lemon pie. It was a monument to food technology, yellow enough to give you a headache, sweet enough to make your eyeballs roll up into your head—everything, in short, you could want in a pie so long as taste and quality didn't enter into your requirements. I was just plunging into it when Katz broke a long silence by saying, with a strange kind of nervousness, "You know what I keep doing? I keep looking up to see if Mary Ellen's coming through the door."

I paused, a forkful of shimmering goo halfway to my mouth, and noticed with passing disbelief that his dessert plate was already empty. "You're not going to tell me you miss her, Stephen?" I said dryly and pushed the food home.

"No," he responded tartly, not taking this as a joke at all. He took on a frustrated look from trying to find words to express his complex emotions. "We did kind of ditch her, you know," he finally blurted.

I considered the charge. "Actually, we didn't kind of ditch her. We ditched her." I wasn't with him at all on this. "So?"

"Well, I just, I just feel kind of bad—just *kind* of bad—that we left her out in the woods on her own." Then he crossed his arms as if to say: "There. I've said it."

I put my fork down and considered the point. "She came into the woods on her own," I said. "We're not actually responsible for her, you know. I mean, it's not as if we signed a contract to look after her."

Even as I said these things, I realized with a kind of horrible, seeping awareness that he was right. We had ditched her, left her to the bears and wolves and chortling mountain men. I had been so completely preoccupied with my own savage lust for food and a real bed that I had not paused to consider what our abrupt departure would mean for her—a night alone among the whispering trees, swaddled in darkness, listening with involuntary keenness for the telltale crack of branch or stick under a heavy foot or paw. It wasn't something I would wish on anyone. My gaze fell on my pie, and I realized I didn't want it any longer. "Maybe she'll have found somebody else to camp with," I suggested lamely, and pushed the pie away.

"Did *you* see anybody today?"

He was right. We had seen hardly a soul.

"She's probably still walking right now," Katz said with a hint of sudden heat. "Wondering where the hell we got to. Scared out of her chubby little wits."

"Oh, don't," I half pleaded, and distractedly pushed the pie a half inch farther away.

He nodded an emphatic, busy, righteous little nod, and looked at me with a strange, glowing, accusatory expression that said, "And if she dies, let it be on *your* conscience." And he was right; I was the ringleader here. This was my fault.

Then he leaned closer and said in a completely different tone of voice, "If you're not going to eat that pie, can I have it?"

In the morning we breakfasted at a Hardees across the street and paid for a taxi to take us back to the trail. We didn't speak about Mary Ellen or much of anything else. Returning to the trail after a night's comforts in a town always left us disinclined to talk.

We were greeted with an immediate steep climb and walked slowly, almost gingerly. I always felt terrible on the trail the first day after a break. Katz, on the other hand, just always felt terrible. Whatever restorative effects a town visit offered always vanished with astounding swiftness on the trail. Within two minutes it was as if we had never been away—actually worse, because on a normal day I would not be laboring up a steep hill with a greasy, leaden Hardees breakfast threatening at every moment to come up for air.

We had been walking for about half an hour when another hiker—a fit-looking middle-aged guy—came along from the other direction. We asked him if he had seen a girl named Mary Ellen in a red jacket with kind of a loud voice.

He made an expression of possible recognition and said: "Does she—I'm not being rude here or anything—but does she do this a lot?" and he pinched his nose and made a series of horrible honking noises.

We nodded vigorously.

"Yeah, I stayed with her and two other guys in Plumorchard Gap Shelter last night." He gave us a dubious, sideways look. "She a friend of yours?"

"Oh, no," we said, disavowing her entirely, as any sensible person would. "She just sort of latched on to us for a couple of days."

He nodded in understanding, then grinned. "She's a piece of work, isn't she?"

We grinned, too. "Was it bad?" I said.

He made a look that showed genuine pain, then abruptly, as if putting two and two together, said, "So you must be the guys she was talking about."

"Really?" Katz said. "What'd she say?"

"Oh, nothing," he said, but he was suppressing a small smile in that way that makes you say: "What?"

"Nothing. It was nothing." But he was smiling.

"*What?*"

He wavered. "Oh, all right. She said you guys were a couple of overweight wimps who didn't know the first thing about hiking and that she was tired of carrying you."

"She said *that*?" Katz said, scandalized.

"Actually I think she called you pussies."

"She called us *pussies*?" Katz said. "Now I will kill her."

"Well, I don't suppose you'll have any trouble finding people to hold her down for you," the man said absently, scanning the sky, and added: "Supposed to snow."

I made a crestfallen noise. This was the last thing we wanted. "Really? Bad?"

He nodded. "Six to eight inches. More on the higher elevations." He lifted his eyebrows stoically, agreeing with my dismayed expression. Snow wasn't just discouraging, it was dangerous.

He let the prospect hang there for a moment, then said, "Well, better keep moving." I nodded in understanding, for that was what we did in these hills. I watched him go, then turned to Katz, who was shaking his head.

"Imagine her saying that after all we did for her," he said, then noticed me staring at him, and said in a kind of squirmy way, "What?" and then, more squirmily, "*What?*"

"Don't you ever, *ever*, spoil a piece of pie for me again. Do you understand? "

He winced. "Yeah, all right. Jeez," he said and trudged on, muttering.

Two days later we heard that Mary Ellen had dropped out with blisters after trying to do thirty-five miles in two days. Big mistake.

from Deliverance
by James Dickey

Deliverance is a novel written by a poet—James Dickey (1923–1997)—and it shows. Four men take canoes through a canyon that soon will disappear (another dam). They quickly stumble upon things they've hidden away: fear, shame, anger, violence. Here, the men have voted to keep secret Lewis' killing of one of two hill people who waylaid and assaulted Bobby and Ed (the narrator). Now the friends must hide the body, and the woods at the river's edge suddenly seem different.

A ll right then," Lewis said, and reached for the dead man's shoulder. He rolled him over, took hold of the arrow shaft where it came out of the chest and began to pull. He added his other hand and jerked to get it started out and then hauled strongly with one hand again as the arrow slowly slithered from the body, painted a dark uneven red. Lewis stood up, went to the river and washed it, then came back. He clipped the shaft into his bow quiver.

I handed the shotgun to Bobby and went and got my belt and the knife and rope. Then Drew and I bent to the shoulders and lifted, and Bobby and Lewis took a foot apiece, with their free hands carrying the gun and the bow and an entrenching tool from the loaded canoe. The corpse sagged between us, extremely heavy, and the full meaning of the words *dead weight* dragged at me as I tried to straighten. We moved toward the place where Lewis had come from.

Before we had gone twenty yards Drew and I were staggering, our feet going any way they could through the dry grass. Once I heard a racheting I was sure was a rattlesnake, and looked right and left of the body sliding feet-first ahead of me into the woods. The man's head hung back and rolled between Drew and me, dragging at everything it could touch.

It was not believable. I had never done anything like it even in my mind. To say that it was like a game would not describe exactly how it felt. I knew it was not a game, and yet, whenever I could, I glanced at the corpse to see if it would come out of the phony trance it was in, and stand up and shake hands all around, someone new we'd met in the woods, who could give us some idea where we were. But the head kept dropping back and we kept having to keep it up, clear of the weeds and briars, so that we could go wherever we were going with it.

We came out finally at the creek bank near Lewis' canoe. The water was pushing through the leaves, and the whole stream looked as though it was about half slow water and half bushes and branches. There was nothing in my life like it, but I was there. I helped Lewis and the others put the body into the canoe. The hull rode deep and low in the leafy water, and we began to push it up the creek, deeper into the woods. I could feel every pebble through the city rubber of my tennis shoes, and the creek flowed as untouchable as a shadow around my legs. There was nothing else to do except what we were doing.

Lewis led, drawing the canoe by the bow painter, plodding bent-over upstream with the veins popping, the rope over his shoulder like a bag of gold. The trees, mostly mountain laurel and rhododendron, made an arch over the creek, so that at times we had to get down on one knee or both knees and grope through leaves and branches, going right into the most direct push of water against our chests as it came through the foliage. At some places it was like a tunnel where nothing human had ever been expected to come, and at others it was like a long green hall where the water changed tones and temperatures and was much quieter than it would have been in the open.

In this endless water-floored cave of leaves we kept going for twenty minutes by my watch, until the only point at all was to keep going, to find the creek our feet were in when the leaves of rhododendrons dropped in our faces and hid it. I wondered what on earth I would do if the others disappeared, the creek disappeared and left only me and the woods and the corpse. Which way would I go? Without the creek to go back down, could I find the river? Probably not, and I bound myself with my brain and heart to the others; with them was the only way I would ever get out.

Every now and then I looked into the canoe and saw the body riding there, slumped back with its hand over its face and its feet crossed, a caricature of the southern small-town bum too lazy to do anything but sleep.

Lewis held up his hand. We all straightened up around the canoe, holding it lightly head-on into the current. Lewis went up the far bank like a creature. Drew and Bobby and I stood with the canoe at our hips and the sleeping man rocking softly between. Around us the woods were so thick that there would have been trouble putting an arm into it in places. We could have been watched from anywhere, any angle, any tree or bush, but nothing happened. I could feel the others' hands on the canoe, keeping it steady.

In about ten minutes Lewis came back, lifting a limb out of the water and appearing. It was as though the tree raised its own limb out of the water like a man. I had the feeling that such things happened all the time to branches in woods that were deep enough. The leaves lifted carefully but decisively, and Lewis Medlock came through.

We tied the canoe to a bush and picked up the body, each of us having the same relationship to it as before. I don't believe I could have brought myself to take hold of it in any other way.

Lewis had not found a path, but he had come on an opening between trees that went back inland and, he said, upstream. That was good enough; it was as good as anything. We hauled and labored away from the creek between the big water oak trunks and the sweetgums standing there forever, falling down, lurching this way and the other with the corpse, thick and slick with sweat, trying to make good a senselessly complicated pattern of movement between the bushes and trees. After the first few turns I had no idea where we were, and in a curious way I enjoyed being *that* lost. If you were in something as deep as we were in, it was better to go all the way. When I quit hearing the creek I knew I was lost, wandering foolishly in the woods holding a corpse by the sleeve.

Lewis lifted his hand again, and we let the body down onto the ground. We were by a sump of some kind, a blue-black seepage of rotten water that had either crawled in from some other place or came up from the ground where it was. The earth around it was soft and squelchy, and I kept backing off from it, even though I had been walking in the creek with the others.

Lewis motioned to me. I went up to him and he took the arrow he had killed the man with out of his quiver. I expected it to vibrate, but it didn't; it was like the others—civilized and expert. I tested it; it was straight. I handed it back, but for some reason didn't feel like turning loose of it. Lewis made an odd motion with his head, somewhere between disbelief and determination, and we stood holding the arrow. There was no blood on it, but the feathers were still wet from the river where he had washed it off. It looked just like any arrow that had been carried in the rain, or in heavy dew or fog. I let go.

Lewis put it on the string of his bow. He came back to full draw as I had seen him do hundreds of times, in his classic, knowledgeable form so much more functional and accurate than the form of an archer on an urn, and stood, concentrating. There was nothing there but the black water, but he was aiming at a definite part of it: a single drop, maybe, as it moved and would have to stop, sooner or later, for an instant.

It went. The arrow leapt with a breathtaking instant silver and disappeared at almost the same time, while Lewis held his follow-through, standing with the bow as though the arrow were still in it. There was no sense of the arrow's being stopped by anything under the water—log or rock. It was gone, and could have been traveling down through muck to the soft center of the earth.

We picked up the body and went on. In a while more we came out against the side of a bank that shelved up, covered with ferns and leaves that were mulchy like shit. Lewis turned to us and narrowed one eye. We put the body down. One of its arms was wrenched around backwards, and it seemed odd and more terrible than anything that had happened that such a position didn't hurt it.

Lewis fell. He started to dig with the collapsible GI shovel we had brought for digging latrines. The ground came up easily, or what was on the ground. There was no earth; it was all leaves and rotten stuff. It had the smell of generations of mold. They might as well let the water in on it, I thought; this stuff is no good to anybody.

Drew and I got down and helped with our hands. Bobby stood looking off into the trees. Drew dug in, losing himself in a practical job, figuring the best way to do it. The sweat stood in the holes of his blocky, pitted face, and his black hair, solid with thickness and hair lotion, shone sideways, hanging over one ear.

It was a dark place, quiet and almost airless. When we were finished with the hole there was not a dry spot anywhere on my nylon. We had hollowed out a narrow trench about two feet deep.

We hauled the body over and rolled it in on its side, unbelievably far from us. Lewis reached his hand and Bobby handed him the shotgun. Lewis put the gun in and pulled back his hands to his knees, looking. Then his right hand went back into the grave, and he gave the gun a turn, arranging it in some kind of way.

"OK," he said.

We shoveled and scrambled the dirt back in, working wildly. I kept throwing the stuff in his face, to get it covered up quick. But it was easy, in double handfuls. He disappeared slowly, into the general sloppiness and uselessness of the woods. When he was gone, Lewis smoothed out the leaf mold over him.

We stood on our knees. We leaned forward, panting, our hands on the fronts of our thighs or on the ground. I had a tremendous driving moment of wanting to dig him up again, of siding with Drew. Now, if not later, we knew where he was. But there was already too much to explain: the dirt, the delay, and the rest of it. Or should we take him and wash him in the river? The thought of doing that convinced me; it was impossible, and I stood up with the others.

"Ferns'll be growing here in a few days," Lewis said. It was good to hear a voice, especially his. "Nobody'd ever come on him in a million years. I doubt if we could even find this place again."

"There's still time, Lewis," Drew said. "You better be sure you know what you're doing."

"I'm sure," Lewis said. "The first rain will kill every sign we made. There's not a dog can follow us here. When we get off this river, we'll be all right. Believe me."

We started back. I couldn't tell anything about our back trail, but Lewis kept stopping and looking at a wrist compass, and it seemed to me that we were going more or less in the right direction; it was the direction I would have followed if I had been by myself.

We came out upstream of where the canoe was. The water was running toward the river, and we went with it, down the secret pebbles of the creek-bed, stooping under the leaves of low branches, mumbling to ourselves. I felt separated from the others, and especially from Lewis. There was no feeling any longer of helping each other; I believed that if I had stepped into a hole and disappeared the others would not have noticed, but would have gone on faster and faster. Each of us wanted to get out of the woods in the quickest way he could. I know I did, and it would have taken a great physical effort for me to turn back and take one step upstream, no matter what trouble one of the others was in.

To Build a Fire
by Jack London

Jack London (1876–1916) knew that most people who get in trouble in the wild are surprised. It's hard to believe—or even to remember between visits—that the wilderness just doesn't care what happens to us. That's one reason we go there: It's good to be reminded that we don't matter much. Still, we matter to us. Got a light?

Day had broken cold and gray, exceedingly cold and gray, when the man turned aside from the main Yukon trail and climbed the high earth-bank, where a dim and little-travelled trail led eastward through the fat spruce timberland. It was a steep bank, and he paused for breath at the top, excusing the act to himself by looking at his watch. It was nine o'clock. There was no sun nor hint of sun, though there was not a cloud in the sky. It was a clear day, and yet there seemed an intangible pall over the face of things, a subtle gloom that made the day dark, and that was due to the absence of sun. This fact did not worry the man. He was used to the lack of sun. It had been days since he had seen the sun, and he knew that a few more days must pass before that cheerful orb, due south, would just peep above the sky-line and dip immediately from view.

The man flung a look back along the way he had come. The Yukon lay a mile wide and hidden under three feet of ice. On top of this ice were as many feet of snow. It was all pure white, rolling in gentle undulations where the ice-jams of the freeze-up had formed. North and south, as far as his eye could see, it was unbroken white, save for a dark hair-line that curved and twisted from around the spruce-covered island to the south, and that curved and twisted away into the north, where it disappeared behind another spruce-covered island. This dark hair-line was the trail—the main trail—that led south five hundred miles to the Chilcoot Pass, Dyea, and salt water; and that led north seventy miles to Dawson, and still on to the north a thousand miles to Nulato, and finally to St. Michael on Bering Sea, a thousand miles and half a thousand more.

But all this—the mysterious, far-reaching hair-line trail, the absence of sun from the sky, the tremendous cold, and the strangeness and weirdness of it all—made no impression on the man. It was not because he was long used to it. He was a newcomer in the land, a *chechaquo*, and this was his first winter. The trouble with him was that he was without imagination. He was quick and alert in the things of life, but only in the things, and not in the significances. Fifty degrees below zero meant eighty-odd degrees of frost. Such fact impressed him as being cold and uncomfortable, and that was all. It did not lead him to meditate upon his frailty as a creature of temperature, and upon man's frailty in general, able only to live within certain narrow limits of heat and cold; and from there on it did not lead him to the conjectural field of immortality and man's place in the universe. Fifty degrees below zero stood for a bite of frost that hurt and that must be guarded against by the use of mittens, ear-flaps, warm moccasins, and thick socks. Fifty degrees below zero was to him just precisely fifty degrees below zero. That there should be anything more to it than that was a thought that never entered his head.

As he turned to go on, he spat speculatively. There was a sharp, explosive crackle that startled him. He spat again. And again, in the air, before it could fall to the snow, the spittle crackled. He knew that at fifty below spittle crackled on the snow, but this spittle had crackled in the air. Undoubtedly it was colder than fifty below—how much colder he did not know. But the temperature did not matter. He was bound for the old claim on the left fork of Henderson Creek, where the boys were already. They had come over across the divide from the Indian Creek country, while he had come the roundabout way to take a look at the possibilities of getting out logs in the spring from the islands in the Yukon. He would be in to camp by six o'clock; a bit after dark, it was true, but the boys would be there, a fire would be going, and a hot supper would be ready. As for lunch, he pressed his hand against the protruding bundle under his jacket. It was also under his shirt, wrapped up in a handkerchief and lying against the naked skin. It was the only way to keep the biscuits from freezing. He smiled agreeably to himself as he thought of those biscuits, each cut open and sopped in bacon grease, and each enclosing a generous slice of fried bacon.

He plunged in among the big spruce trees. The trail was faint. A foot of snow had fallen since the last sled had passed over, and he was glad he was without a sled, travelling light. In fact, he carried nothing but the lunch wrapped in the handkerchief. He was surprised, however, at the cold. It certainly was cold, he concluded, as he rubbed his numb nose and cheek-bones with his mittened hand. He was a warm whiskered man, but the hair on his face did not protect the high cheek-bones and the eager nose that thrust itself aggressively into the frosty air.

At the man's heels trotted a dog, a big native husky, the proper wolf-dog, gray-coated and without any visible or temperamental difference from its brother, the wild wolf. The animal was depressed by the tremendous cold. It knew that it was no time for travelling. Its instinct told it a truer tale than was told to the man by the man's judgment. In reality, it was not merely colder than fifty below zero; it was colder than sixty below, than seventy below. It was seventy-five below zero. Since the freezing-point is thirty-two above zero, it meant that one hundred and seven degrees of frost obtained. The dog did not know anything about thermometers. Possibly in its brain there was no sharp consciousness of a condition of very cold such as was in the man's brain. But the brute had its instinct. It experienced a vague but menacing apprehension that subdued it and made it slink along at the man's heels, and that made it question eagerly every unwonted movement of the man as if expecting him to go into camp or to seek shelter somewhere and build a fire. The dog had learned fire, and it wanted fire, or else to burrow under the snow and cuddle its warmth away from the air.

The frozen moisture of its breathing had settled on its fur in a fine powder of frost, and especially were its jowls, muzzle, and eyelashes whitened by its crystalled breath. The man's red beard and mustache were likewise frosted, but more solidly, the deposit taking the form of ice and increasing with every warm, moist breath he exhaled. Also, the man was chewing tobacco, and the muzzle of ice held his lips so rigidly that he was unable to clear his chin when he expelled the juice. The result was that a crystal beard of the color and solidity of amber was increasing its length on his chin. If he fell down it would shatter itself, like glass, into brittle fragments. But he did not mind the appendage. It was the penalty all tobacco-chewers paid in that country, and he had been out before in two cold snaps. They had not been so cold as this, he knew, but by the spirit thermometer at Sixty Mile he knew they had been registered at fifty below and at fifty-five.

He held on through the level stretch of woods for several miles, crossed a wide flat of niggerheads, and dropped down a bank to the frozen bed of a small stream. This was Henderson Creek, and he knew he was ten miles from the forks. He looked at his watch. It was ten o'clock. He was making four miles an hour, and he calculated that he would arrive at the forks at half-past twelve. He decided to celebrate that event by eating his lunch there.

The dog dropped in again at his heels, with a tail drooping discouragement, as the man swung along the creek-bed. The furrow of the old sled-trail was plainly visible, but a dozen inches of snow covered the marks of the last runners. In a month no man had come up or down that silent creek. The man held steadily on. He was not much given to thinking, and just then particularly he had nothing to think about save that he would eat lunch at the forks and that at six o'clock he would be in camp with the boys. There was nobody to talk to; and, had there been, speech would have been impossible because of the ice-muzzle on his mouth. So he continued monotonously to chew tobacco and to increase the length of his amber beard.

Once in a while the thought reiterated itself that it was very cold and that he had never experienced such cold. As he walked along he rubbed his cheek-bones and nose with the back of his mittened hand. He did this automatically, now and again changing hands. But rub as he would, the instant he stopped his cheek-bones went numb, and the following instant the end of his nose went numb. He was sure to frost his cheeks; he knew that, and experienced a pang of regret that he had not devised a nose-strap of the sort Bud wore in cold snaps. Such a strap passed across the cheeks, as well, and saved them. But it didn't matter much, after all. What were frosted cheeks? A bit painful, that was all; they were never serious.

Empty as the man's mind was of thoughts, he was keenly observant, and he noticed the changes in the creek, the curves and bends and timber-jams, and always he sharply noted where he placed his feet. Once, coming around a bend, he shied abruptly, like a startled horse, curved away from the place where he had been walking, and retreated several paces back along the trail. The creek he knew was frozen clear to the bottom,—no creek could contain water in that arctic winter,—but he knew also that there were springs that bubbled out from the hillsides and ran along under the snow and on top the ice of the creek. He knew that the coldest snaps never froze these springs, and he knew likewise their danger. They were traps. They hid pools of water under the snow that might be three inches deep, or three feet. Sometimes a skin of ice half an inch thick covered them, and in turn was covered by the snow. Sometimes there were alternate layers of water and ice-skin, so that when one broke through he kept on breaking through for a while, sometimes wetting himself to the waist.

That was why he had shied in such panic. He had felt the give under his feet and heard the crackle of a snow-hidden ice-skin. And to get his feet wet in such a temperature meant trouble and danger. At the very least it meant delay, for he would be forced to stop and build a fire, and under its protection to bare his feet while he dried his socks and moccasins. He stood and studied the creek-bed and its banks, and decided that the flow of water came from the right. He reflected awhile, rubbing his nose and cheeks, then skirted to the left, stepping gingerly and testing the footing for each step. Once clear of the danger, he took a fresh chew of tobacco and swung along at his four-mile gait.

In the course of the next two hours he came upon several similar traps. Usually the snow above the hidden pools had a sunken, candied appearance that advertised the danger. Once again, however, he had a close call; and once, suspecting danger, he compelled the dog to go on in front. The dog did not want to go. It hung back until the man shoved it forward, and then it went quickly across the white, unbroken surface. Suddenly it broke through, floundered to one side, and got away to firmer footing. It had wet its forefeet and legs, and almost immediately the water that clung to it turned to ice. It made quick efforts to lick the ice off its legs, then dropped down in the snow and began to bite out the ice that had formed between the toes. This was a matter of instinct. To permit the ice to remain would mean sore feet. It did not know this. It merely obeyed the mysterious prompting that arose from the deep crypts of its being. But the man knew, having achieved a judgment on the subject, and he removed the mitten from his right hand and helped tear out the ice-particles. He did not expose his fingers more than a minute, and was astonished at the swift numbness that smote them. It certainly was cold. He pulled on the mitten hastily, and beat the hand savagely across his chest.

At twelve o'clock the day was at its brightest. Yet the sun was too far south on its winter journey to clear the horizon. The bulge of the earth intervened between it and Henderson Creek, where the man walked under a clear sky at noon and cast no shadow. At half-past twelve, to the minute, he arrived at the forks of the creek. He was pleased at the speed he had made. If he kept it up, he would certainly be with the boys by six. He unbuttoned his jacket and shirt and drew forth his lunch. The action consumed no more than a quarter of a minute, yet in that brief moment the numbness laid hold of the exposed fingers. He did not put the mitten on, but, instead, struck the fingers a dozen sharp smashes against his leg. Then he sat down on a snow-covered log to eat. The sting that followed upon the striking of his fingers against his leg ceased so quickly that he was startled. He had had no chance to take a bite of biscuit. He struck the fingers repeatedly and returned them to the mitten, baring the other hand for the purpose of eating. He tried to take a mouthful, but the ice-muzzle prevented. He had forgotten to build a fire and thaw out. He chuckled at his foolishness, and as he chuckled he noted the numbness creeping into the exposed fingers. Also, he noted that the stinging which had first come to his toes when he sat down was already passing away. He wondered whether the toes were warm or numb. He moved them inside the moccasins and decided that they were numb.

He pulled the mitten on hurriedly and stood up. He was a bit frightened. He stamped up and down until the stinging returned into the feet. It certainly was cold, was his thought. That man from Sulphur Creek had spoken the truth when telling how cold it sometimes got in the country. And he had laughed at him at the time! That showed one must not be too sure of things. There was no mistake about it, it *was* cold. He strode up and down, stamping his feet and threshing his arms, until reassured by the returning warmth. Then he got out matches and proceeded to make a fire. From the undergrowth, where high water of the previous spring had lodged a supply of seasoned twigs, he got his fire-wood. Working carefully from a small beginning, he soon had a roaring fire, over which he thawed the ice from his face and in the protection of which he ate his biscuits. For the moment the cold of space was outwitted. The dog took satisfaction in the fire, stretching out close enough for warmth and far enough away to escape being singed.

When the man had finished, he filled his pipe and took his comfortable time over a smoke. Then he pulled on his mittens, settled the ear-flaps of his cap firmly about his ears, and took the creek trail up the left fork. The dog was disappointed and yearned back toward the fire. This man did not know cold. Possibly all the generations of his ancestry had been ignorant of cold, of real cold, of cold one hundred and seven degrees below freezing-point. But the dog knew; all its ancestry knew, and it had inherited the knowledge. And it knew that it was not good to walk abroad in such fearful cold. It was the time to lie snug in a hole in the snow and wait for a curtain of cloud to be drawn across the face of outer space whence this cold came. On the other hand, there was no keen intimacy between the dog and the man. The one was the toil-slave of the other, and the only caresses it had ever received were the caresses of the whip-lash and of harsh and menacing throat-sounds that threatened the whip-lash. So the dog made no effort to communicate its apprehension to the man. It was not concerned in the welfare of the man; it was for its own sake that it yearned back toward the fire. But the man whistled, and spoke to it with the sound of whip-lashes, and the dog swung in at the man's heels and followed after.

The man took a chew of tobacco and proceeded to start a new amber beard. Also, his moist breath quickly powdered with white his mustache, eyebrows, and lashes. There did not seem to be so many springs on the left fork of the Henderson, and for half an hour the man saw no signs of any. And then it happened. At a place where there were no signs, where the soft, unbroken snow seemed to advertise solidity beneath, the man broke through. It was not deep. He wet himself halfway to the knees before he floundered out to the firm crust.

He was angry, and cursed his luck aloud. He had hoped to get into camp with the boys at six o'clock, and this would delay him an hour, for he would have to build a fire and dry out his foot-gear. This was imperative at that low temperature—he knew that much; and he turned aside to the bank, which he climbed. On top, tangled in the underbrush about the trunks of several small spruce trees, was a high-water deposit of dry fire-wood—sticks and twigs, principally, but also larger portions of seasoned branches and fine, dry, last-year's grasses. He threw down several large pieces on top of the snow. This served for a foundation and prevented the young flame from drowning itself in the snow it otherwise would melt. The flame he got by touching a match to a small shred of birch-bark that he took from his pocket. This burned even more readily than paper. Placing it on the foundation, he fed the young flame with wisps of dry grass and with the tiniest dry twigs.

He worked slowly and carefully, keenly aware of his danger. Gradually, as the flame grew stronger, he increased the size of the twigs with which he fed it. He squatted in the snow, pulling the twigs out from their entanglement in the brush and feeding directly to the flame. He knew there must be no failure. When it is seventy-five below zero, a man must not fail in his first attempt to build a fire—that is, if his feet are wet. If his feet are dry, and he fails, he can run along the trail for half a mile and restore his circulation. But the circulation of wet and freezing feet cannot be restored by running when it is seventy-five below. No matter how fast he runs, the wet feet will freeze the harder.

All this the man knew. The old-timer on Sulphur Creek had told him about it the previous fall, and now he was appreciating the advice. Already all sensation had gone out of his feet. To build the fire he had been forced to remove his mittens, and the fingers had quickly gone numb. His pace of four miles an hour had kept his heart pumping blood to the surface of his body and to all the extremities. But the instant he stopped, the action of the pump eased down. The cold of space smote the unprotected tip of the planet, and he, being on that unprotected tip, received the full force of the blow. The blood of his body recoiled before it. The blood was alive, like the dog, and like the dog it wanted to hide away and cover itself up from the fearful cold. So long as he walked four miles an hour, he pumped that blood, willy-nilly, to the surface; but now it ebbed away and sank down into the recesses of his body. The extremities were the first to feel its absence. His wet feet froze the faster, and his exposed fingers numbed the faster, though they had not yet begun to freeze. Nose and cheeks were already freezing, while the skin of all his body chilled as it lost its blood.

But he was safe. Toes and nose and cheeks would be only touched by the frost, for the fire was beginning to burn with strength. He was feeding it with twigs the size of his finger. In another minute he would be able to feed it with branches the size of his wrist, and then he could remove his wet foot gear, and, while it dried, he could keep his naked feet warm by the fire, rubbing them at first, of course, with snow. The fire was a success. He was safe. He remembered the advice of the old-timer on Sulphur Creek, and smiled. The old-timer had been very serious in laying down the law that no man must travel alone in the Klondike after fifty below. Well, here he was; he had had the accident; he was alone; and he had saved himself. Those old-timers were rather womanish, some of them, he thought. All a man had to do was to keep his head, and he was all right. Any man who was a man could travel alone. But it was surprising, the rapidity with which his cheeks and nose were freezing. And he had not thought his fingers could go lifeless in so short a time. Lifeless they were, for he could scarcely make them move together to grip a twig, and they seemed remote from his body and from him. When he touched a twig, he had to look and see whether or not he had hold of it. The wires were pretty well down between him and his finger-ends.

All of which counted for little. There was the fire, snapping and crackling and promising life with every dancing flame. He started to untie his moccasins. They were coated with ice; the thick German socks were like sheaths of iron halfway to the knees; and the moccasin strings were like rods of steel all twisted and knotted as by some conflagration. For a moment he tugged with his numb fingers, then, realizing the folly of it, he drew his sheath-knife.

But before he could cut the strings, it happened. It was his own fault or, rather, his mistake. He should not have built the fire under the spruce tree. He should have built it in the open. But it had been easier to pull the twigs from the brush and drop them directly on the fire. Now the tree under which he had done this carried a weight of snow on its boughs. No wind had blown for weeks, and each bough was fully freighted. Each time he had pulled a twig he had communicated a slight agitation to the tree—an imperceptible agitation, so far as he was concerned, but an agitation sufficient to bring about the disaster. High up in the tree one bough capsized its load of snow. This fell on the boughs beneath, capsizing them. This process continued, spreading out and involving the whole tree. It grew like an avalanche, and it descended without warning upon the man and the fire, and the fire was blotted out! Where it had burned was a mantle of fresh and disordered snow.

The man was shocked. It was as though he had just heard his own sentence of death. For a moment he sat and stared at the spot where the fire had been. Then he grew very calm. Perhaps the old-timer on Sulphur Creek was right. If he had only had a trail-mate he would have been in no danger now. The trail-mate could have built the fire. Well, it was up to him to build the fire over again, and this second time there must be no failure. Even if he succeeded, he would most likely lose some toes. His feet must be badly frozen by now, and there would be some time before the second fire was ready.

Such were his thoughts, but he did not sit and think them. He was busy all the time they were passing through his mind. He made a new foundation for a fire, this time in the open, where no treacherous tree could blot it out. Next, he gathered dry grasses and tiny twigs from the high-water flotsam. He could not bring his fingers together to pull them out, but he was able to gather them by the handful. In this way he got many rotten twigs and bits of green moss that were undesirable, but it was the best he could do. He worked methodically, even collecting an armful of the larger branches to be used later when the fire gathered strength. And all the while the dog sat and watched him, a certain yearning wistfulness in its eyes, for it looked upon him as the fire-provider, and the fire was slow in coming.

When all was ready, the man reached in his pocket for a second piece of birch-bark. He knew the bark was there, and, though he could not feel it with his fingers, he could hear its crisp rustling as he fumbled for it. Try as he would, he could not clutch hold of it. And all the time, in his consciousness, was the knowledge that each instant his feet were freezing. This thought tended to put him in a panic, but he fought against it and kept calm. He pulled on his mittens with his teeth, and threshed his arms back and forth, beating his hands with all his might against his sides. He did this sitting down, and he stood up to do it; and all the while the dog sat in the snow, its wolf-brush of a tail curled around warmly over its forefeet, its sharp wolf-ears pricked forward intently as it watched the man. And the man, as he beat and threshed with his arms and hands, felt a great surge of envy as he regarded the creature that was warm and secure in its natural covering.

After a time he was aware of the first faraway signals of sensation in his beaten fingers. The faint tingling grew stronger till it evolved into a stinging ache that was excruciating, but which the man hailed with satisfaction. He stripped the mitten from his right hand and fetched forth the birch-bark. The exposed fingers were quickly going numb again. Next he brought out his bunch of sulphur matches. But the tremendous cold had already driven the life out of his fingers. In his effort to separate one match from the others, the whole bunch fell in the snow. He tried to pick it out of the snow, but failed. The dead fingers could neither touch nor clutch. He was very careful. He drove the thought of his freezing feet, and nose, and cheeks, out of his mind, devoting his whole soul to the matches. He watched, using the sense of vision in place of that of touch, and when he saw his fingers on each side the bunch, he closed them—that is, he willed to close them, for the wires were down, and the fingers did not obey. He pulled the mitten on the right hand, and beat it fiercely against his knee. Then, with both mittened hands, he scooped the bunch of matches, along with much snow, into his lap. Yet he was no better off.

After some manipulation he managed to get the bunch between the heels of his mittened hands. In this fashion he carried it to his mouth. The ice crackled and snapped when by a violent effort he opened his mouth. He drew the lower jaw in, curled the upper lip out of the way, and scraped the bunch with his upper teeth in order to separate a match. He succeeded in getting one, which he dropped on his lap. He was no better off. He could not pick it up. Then he devised a way. He picked it up in his teeth and scratched it on his leg. Twenty times he scratched before he succeeded in lighting it. As it flamed he held it with his teeth to the birch-bark. But the burning brimstone went up his nostrils and into his lungs, causing him to cough spasmodically. The match fell into the snow and went out.

The old-timer on Sulphur Creek was right, he thought in the moment of controlled despair that ensued: after fifty below, a man should travel with a partner. He beat his hands, but failed in exciting any sensation. Suddenly he bared both hands, removing the mittens with his teeth. He caught the whole bunch between the heels of his hands. His arm-muscles not being frozen enabled him to press the hand-heels tightly against the matches. Then he scratched the bunch along his leg. It flared into flame, seventy sulphur matches at once! There was no wind to blow them out. He kept his head to one side to escape the strangling fumes, and held the blazing bunch to the birch-bark. As he so held it, he became aware of sensation in his hand. His flesh was burning. He could smell it. Deep down below the surface he could feel it. The sensation developed into pain that grew acute. And still he endured it, holding the flame of the matches clumsily to the bark that would not light readily because his own burning hands were in the way, absorbing most of the flame.

At last, when he could endure no more, he jerked his hands apart. The blazing matches fell sizzling into the snow, but the birch-bark was alight. He began laying dry grasses and the tiniest twigs on the flame. He could not pick and choose, for he had to lift the fuel between the heels of his hands. Small pieces of rotten wood and green moss clung to the twigs, and he bit them off as well as he could with his teeth. He cherished the flame carefully and awkwardly. It meant life, and it must not perish. The withdrawal of blood from the surface of his body now made him begin to shiver, and he grew more awkward. A large piece of green moss fell squarely on the little fire. He tried to poke it out with his fingers, but his shivering frame made him poke too far, and he disrupted the nucleus of the little fire, the burning grasses and tiny twigs separating and scattering. He tried to poke them together again, but in spite of the tenseness of the effort, his shivering got away with him, and the twigs were hopelessly scattered. Each twig gushed a puff of smoke and went out. The fire-provider had failed. As he looked apathetically about him, his eyes chanced on the dog, sitting across the ruins of the fire from him, in the snow, making restless, hunching movements, slightly lifting one forefoot and then the other, shifting its weight back and forth on them with wistful eagerness.

The sight of the dog put a wild idea into his head. He remembered the tale of the man, caught in a blizzard, who killed a steer and crawled inside the carcass, and so was saved. He would kill the dog and bury his hands in the warm body, until the numbness went out of them. Then he could build another fire. He spoke to the dog, calling it to him; but in his voice was a strange note of fear that frightened the animal, who had never known the man to speak in such way before. Something was the matter, and its suspicious nature sensed danger—it knew not what danger, but somewhere, somehow, in its brain arose an apprehension of the man. It flattened its ears down at the sound of the man's voice, and its restless, hunching movements and the liftings and shiftings of its forefeet became more pronounced; but it would not come to the man. He got on his hands and knees and crawled toward the dog. This unusual posture again excited suspicion, and the animal sidled mincingly away.

The man sat up in the snow for a moment and struggled for calmness. Then he pulled on his mittens, by means of his teeth, and got upon his feet. He glanced down at first in order to assure himself that he was really standing up, for the absence of sensation in his feet left him unrelated to the earth. His erect position in itself started to drive the webs of suspicion from the dog's mind; and when he spoke peremptorily, with the sound of whip-lashes in his voice, the dog rendered its customary allegiance and came to him. As it came within reaching distance, the man lost his control. His arms flashed out to the dog, and he experienced genuine surprise when he discovered that his hands could not clutch, that there was neither bend nor feeling in the fingers. He had forgotten for the moment that they were frozen and that they were freezing more and more. All this happened quickly, and before the animal could get away, he encircled its body with his arms. He sat down in the snow, and in this fashion held the dog, while it snarled and whined and struggled.

But it was all he could do, hold its body encircled in his arms and sit there. He realized that he could not kill the dog. There was no way to do it. With his helpess hands he could neither draw nor hold his sheath-knife nor throttle the animal. He released it, and it plunged wildly away, with tail between its legs, and still snarling. It halted forty feet away and surveyed him curiously, with ears sharply pricked forward. The man looked down at his hands in order to locate them, and found them hanging on the ends of his arms. It struck him as curious that one should have to use his eyes in order to find out where his hands were. He began threshing his arms back and forth, beating the mittened hands against his sides. He did this for five minutes, violently, and his heart pumped enough blood up to the surface to put a stop to his shivering. But no sensation was aroused in the hands. He had an impression that they hung like weights on the ends of his arms, but when he tried to run the impression down, he could not find it.

A certain fear of death, dull and oppressive, came to him. This fear quickly became poignant as he realized that it was no longer a mere matter of freezing his fingers and toes, or of losing his hands and feet, but that it was a matter of life and death with the chances against him. This threw him into a panic, and he turned and ran up the creek-bed along the old, dim trail. The dog joined in behind and kept up with him. He ran blindly, without intention, in fear such as he had never known in his life. Slowly, as he ploughed and floundered through the snow, he began to see things again,—the banks of the creek, the old timber-jams, the leafless aspens, and the sky. The running made him feel better. He did not shiver. Maybe, if he ran on, his feet would thaw out; and, anyway, if he ran far enough, he would reach camp and the boys. Without doubt he would lose some fingers and toes and some of his face; but the boys would take care of him, and save the rest of him when he got there. And at the same time there was another thought in his mind that said he would never get to the camp and the boys; that it was too many miles away, that the freezing had too great a start on him, and that he would soon be stiff and dead. This thought he kept in the background and refused to consider. Sometimes it pushed itself forward and demanded to be heard, but he thrust it back and strove to think of other things.

It struck him as curious that he could run at all on feet so frozen that he could not feel them when they struck the earth and took the weight of his body. He seemed to himself to skim along above the surface, and to have no connection with the earth. Somewhere he had once seen a winged Mercury, and he wondered if Mercury felt as he felt when skimming over the earth.

His theory of running until he reached camp and the boys had one flaw in it: he lacked the endurance. Several times he stumbled, and finally he tottered, crumpled up, and fell. When he tried to rise, he failed. He must sit and rest, he decided, and next time he would merely walk and keep on going. As he sat and regained his breath, he noted that he was feeling quite warm and comfortable. He was not shivering, and it even seemed that a warm glow had come to his chest and trunk. And yet, when he touched his nose or cheeks, there was no sensation. Running would not thaw them out. Nor would it thaw out his hands and feet. Then the thought came to him that the frozen portions of his body must be extending. He tried to keep this thought down, to forget it, to think of something else; he was aware of the panicky feeling that it caused, and he was afraid of the panic. But the thought asserted itself, and persisted, until it produced a vision of his body totally frozen. This was too much, and he made another wild run along the trail. Once he slowed down to a walk, but the thought of the freezing extending itself made him run again.

And all the time the dog ran with him, at his heels. When he fell down a second time, it curled its tail over its forefeet and sat in front of him, facing him, curiously eager and intent. The warmth and security of the animal angered him, and he cursed it till it flattened down its ears appeasingly. This time the shivering came more quickly upon the man. He was losing in his battle with the frost. It was creeping into his body from all sides. The thought of it drove him on, but he ran no more than a hundred feet, when he staggered and pitched headlong. It was his last panic. When he had recovered his breath and control, he sat up and entertained in his mind the conception of meeting death with dignity. However, the conception did not come to him in such terms. His idea of it was that he had been making a fool of himself, running around like a chicken with its head cut off—such was the simile that occurred to him. Well, he was bound to freeze anyway, and he might as well take it decently. With this new-found peace of mind came the first glimmerings of drowsiness. A good idea, he thought, to sleep off to death. It was like taking an anesthetic. Freezing was not so bad as people thought. There were lots worse ways to die.

He pictured the boys finding his body next day. Suddenly he found himself with them, coming along the trail and looking for himself. And, still with them, he came around a turn in the trail and found himself lying in the snow. He did not belong with himself any more, for even then he was out of himself, standing with the boys and looking at himself in the snow. It certainly was cold, was his thought. When he got back to the States he could tell the folks what real cold was. He drifted on from this to a vision of the old-timer on Sulphur Creek. He could see him quite clearly, warm and comfortable, and smoking a pipe.

"You were right, old hoss; you were right," the man mumbled to the old-timer of Sulphur Creek.

Then the man drowsed off into what seemed to him the most comfortable and satisfying sleep he had ever known. The dog sat facing him and waiting. The brief day drew to a close in a long, slow twilight. There were no signs of a fire to be made, and, besides, never in the dog's experience had it known a man to sit like that in the snow and make no fire. As the twilight drew on, its eager yearning for the fire mastered it, and with a great lifting and shifting of forefeet, it whined softly, then flattened its ears down in anticipation of being chidden by the man. But the man remained silent. Later, the dog whined loudly. And still later it crept close to the man and caught the scent of death. This made the animal bristle and back away. A little longer it delayed, howling under the stars that leaped and danced and shone brightly in the cold sky. Then it turned and trotted up the trail in the direction of the camp it knew, where were the other food-providers and fire-providers.

The Willows

by Algernon Blackwood

There is something tame about some current notions of the wilderness, which we often represent as a place to orient ourselves and somehow become whole. In this story, Algernon Blackwood (1869–1951) reminds us that the wild has the power to threaten our sanity as well as to preserve or restore it—that the wilderness is our closest link to darkness as well as light.

After leaving Vienna, and long before you come to BudaPesth, the Danube enters a region of singular loneliness and desolation, where its waters spread away on all sides regardless of a main channel, and the country becomes a swamp for miles upon miles, covered by a vast sea of low willow-bushes. On the big maps this deserted area is painted in a fluffy blue, growing fainter in color as it leaves the banks, and across it may be seen in large straggling letters the word *Sümpfe*, meaning marshes.

In high flood this great acreage of sand, shingle-beds, and willow-grown islands is almost topped by the water, but in normal seasons the bushes bend and rustle in the free winds, showing their silver leaves to the sunshine in an ever-moving plain of bewildering beauty. These willows never attain to the dignity of trees; they have no rigid trunks; they remain humble bushes, with rounded tops and soft outline, swaying on slender stems that answer to the least pressure of the wind; supple as grasses, and so continually shifting that they somehow give the impression that the entire plain is moving and *alive*. For the wind sends waves rising and falling over the whole surface, waves of leaves instead of waves of water, green swells like the sea, too, until the branches turn and lift, and then silvery white as their under-side turns to the sun.

Happy to slip beyond the control of stern banks, the Danube here wanders about at will among the intricate network of channels intersecting the islands everywhere with broad avenues down which the waters pour with a shouting sound; making whirlpools, eddies, and foaming rapids; tearing at the sandy banks; carrying away masses of shore and willow-clumps; and forming new islands innumerable which shift daily in size and shape and possess at best an impermanent life, since the flood-time obliterates their very existence.

Properly speaking, this fascinating part of the river's life begins soon after leaving Pressburg, and we, in our Canadian canoe, with gipsy tent and frying-pan on board, reached it on the crest of a rising flood about mid-July. That very same morning, when the sky was reddening before sunrise, we had slipped swiftly through still-sleeping Vienna, leaving it a couple of hours later a mere patch of smoke against the blue hills of the Wienerwald on the horizon; we had breakfasted below Fischamend under a grove of birch trees roaring in the wind; and had then swept on the tearing current past Orth, Hainburg, Petronell (the old Roman Carnuntum of Marcus Aurelius), and so under the frowning heights of Theben on a spur of the Carpathians, where the March steals in quietly from the left and the frontier is crossed between Austria and Hungary.

Racing along at twelve kilometers an hour soon took us well into Hungary, and the muddy waters—sure sign of flood—sent us aground on many a shingle-bed, and twisted us like a cork in many a sudden belching whirlpool before the towers of Pressburg (Hungarian, Poszóny) showed against the sky; and then the canoe, leaping like a spirited horse, flew at top speed under the gray walls, negotiated safely the sunken chain of the Fliegende Brücke ferry, turned the corner sharply to the left, and plunged on yellow foam into the wilderness of islands, sand-banks, and swamp-land beyond—the land of the willows.

The change came suddenly, as when a series of bioscope pictures snaps down on the streets of a town and shifts without warning into the scenery of lake and forest. We entered the land of desolation on wings, and in less than half an hour there was neither boat nor fishing-hut nor red roof, nor any single sign of human habitation and civilization within sight. The sense of remoteness from the world of human kind, the utter isolation, the fascination of this singular world of willows, winds, and waters, instantly laid its spell upon us both, so that we allowed laughingly to one another that we ought by rights to have held some special kind of passport to admit us, and that we had, somewhat audaciously, come without asking leave into a separate little kingdom of wonder and magic—a kingdom that was reserved for the use of others who had a right to it, with everywhere unwritten warnings to trespassers for those who had the imagination to discover them.

Though still early in the afternoon, the ceaseless buffetings of a most tempestuous wind made us feel weary, and we at once began casting about for a suitable camping-ground for the night. But the bewildering character of the islands made landing difficult; the swirling flood carried us in-shore and then swept us out again; the willow branches tore our hands as we seized them to stop the canoe, and we pulled many a yard of sandy bank into the water before at length we shot with a great sideways blow from the wind into a backwater and managed to beach the bows in a cloud of spray. Then we lay panting and laughing after our exertions on hot yellow sand, sheltered from the wind, and in the full blaze of a scorching sun, a cloudless blue sky above, and an immense army of dancing, shouting willow bushes, closing in from all sides, shining with spray and clapping their thousand little hands as though to applaud the success of our efforts.

"What a river!" I said to my companion, thinking of all the way we had traveled from the source in the Black Forest, and how we had often been obliged to wade and push in the upper shallows at the beginning of June.

"Won't stand much nonsense now, will it?" he said, pulling the canoe a little farther into safety up the sand, and then composing himself for a nap.

I lay by his side, happy and peaceful in the bath of the elements—water, wind, sand, and the great fire of the sun—thinking of the long journey that lay behind us, and of the great stretch before us to the Black Sea, and how lucky I was to have such a delightful and charming traveling companion as my friend, the Swede.

We had made many similar journeys together, but the Danube, more than any other river I knew, impressed us from the very beginning with its *aliveness*. From its tiny bubbling entry into the world among the pinewood gardens of Donaueschingen, until this moment when it began to play the great river-game of losing itself among the deserted swamps, unobserved, unrestrained, it had seemed to us like following the growth of some living creature. Sleepy at first, but later developing violent desires as it became conscious of its deep soul, it rolled, like some huge fluid being, through all the countries we had passed, holding our little craft on its mighty shoulders, playing roughly with us sometimes, yet always friendly and well-meaning, till at length we had come inevitably to regard it as a Great Personage.

How, indeed, could it be otherwise, since it told us so much of its secret life? At night we heard it singing to the moon as we lay in our tent, uttering that odd sibilant note peculiar to itself and said to be caused by the rapid tearing of the pebbles along its bed, so great is its hurrying speed. We knew, too, the voice of its gurgling whirlpools, suddenly bubbling up on a surface previously quite calm; the roar of its shallows and swift rapids; its constant steady thundering below all mere surface sounds; and that ceaseless tearing of its icy waters at the banks. How it stood up and shouted when the rains fell flat upon its face! And how its laughter roared out when the wind blew upstream and tried to stop its growing speed! We knew all its sounds and voices, its tumblings and foamings, its unnecessary splashing against the bridges; that self-conscious chatter when there were hills to look on; the affected dignity of its speech when it passed through the little towns, far too important to laugh; and all these faint, sweet whisperings when the sun caught it fairly in some slow curve and poured down upon it till the steam rose.

It was full of tricks, too, in its early life before the great world knew it. There were places in the upper reaches among the Swabian forests, when yet the first whispers of its destiny had not reached it, where it elected to disappear through holes in the ground, to appear again on the other side of the porous limestone hills and start a new river with another name; leaving, too, so little water in its own bed that we had to climb out and wade and push the canoe through miles of shallows!

And a chief pleasure, in those early days of its irresponsible youth, was to lie low, like Brer Fox, just before the little turbulent tributaries came to join it from the Alps, and to refuse to acknowledge them when in, but to run for miles side by side, the dividing line well marked, the very levels different, the Danube utterly declining to recognize the newcomer. Below Passau, however, it gave up this particular trick, for there the Inn comes in with a thundering power impossible to ignore, and so pushes and incommodes the parent river that there is hardly room for them in the long twisting gorge that follows, and the Danube is shoved this way and that against the cliffs, and forced to hurry itself with great waves and much dashing to and fro in order to get through in time. And during the fight our canoe slipped down from its shoulder to its breast, and had the time of its life among the struggling waves. But the Inn taught the old river a lesson, and after Passau it no longer pretended to ignore new arrivals.

This was many days back, of course, and since then we had come to know other aspects of the great creature, and across the Bavarian wheat plain of Straubing she wandered so slowly under the blazing June sun that we could well imagine only the surface inches were water, while below there moved, concealed as by a silken mantle, a whole army of Undines, passing silently and unseen down to the sea, and very leisurely too, lest they be discovered.

Much, too, we forgave her because of her friendliness to the birds and animals that haunted the shores. Cormorants lined the banks in lonely places in rows like short black palings; gray crows crowded the shingle-beds; storks stood fishing in the vistas of shallower water that opened up between the islands, and hawks, swans, and marsh birds of all sorts filled the air with glinting wings and singing, petulant cries. It was impossible to feel annoyed with the river's vagaries after seeing a deer leap with a splash into the water at sunrise and swim past the bows of the canoe; and often we saw fawns peering at us from the underbrush, or looked straight into the brown eyes of a stag as we charged full tilt round a corner and entered another reach of the river. Foxes, too, everywhere haunted the banks, tripping daintily among the driftwood and disappearing so suddenly that it was impossible to see how they managed it.

But now, after leaving Pressburg, everything changed a little, and the Danube became more serious. It ceased trifling. It was half-way to the Black Sea, within scenting distance almost of other, stranger countries where no tricks would be permitted or understood. It became suddenly grown-up, and claimed our respect and even our awe. It broke out into three arms, for one thing, that only met again a hundred kilometers farther down, and for a canoe there were no indications which one was intended to be followed.

"If you take a side channel," said the Hungarian officer we met in the Pressburg shop while buying provisions, "you may find yourselves, when the flood subsides, forty miles from anywhere, high and dry, and you may easily starve. There are no people, no farms, no fishermen. I warn you not to continue. The river, too, is still rising, and this wind will increase."

The rising river did not alarm us in the least, but the matter of being left high and dry by a sudden subsidence of the waters might be serious, and we had consequently laid in an extra stock of provisions. For the rest, the officer's prophecy held true, and the wind, blowing down a perfectly clear sky, increased steadily till it reached the dignity of a westerly gale.

It was earlier than usual when we camped, for the sun was a good hour or two from the horizon, and leaving my friend still asleep on the hot sand, I wandered about in desultory examination of our hotel. The island, I found, was less than an acre in extent, a mere sandy bank standing some two or three feet above the level of the river. The far end, pointing into the sunset, was covered with flying spray which the tremendous wind drove off the crests of the broken waves. It was triangular in shape, with the apex upstream.

I stood there for several minutes, watching the impetuous crimson flood bearing down with a shouting roar, dashing in waves against the bank as though to sweep it bodily away, and then swirling by in two foaming streams on either side. The ground seemed to shake with the shock and rush, while the furious movement of the willow bushes as the wind poured over them increased the curious illusion that the island itself actually moved. Above, for a mile or two, I could see the great river descending upon me: it was like looking up the slope of a sliding hill, white with foam, and leaping up everywhere to show itself to the sun.

The rest of the island was too thickly grown with willows to make walking pleasant, but I made the tour, nevertheless. From the lower end the light, of course, changed, and the river looked dark and angry. Only the backs of the flying waves were visible, streaked with foam, and pushed forcibly by the great puffs of wind that fell upon them from behind. For a short mile it was visible, pouring in and out among the islands, and then disappearing with a huge sweep into the willows, which closed about it like a herd of monstrous antediluvian creatures crowding down to drink. They made me think of gigantic sponge-like growths that sucked the river up into themselves. They caused it to vanish from sight. They herded there together in such overpowering numbers.

Altogether it was an impressive scene, with its utter loneliness, its bizarre suggestion; and as I gazed, long and curiously, a singular emotion began to stir somewhere in the depths of me. Midway in my delight of the wild beauty, there crept, unbidden and unexplained, a curious feeling of disquietude, almost of alarm.

A rising river, perhaps, always suggests something of the ominous: many of the little islands I saw before me would probably have been swept away by the morning; this resistless, thundering flood of water touched the sense of awe. Yet I was aware that my uneasiness lay deeper far than the emotions of awe and wonder. It was not that I felt. Nor had it directly to do with the power of the driving wind—this shouting hurricane that might almost carry up a few acres of willows into the air and scatter them like so much chaff over the landscape. The wind was simply enjoying itself, for nothing rose out of the flat landscape to stop it, and I was conscious of sharing its great game with a kind of pleasurable excitement. Yet this novel emotion had nothing to do with the wind. Indeed, so vague was the sense of distress I experienced, that it was impossible to trace it to its source and deal with it accordingly, though I was aware somehow that it had to do with my realization of our utter insignificance before this unrestrained power of the elements about me. The huge-grown river had something to do with it too—a vague, unpleasant idea that we had somehow trifled with these great elemental forces in whose power we lay helpless every hour of the day and night. For here, indeed, they were gigantically at play together, and the sight appealed to the imagination.

But my emotion, so far as I could understand it, seemed to attach itself more particularly to the willow bushes, to these acres and acres of willows, crowding, so thickly growing there, swarming everywhere the eye could reach, pressing upon the river as though to suffocate it, standing in dense array mile after mile beneath the sky, watching, waiting, listening. And, apart quite from the elements, the willows connected themselves subtly with my malaise, attacking the mind insidiously somehow by reason of their vast numbers, and contriving in some way or other to represent to the imagination a new and mighty power, a power, moreover, not altogether friendly to us.

Great revelations of nature, of course, never fail to impress in one way or another, and I was no stranger to moods of the kind. Mountains overawe and oceans terrify, while the mystery of great forests exercises a spell peculiarly its own. But all these, at one point or another, somewhere link on intimately with human life and human experience. They stir comprehensible, even if alarming, emotions. They tend on the whole to exalt.

With this multitude of willows, however, it was something far different, I felt. Some essence emanated from them that besieged the heart. A sense of awe awakened, true, but of awe touched somewhere by a vague terror. Their serried ranks, growing everywhere darker about me as the shadows deepened, moving furiously yet softly in the wind, woke in me the curious and unwelcome suggestion that we had trespassed here upon the borders of an alien world, a world where we were intruders, a world where we were not wanted or invited to remain— where we ran grave risks perhaps!

The feeling, however, though it refused to yield its meaning entirely to analysis, did not at the time trouble me by passing into menace. Yet it never left me quite, even during the very practical business of putting up the tent in a hurricane of wind and building a fire for the stew-pot. It remained, just enough to bother and perplex, and to rob a most delightful camping-ground of a good portion of its charm. To my companion, however, I said nothing, for he was a man I considered devoid of imagination. In the first place, I could never have explained to him what I meant, and in the second, he would have laughed stupidly at me if I had.

There was a slight depression in the center of the island, and here we pitched the tent. The surrounding willows broke the wind a bit.

"A poor camp," observed the imperturbable Swede when at last the tent stood upright; "no stones and precious little firewood. I'm for moving on early tomorrow—eh? This sand won't hold anything."

But the experience of a collapsing tent at midnight had taught us many devices, and we made the cozy gipsy house as safe as possible, and then set about collecting a store of wood to last till bedtime. Willow bushes drop no branches, and driftwood was our only source of supply. We hunted the shores pretty thoroughly. Everywhere the banks were crumbling as the rising tide flood tore at them and carried away great portions with a splash and a gurgle.

"The island's much smaller than when we landed," said the accurate Swede. "It won't last long at this rate. We'd better drag the canoe close to the tent, and be ready to start at a moment's notice. *I* shall sleep in my clothes."

He was a little distance off, climbing along the bank, and I heard his rather jolly laugh as he spoke.

"By Jove!" I heard him call, a moment later, and turned to see what had caused his exclamation. But for the moment he was hidden by the willows, and I could not find him.

"What in the world's this?" I heard him cry again, and this time his voice had become serious.

I ran up quickly and joined him on the bank. He was looking over the river, pointing at something in the water.

"Good Heavens, it's a man's body!" he cried excitedly. "Look!"

A black thing, turning over and over in the foaming waves, swept rapidly past. It kept disappearing and coming up to the surface again. It was about twenty feet from the shore, and just as it was opposite to where we stood it lurched round and looked straight at us. We saw its eyes reflecting the sunset, and gleaming an odd yellow as the body turned over. Then it gave a swift, gulping plunge, and dived out of sight in a flash.

"An otter, by gad!" we exclaimed in the same breath, laughing.

It *was* an otter, alive, and out on the hunt; yet it had looked exactly like the body of a drowned man turning helplessly in the current. Far below it came to the surface once again, and we saw its black skin, wet and shining in the sunlight.

Then, too, just as we turned back, our arms full of driftwood, another thing happened to recall us to the river bank. This time it really was a man, and what was more, a man in a boat. Now a small boat on the Danube was an unusual sight at any time, but here in this deserted region, and at flood time, it was so unexpected as to constitute a real event. We stood and stared.

Whether it was due to the slanting sunlight, or the refraction from the wonderfully illumined water, I cannot say, but, whatever the cause, I found it difficult to focus my sight properly upon the flying apparition. It seemed, however, to be a man standing upright in a sort of flat-bottomed boat, steering with a long oar, and being carried down the opposite shore at a tremendous pace. He apparently was looking across in our direction, but the distance was too great and the light too uncertain for us to make out very plainly what he was about. It seemed to me that he was gesticulating and making signs at us. His voice came across the water to us shouting something furiously, but the wind drowned it so that no single word was audible. There was something curious about the whole appearance—man, boat, signs, voice—that made an impression on me out of all proportion to its cause.

"He's crossing himself!" I cried. "Look, he's making the sign of the Cross!"

"I believe you're right," the Swede said, shading his eyes with his hand and watching the man out of sight. He seemed to be gone in a moment, melting away down there into the sea of willows where the sun caught them in the bend of the river and turned them into a great crimson wall of beauty. Mist, too, had begun to rise, so that the air was hazy.

"But what in the world is he doing at night-fall on this flooded river?" I said, half to myself. "Where is he going at such a time, and what did he mean by his signs and shouting? D'you think he wished to warn us about something?"

"He saw our smoke, and thought we were spirits probably," laughed my companion. "These Hungarians believe in all sorts of rubbish: you remember the shopwoman at Pressburg warning us that no one ever landed here because it belonged to some sort of beings outside man's world! I suppose they believe in fairies and elementals, possibly demons too. That peasant in the boat saw people on the islands for the first time in his life," he added, after a slight pause, "and it scared him, that's all."

The Swede's tone of voice was not convincing, and his manner lacked something that was usually there. I noted the change instantly while he talked, though without being able to label it precisely.

"If they had enough imagination," I laughed loudly—I remember trying to make as much *noise* as I could—"they might well people a place like this with the old gods of antiquity. The Romans must have haunted all this region more or less with their shrines and sacred groves and elemental deities."

The subject dropped and we returned to our stew-pot, for my friend was not given to imaginative conversation as a rule. Moreover, just then I remember feeling distinctly glad that he was *not* imaginative; his stolid, practical nature suddenly seemed to me welcome and comforting. It was an admirable temperament, I felt: he could steer down rapids like a red Indian, shoot dangerous bridges and whirlpools better than any white man I ever saw in a canoe. He was a grand fellow for an adventurous trip, a tower of strength when untoward things happened. I looked at his strong face and light curly hair as he staggered along under his pile of driftwood (twice the size of mine!), and I experienced a feeling of relief. Yes, I was distinctly glad just then that the Swede was—what he was, and that he never made remarks that suggested more than they said.

"The river's still rising," he added, as if following out some thoughts of his own, and dropping his load with a gasp. "This island will be under water in two days if it goes on."

"I wish the *wind* would go down," I said. "I don't care a fig for the river."

The flood, indeed, had no terrors for us; we could get off at ten minutes' notice, and the more water the better we liked it. It meant an increasing current and the obliteration of the treacherous shingle-beds that so often threatened to tear the bottom out of our canoe.

Contrary to our expectations, the wind did not go down with the sun. It seemed to increase with the darkness, howling overhead and shaking the willows round us like straws. Curious sounds accompanied it sometimes, like the explosion of heavy guns, and it fell upon the water and the island in great flat blows of immense power. It made me think of the sounds a planet must make, could we only hear it, driving along through space.

But the sky kept wholly clear of clouds, and soon after supper the full moon rose up in the east and covered the river and the plain of shouting willows with a light like the day.

We lay on the sandy patch beside the fire, smoking, listening to the noises of the night round us, and talking happily of the journey we had already made, and of our plans ahead. The map lay spread in the door of the tent, but the high wind made it hard to study, and presently we lowered the curtain and extinguished the lantern. The firelight was enough to smoke and see each other's faces by, and the sparks flew about overhead like fireworks. A few yards beyond, the river gurgled and hissed, and from time to time a heavy splash announced the falling away of further portions of the bank.

Our talk, I noticed, had to do with the far-away scenes and incidents of our first camps in the Black Forest, or of other subjects altogether remote from the present setting, for neither of us spoke of the actual moment more than was necessary—almost as though we had agreed tacitly to avoid discussion of the camp and its incidents. Neither the otter nor the boatman, for instance, received the honor of a single mention, though ordinarily these would have furnished discussion for the greater part of the evening. They were, of course, distinct events in such a place.

The scarcity of wood made it a business to keep the fire going, for the wind, that drove the smoke in our faces wherever we sat, helped at the same time to make a forced draught. We took it in turn to make foraging expeditions into the darkness, and the quantity the Swede brought back always made me feel that he took an absurdly long time finding it; for the fact was I did not care much about being left alone, and yet it always seemed to be my turn to grub about among the bushes or scramble along the slippery banks in the moonlight. The long day's battle with wind and water—such wind and such water!—had tired us both, and an early bed was the obvious program. Yet neither of us made the move for the tent. We lay there, tending the fire, talking in desultory fashion, peering about us into the dense willow bushes, and listening to the thunder of wind and river. The loneliness of the place had entered our very bones, and silence seemed natural, for after a bit the sound of our voices became a trifle unreal and forced; whispering would have been the fitting mode of communication, I felt, and the human voice, always rather absurd amid the roar of the elements, now carried with it something almost illegitimate. It was like talking out loud in church, or in some place where it was not lawful, perhaps not quite *safe*, to be overheard.

The eeriness of this lonely island, set among a million willows, swept by a hurricane, and surrounded by hurrying deep waters, touched us both, I fancy. Untrodden by man, almost unknown to man, it lay there beneath the moon, remote from human influence, on the frontier of another world, an alien world, a world tenanted by willows only and the souls of willows. And we, in our rashness, had dared to invade it, even to make use of it! Something more than the power of its mystery stirred in me as I lay on the sand, feet to fire, and peered up through the leaves at the stars. For the last time I rose to get firewood.

"When this has burnt up," I said firmly, "I shall turn in," and my companion watched me lazily as I moved off into the surrounding shadows.

For an unimaginative man I thought he seemed unusually receptive that night, unusually open to suggestion of things other than sensory. He too was touched by the beauty and loneliness of the place. I was not altogether pleased, I remember, to recognize this slight change in him, and instead of immediately collecting sticks, I made my way to the far point of the island where the moonlight on plain and river could be seen to better advantage. The desire to be alone had come suddenly upon me; my former dread returned in force; there was a vague feeling in me I wished to face and probe to the bottom.

When I reached the point of sand jutting out among the waves, the spell of the place descended upon me with a positive shock. No mere "scenery" could have produced such an effect. There was something more here, something to alarm.

I gazed across the waste of wild waters; I watched the whispering willows; I heard the ceaseless beating of the tireless wind; and, one and all, each in its own way, stirred in me this sensation of a strange distress. But the *willows* especially: for ever they went on chattering and talking among themselves, laughing a little, shrilly crying out, sometimes sighing—but what it was they made so much to-do about belonged to the secret life of the great plain they inhabited. And it was utterly alien to the world I knew, or to that of the wild yet kindly elements. They made me think of a host of beings from another plane of life, another evolution altogether, perhaps, all discussing a mystery known only to themselves. I watched them moving busily together, oddly shaking their big bushy heads, twirling their myriad leaves even when there was no wind. They moved of their own will as though alive, and they touched, by some incalculable method, my own keen sense of the *horrible*.

There they stood in the moonlight, like a vast army surrounding our camp, shaking their innumerable silver spears defiantly, formed all ready for an attack.

The psychology of places, for some imaginations at least, is very vivid; for the wanderer, especially, camps have their "note" either of welcome or rejection. At first it may not always be apparent, because the busy preparations of tent and cooking prevent, but with the first pause—after supper usually—it comes and announces itself. And the note of this willow-camp now became unmistakably plain to me: we were interlopers, trespassers; we were not welcomed. The sense of unfamiliarity grew upon me as I stood there watching. We touched the frontier of a region where our presence was resented. For a night's lodging we might perhaps be tolerated; but for a prolonged and inquisitive stay—No! by all the gods of the trees and the wilderness, no! We were the first human influences upon this island, and we were not wanted. *The willows were against us.*

Strange thoughts like these, bizarre fancies, borne I know not whence, found lodgment in my mind as I stood listening. What, I thought, if, after all, these crouching willows proved to be alive; if suddenly they should rise up, like a swarm of living creatures, marshaled by the gods whose territory we had invaded, sweep toward us off the vast swamps, booming overhead in the night—and then *settle* down! As I looked it was so easy to imagine they actually moved, crept nearer, retreated a little, huddled together in masses, hostile, waiting for the great wind that should finally start them a-running. I could have sworn their aspect changed a little, and their ranks deepened and pressed more closely together.

The melancholy shrill cry of a night-bird sounded overhead, and suddenly I nearly lost my balance as the piece of bank I stood upon fell with a great splash into the river, undermined by the flood. I stepped back just in time, and went on hunting for firewood again, half laughing at the odd fancies that crowded so thickly into my mind and cast their spell upon me. I recalled the Swede's remark about moving on next day, and I was just thinking that I fully agreed with him, when I turned with a start and saw the subject of my thoughts standing immediately in front of me. He was quite close. The roar of the elements had covered his approach.

"You've been gone so long," he shouted above the wind, "I thought something must have happened to you."

But there was that in his tone, and a certain look in his face as well, that conveyed to me more than his actual words, and in a flash I understood the real reason for his coming. It was because the spell of the place had entered his soul too, and he did not like being alone.

"River still rising," he cried, pointing to the flood in the moonlight, "and the wind's simply awful."

He always said the same things, but it was the cry for companionship that gave the real importance to his words.

"Lucky," I cried back, "our tent's in the hollow. I think it'll hold all right." I added something about the difficulty of finding wood, in order to explain my absence, but the wind caught my words and flung them across the river, so that he did not hear, but just looked at me through the branches, nodding his head.

"Lucky if we get away without disaster!" he shouted, or words to that effect; and I remember feeling half angry with him for putting the thought into words, for it was exactly what I felt myself. There was disaster impending somewhere, and the sense of presentiment lay unpleasantly upon me.

We went back to the fire and made a final blaze, poking it up with our feet. We took a last look round. But for the wind the heat would have been unpleasant. I put this thought into words, and I remember my friend's reply struck me oddly: that he would rather have the heat, the ordinary July weather than this "diabolical wind."

Everything was snug for the night; the canoe lying turned over beside the tent, with both yellow paddles beneath her; the provision sack hanging from a willow-stem, and the washed-up dishes removed to a safe distance from the fire, all ready for the morning meal.

We smothered the embers of the fire with sand, and then turned in. The flap of the tent door was up, and I saw the branches and the stars and the white moonlight. The shaking willows and the heavy buffetings of the wind against our taut little house were the last things I remembered as sleep came down and covered all with its soft and delicious forgetfulness.

Suddenly I found myself lying awake, peering from my sandy mattress through the door of the tent. I looked at my watch pinned against the canvas, and saw by the bright moonlight that it was past twelve o'clock—the threshold of a new day—and I had therefore slept a couple of hours. The Swede was asleep still beside me; the wind howled as before; something plucked at my heart and made me feel afraid. There was a sense of disturbance in my immediate neighborhood.

I sat up quickly and looked out. The trees were swaying violently to and fro as the gusts smote them, but our little bit of green canvas lay snugly safe in the hollow, for the wind passed over it without meeting enough resistance to make it vicious. The feeling of disquietude did not pass, however, and I crawled quietly out of the tent to see if our belongings were safe. I moved carefully so as not to waken my companion. A curious excitement was on me.

I was halfway out, kneeling on all fours, when my eye first took in that the tops of the bushes opposite, with their moving tracery of leaves, made shapes against the sky. I sat back on my haunches and stared. It was incredible, surely, but there, opposite and slightly above me, were shapes of some indeterminate sort among the willows, and as the branches swayed in the wind they seemed to group themselves about these shapes, forming a series of monstrous outlines that shifted rapidly beneath the moon. Close, about fifty feet in front of me, I saw these things.

My first instinct was to waken my companion, that he too might see them, but something made me hesitate—the sudden realization, probably, that I should not welcome corroboration; and meanwhile I crouched there staring in amazement with smarting eyes. I was wide awake. I remember saying to myself that I was *not* dreaming.

They first became properly visible, these huge figures, just within the tops of the bushes—immense, bronze-colored, moving, and wholly independent of the swaying of the branches. I saw them plainly and noted, now I came to examine them more calmly, that they were very much larger than human, and indeed that something in their appearance proclaimed them to be *not human* at all. Certainly they were not merely the moving tracery of the branches against the moonlight. They shifted independently. They rose upward in a continuous stream from earth to sky, vanishing utterly as soon as they reached the dark of the sky. They were interlaced one with another, making a great column, and I saw their limbs and huge bodies melting in and out of each other, forming this serpentine line that bent and swayed and twisted spirally with the contortions of the wind-tossed trees. They were nude, fluid shapes, passing up the bushes, *within* the leaves almost—rising up in a living column into the heavens. Their faces I never could see. Unceasingly they poured upward, swaying in great bending curves, with a hue of dull bronze upon their skins.

I stared, trying to force every atom of vision from my eyes. For a long time I thought they *must* every moment disappear and resolve themselves into the movements of the branches and prove to be an optical illusion. I searched everywhere for a proof of reality, when all the while I understood quite well that the standard of reality had changed. For the longer I looked the more certain I became that these figures were real and living, though perhaps not according to the standards that the camera and the biologist would insist upon.

Far from feeling fear, I was possessed with a sense of awe and wonder such as I have never known. I seemed to be gazing at the personified elemental forces of this haunted and primeval region. Our intrusion had stirred the powers of the place into activity. It was we who were the cause of the disturbance, and my brain filled to bursting with stories and legends of the spirits and deities of places that have been acknowledged and worshipped by men in all ages of the world's history. But, before I could arrive at any possible explanation, something impelled me to go farther out, and I crept forward on to the sand and stood upright. I felt the ground still warm under my bare feet; the wind tore at my hair and face; and the sound of the river burst upon my ears with a sudden roar. These things, I knew, were real, and proved that my senses were acting normally. Yet the figures still rose from earth to heaven, silent, majestically, in a great spiral of grace and strength that overwhelmed me at length with a genuine deep emotion of worship. I felt that I must fall down and worship—absolutely worship.

Perhaps in another minute I might have done so, when a gust of wind swept against me with such force that it blew me sideways, and I nearly stumbled and fell. It seemed to shake the dream violently out of me. At least it gave me another point of view somehow. The figures still remained, still ascended into heaven from the heart of the night, but my reason at last began to assert itself. It must be a subjective experience, I argued—none the less real for that, but still subjective. The moonlight and the branches combined to work out these pictures upon the mirror of my imagination, and for some reason I projected them outward and made them appear objective. I knew this must be the case, of course. I was the subject of a vivid and interesting hallucination. I took courage, and began to move forward across the open patches of sand. By Jove, though, was it all hallucination? Was it merely subjective? Did not my reason argue in the old futile way from the little standard of the known?

I only know that great column of figures ascended darkly into the sky for what seemed a very long period of time, and with a very complete measure of reality as most men are accustomed to gauge reality. Then suddenly they were gone!

And, once they were gone and the immediate wonder of their great presence had passed, fear came down upon me with a cold rush. The esoteric meaning of this lonely and haunted region suddenly flamed up within me, and I began to tremble dreadfully. I took a quick look round—a look of horror that came near to panic—calculating vainly ways of escape; and then, realizing how helpless I was to achieve anything really effective, I crept back silently into the tent and lay down again upon my sandy mattress, first lowering the door-curtain to shut out the sight of the willows in the moonlight, and then burying my head as deeply as possible beneath the blankets to deaden the sound of the terrifying wind.

As though further to convince me that I had not been dreaming, I remember that it was a long time before I fell again into a troubled and restless sleep; and even then only the upper crust of me slept, and underneath there was something that never quite lost consciousness, but lay alert and on the watch.

But this second time I jumped up with a genuine start of terror. It was neither the wind nor the river that woke me, but the slow approach of something that caused the sleeping portion of me to grow smaller and smaller till at last it vanished altogether, and I found myself sitting bolt upright—listening.

Outside there was a sound of multitudinous little patterings. They had been coming, I was aware, for a long time, and in my sleep they had first become audible. I sat there nervously wide awake as though I had not slept at all. It seemed to me that my breathing came with difficulty, and that there was a great weight upon the surface of my body. In spite of the hot night, I felt clammy with cold and shivered. Something surely was pressing steadily against the sides of the tent and weighing down upon it from above. Was it the body of the wind? Was this the pattering rain, the dripping of the leaves? The spray blown from the river by the wind and gathering in big drops? I thought quickly of a dozen things.

Then suddenly the explanation leaped into my mind: a bough from the poplar, the only large tree on the island, had fallen with the wind. Still half caught by the other branches, it would fall with the next gust and crush us, and meanwhile its leaves brushed and tapped upon the tight canvas surface of the tent. I raised the loose flap and rushed out, calling to the Swede to follow.

But when I got out and stood upright I saw that the tent was free.

There was no hanging bough; there was no rain or spray; nothing approached.

A cold, gray light filtered down through the bushes and lay on the faintly gleaming sand. Stars still crowded the sky directly overhead, and the wind howled magnificently, but the fire no longer gave out any glow, and I saw the east reddening in streaks through the trees. Several hours must have passed since I stood there before watching the ascending figures, and the memory of it now came back to me horribly, like an evil dream. Oh, how tired it made me feel, that ceaseless raging wind! Yet, though the deep lassitude of a sleepless night was on me, my nerves were tingling with the activity of an equally tireless apprehension, and all idea of repose was out of the question. The river I saw had risen further. Its thunder filled the air, and a fine spray made itself felt through my thin sleeping shirt.

Yet nowhere did I discover the slightest evidences of anything to cause alarm. This deep, prolonged disturbance in my heart remained wholly unaccounted for.

My companion had not stirred when I called him, and there was no need to waken him now. I looked about me carefully, noting everything: the turned-over canoe; the yellow paddles—two of them, I'm certain; the provision sack and the extra lantern hanging together from the tree; and, crowding everywhere about me, enveloping all, the willows, those endless, shaking willows. A bird uttered its morning cry, and a string of ducks passed with whirring flight overhead in the twilight. The sand whirled, dry and stinging, about my bare feet in the wind.

I walked round the tent and then went out a little way into the bush, so that I could see across the river to the farther landscape, and the same profound yet indefinable emotion of distress seized upon me again as I saw the interminable sea of bushes stretching to the horizon, looking ghostly and unreal in the wan light of dawn. I walked softly here and there, still puzzling over that odd sound of infinite pattering, and of that pressure upon the tent that had wakened me. It *must* have been the wind, I reflected—the wind beating upon the loose, hot sand, driving the dry particles smartly against the taut canvas—the wind dropping heavily upon our fragile roof.

Yet all the time my nervousness and malaise increased appreciably.

I crossed over to the farther shore and noted how the coastline had altered in the night, and what masses of sand the river had torn away. I dipped my hands and feet into the cool current, and bathed my forehead. Already there was a glow of sunrise in the sky and the exquisite freshness of coming day. On my way back I passed purposely beneath the very bushes where I had seen the column of figures rising into the air, and midway among the clumps I suddenly found myself overtaken by a sense of vast terror. From the shadows a large figure went swiftly by. Someone passed me, as sure as ever man did. . . .

It was a great staggering blow from the wind that helped me forward again, and once out in the more open space, the sense of terror diminished strangely. The winds were about and walking, I remember saying to myself; for the winds often move like great presences under the trees. And altogether the fear that hovered about me was such an unknown and immense kind of fear, so unlike anything I had ever felt before, that it woke a sense of awe and wonder in me that did much to counteract its worst effects; and when I reached a high point in the middle of the island from which I could see the wide stretch of river, crimson in the sunrise, the whole magical beauty of it all was so overpowering that a sort of wild yearning woke in me and almost brought a cry up into the throat.

But this cry found no expression, for as my eyes wandered from the plain beyond to the island round me and noted our little tent half hidden among the willows, a dreadful discovery leaped out at me, compared to which my terror of the walking winds seemed as nothing at all.

For a change, I thought, had somehow come about in the arrangement of the landscape. It was not that my point of vantage gave me a different view, but that an alteration had apparently been effected in the relation of the tent to the willows, and of the willows to the tent. Surely the bushes now crowded much closer—unnecessarily, unpleasantly close. *They had moved nearer.*

Creeping with silent feet over the shifting sands, drawing imperceptibly nearer by soft, unhurried movements, the willows had come closer during the night. But had the wind moved them, or had they moved of themselves? I recalled the sound of infinite small patterings and the pressure upon the tent and upon my own heart that caused me to wake in terror. I swayed for a moment in the wind like a tree, finding it hard to keep my upright position on the sandy hillock. There was a suggestion here of personal agency, of deliberate intention, of aggressive hostility, and it terrified me into a sort of rigidity.

Then the reaction followed quickly. The idea was so bizarre, so absurd, that I felt inclined to laugh. But the laughter came no more readily than the cry, for the knowledge that my mind was so receptive to such dangerous imaginings brought the additional terror that it was through our minds and not through our physical bodies that the attack would come, and was coming.

The wind buffeted me about, and, very quickly it seemed, the sun came up over the horizon, for it was after four o'clock, and I must have stood on that little pinnacle of sand longer than I knew, afraid to come down at close quarters with the willows. I returned quietly, creepily, to the tent, first taking another exhaustive look round and—yes, I confess it—making a few measurements. I paced out on the warm sand the distances between the willows and the tent, making a note of the shortest distance particularly.

I crawled stealthily into my blankets. My companion, to all appearances, still slept soundly, and I was glad that this was so. Provided my experiences were not corroborated, I could find strength somehow to deny them, perhaps. With the daylight I could persuade myself that it was all a subjective hallucination, a fantasy of the night, a projection of the excited imagination.

Nothing further came to disturb me, and I fell asleep almost at once, utterly exhausted, yet still in dread of hearing again that weird sound of multitudinous pattering, or of feeling the pressure upon my heart that had made it difficult to breathe.

The sun was high in the heavens when my companion woke me from a heavy sleep and announced that the porridge was cooked and there was just time to bathe. The grateful smell of frizzling bacon entered the tent door.

"River still rising," he said, "and several islands out in midstream have disappeared altogether. Our own island's much smaller."

"Any wood left?" I asked sleepily.

"The wood and the island will finish tomorrow in a dead heat," he laughed, "but there's enough to last us till then."

I plunged in from the point of the island, which had indeed altered a lot in size and shape during the night, and was swept down in a moment to the landing place opposite the tent. The water was icy, and the banks flew by like the country from an express train. Bathing under such conditions was an exhilarating operation, and the terror of the night seemed cleansed out of me by a process of evaporation in the brain. The sun was blazing hot; not a cloud showed itself anywhere; the wind, however, had not abated one little jot.

Quite suddenly then the implied meaning of the Swede's words flashed across me, showing that he no longer wished to leave post-haste, and had changed his mind. "Enough to last till tomorrow"—he assumed we should stay on the island another night. It struck me as odd. The night before he was so positive the other way. How had the change come about?

Great crumblings of the banks occurred at breakfast, with heavy splashings and clouds of spray which the wind brought into our frying-pan, and my fellow-traveler talked incessantly about the difficulty the Vienna-Pesth steamers must have to find the channel in flood. But the state of his mind interested and impressed me far more than the state of the river or the difficulties of the steamers. He had changed somehow since the evening before. His manner was different—a trifle excited, a trifle shy, with a sort of suspicion about his voice and gestures. I hardly know how to describe it now in cold blood, but at the time I remember being quite certain of one thing, viz., that he had become frightened!

He ate very little breakfast, and for once omitted to smoke his pipe. He had the map spread open beside him, and kept studying its markings.

"We'd better get off sharp in an hour," I said presently, feeling for an opening that must bring him indirectly to a partial confession at any rate. And his answer puzzled me uncomfortably: "Rather! If they'll let us."

"Who'll let us? The elements?" I asked quickly, with affected indifference.

"The powers of this awful place, whoever they are," he replied, keeping his eyes on the map. "The gods are here, if they are anywhere at all in the world."

"The elements are always the true immortals," I replied, laughing as naturally as I could manage, yet knowing quite well that my face reflected my true feelings when he looked up gravely at me and spoke across the smoke:

"We shall be fortunate if we get away without further disaster."

This was exactly what I had dreaded, and I screwed myself up to the point of the direct question. It was like agreeing to allow the dentist to extract the tooth; it *had* to come anyhow in the long run, and the rest was all pretense.

"Further disaster! Why, what's happened?"

"For one thing—the steering paddle's gone," he said quietly.

"The steering paddle gone!" I repeated, greatly excited, for this was our rudder, and the Danube in flood without a rudder was suicide. "But what—"

"And there's a tear in the bottom of the canoe," he added, with a genuine little tremor in his voice.

I continued staring at him, able only to repeat the words in his face somewhat foolishly. There, in the heat of the sun, and on this burning sand, I was aware of a freezing atmosphere descending round us. I got up to follow him, for he merely nodded his head gravely and led the way toward the tent a few yards on the other side of the fireplace. The canoe still lay there as I had last seen her in the night, ribs uppermost, the paddles, or rather, *the* paddle, on the sand beside her.

"There's only one," he said, stooping to pick it up. "And here's the rent in the base-board."

It was on the tip of my tongue to tell him that I had clearly noticed *two* paddles a few hours before, but a second impulse made me think better of it, and I said nothing. I approached to see.

There was a long, finely made tear in the bottom of the canoe where a little slither of wood had been neatly taken clean out; it looked as if the tooth of a sharp rock or snag had eaten down her length, and investigation showed that the hole went through. Had we launched out in her without observing it we must inevitably have foundered. At first the water would have made the wood swell so as to close the hole, but once out in midstream the water must have poured in, and the canoe, never more than two inches above the surface, would have filled and sunk very rapidly.

"There, you see, an attempt to prepare a victim for the sacrifice," I heard him saying, more to himself than to me, "two victims rather," he added as he bent over and ran his fingers along the slit.

I began to whistle—a thing I always do unconsciously when utterly nonplussed—and purposely paid no attention to his words. I was determined to consider them foolish.

"It wasn't there last night," he said presently, straightening up from his examination and looking anywhere but at me.

"We must have scratched her in landing, of course," I stopped whistling to say. "The stones are very sharp—"

I stopped abruptly, for at that moment he turned round and met my eye squarely. I knew just as well as he did how impossible my explanation was. There were no stones, to begin with.

"And then there's this to explain too," he added quietly, handing me the paddle and pointing to the blade.

A new and curious emotion spread freezingly over me as I took and examined it. The blade was scraped down all over, beautifully scraped, as though someone had sand-papered it with care, making it so thin that the first vigorous stroke must have snapped it off at the elbow.

"One of us walked in his sleep and did this thing," I said feebly, "or—or it has been filed by the constant stream of sand particles blown against it by the wind, perhaps."

"Ah," said the Swede, turning away, laughing a little, "you can explain everything!"

"The same wind that caught the steering paddle and flung it so near the bank that it fell in with the next lump that crumbled," I called out after him, absolutely determined to find an explanation for everything he showed me.

"I see," he shouted back, turning his head to look at me before disappearing among the willow bushes.

Once alone with these perplexing evidences of personal agency, I think my first thought took the form of "One of us must have done this thing, and it certainly was not I." But any second thought decided how impossible it was to suppose, under all the circumstances, that either of us had done it. That my companion, the trusted friend of a dozen similar expeditions, could have knowingly had a hand in it, was a suggestion not to be entertained for a moment. Equally absurd seemed the explanation that this imperturbable and densely practical nature had suddenly become insane and was busied with insane purposes.

Yet the fact remained that what disturbed me most, and kept my fear actively alive even in this blaze of sunshine and wild beauty, was the clear certainty that some curious alteration had come about in his *mind*—that he was nervous, timid, suspicious, aware of goings on he did not speak about, watching a series of secret and hitherto unmentionable events—waiting, in a word, for a climax that he expected, and, I thought, expected very soon. This grew up in my mind intuitively—I hardly knew how.

I made a hurried examination of the tent and its surroundings, but the measurements of the night remained the same. There were deep hollows formed in the sand, I now noticed for the first time, basin-shaped and of various depths and sizes, varying from that of a tea-cup to a large bowl. The wind, no doubt, was responsible for these mini-ature craters, just as it was for lifting the paddle and tossing it toward the water. The rent in the canoe was the only thing that seemed quite inexplicable; and, after all, it *was* conceivable that a sharp point had caught it when we landed. The examination I made of the shore did not assist this theory, but all the same I clung to it with that diminishing portion of my intelligence which I called my "reason." An explanation of some kind was an absolute necessity, just as some working explanation of the universe is necessary—however absurd—to the happiness of every individual who seeks to do his duty in the world and face the problems of life. The simile seemed to me at the time an exact parallel.

I at once set the pitch melting, and presently the Swede joined me at the work, though under the best conditions in the world the canoe could not be safe for traveling till the following day. I drew his attention casually to the hollows in the sand.

"Yes," he said, "I know. They're all over the island. But *you* can explain them, no doubt!"

"Wind, of course," I answered without hesitation. "Have you never watched those little whirlwinds in the street that twist and twirl everything into a circle? This sand's loose enough to yield, that's all."

He made no reply, and we worked on in silence for a bit. I watched him surreptitiously all the time, and I had an idea he was watching me. He seemed, too, to be always listening attentively to something I could not hear, or perhaps for something that he expected to hear, for he kept turning about and staring into the bushes, and up into the sky, and out across the water where it was visible through the openings among the willows. Sometimes he even put his hand to his ear and held it there for several minutes. He said nothing to me, however, about it, and I asked no questions. And meanwhile, as he mended that torn canoe with the skill and address of a red Indian, I was glad to notice his absorption in the work, for there was a vague dread in my heart that he would speak of the changed aspect of the willows. And, if he had noticed *that*, my imagination could no longer be held a sufficient explanation of it.

At length, after a long pause, he began to talk.

"Queer thing," he added in a hurried sort of voice, as though he wanted to say something and get it over. "Queer thing, I mean, about that otter last night."

I had expected something so totally different that he caught me with surprise, and I looked up sharply.

"Shows how lonely this place is. Otters are awfully shy things—"

"I don't mean that, of course," he interrupted. "I mean—do you think—did you think it really *was* an otter?"

"What else, in the name of Heaven, what else?"

"You know, I saw it before you did, and at first it seemed—so *much* bigger than an otter."

"The sunset as you looked upstream magnified it, or something," I replied.

He looked at me absently a moment, as though his mind were busy with other thoughts.

"It had such extraordinary yellow eyes," he went on half to himself.

"That was the sun too," I laughed, a trifle boisterously. "I suppose you'll wonder next if that fellow in the boat——"

I suddenly decided not to finish the sentence. He was in the act again of listening, turning his head to the wind, and something in the expression of his face made me halt. The subject dropped, and we went on with our calking. Apparently he had not noticed my unfinished sentence. Five minutes later, however, he looked at me across the canoe, the smoking pitch in his hand, his face exceedingly grave.

"I did rather wonder, if you want to know," he said slowly, "what that thing in the boat was. I remember thinking at the time it was not a man. The whole business seemed to rise quite suddenly out of the water."

I laughed again boisterously in his face, but this time there was impatience, and a strain of anger too, in my feeling.

"Look here now," I cried, "this place is quite queer enough without going out of our way to imagine things! That boat was an ordinary boat, and the man in it was an ordinary man, and they were both going downstream as fast as they could lick. And that otter *was* an otter, so don't let's play the fool about it!"

He looked steadily at me with the same grave expression. He was not in the least annoyed. I took courage from his silence.

"And, for Heaven's sake," I went on, "don't keep pretending you hear things, because it only gives me the jumps, and there's nothing to hear but the river and this cursed old thundering wind."

"You *fool*!" he answered in a low, shocked voice, "you utter fool. That's just the way all victims talk. As if you didn't understand just as well as I do!" He sneered with scorn in his voice, and a sort of resignation. "The best thing you can do is to keep quiet and try to hold your mind as firm as possible. This feeble attempt at self-deception only makes the truth harder when you're forced to meet it."

My little effort was over, and I found nothing more to say, for I knew quite well his words were true, and that I was the fool, not *he*. Up to a certain stage in the adventure he kept ahead of me easily, and I think I felt annoyed to be out of it, to be thus proved less psychic, less sensitive than himself to these extraordinary happenings, and half ignorant all the time of what was going on under my very nose. He *knew* from the beginning, apparently. But at the moment I wholly missed the point of his words about the necessity of there being a victim, and that we ourselves were destined to satisfy the want. I dropped all pretense thenceforward, but thenceforward likewise my fear increased steadily to the climax.

"But you're quite right about one thing," he added, before the subject passed, "and that is that we're wiser not to talk about it, or even to think about it, because what one *thinks* finds expression in words, and what one *says*, happens."

That afternoon, while the canoe dried and hardened, we spent trying to fish, testing the leak, collecting wood, and watching the enormous flood of rising water. Masses of driftwood swept near our shores sometimes, and we fished for them with long willow branches. The island grew perceptibly smaller as the banks were torn away with great gulps and splashes. The weather kept brilliantly fine till about four o'clock, and then for the first time for three days the wind showed signs of abating. Clouds began to gather in the south-west, spreading thence slowly over the sky.

This lessening of the wind came as a great relief, for the incessant roaring, banging, and thundering had irritated our nerves. Yet the silence that came about five o'clock with its sudden cessation was in a manner quite as oppressive. The booming of the river had everything its own way then: filled the air with deep murmurs, more musical than the wind noises, but infinitely more monotonous. The wind held many notes, rising, falling, always beating out some sort of great elemental tune; whereas the river's song lay between three notes at most—dull pedal notes, that held a lugubrious quality foreign to the wind, and somehow seemed to me, in my then nervous state, to sound wonderfully well the music of doom.

It was extraordinary, too, how the withdrawal suddenly of bright sunlight took everything out of the landscape that made for cheerfulness; and since this particular landscape had already managed to convey the suggestion of something sinister, the change of course was all the more unwelcome and noticeable. For me, I know, the darkening outlook became distinctly more alarming, and I found myself more than once calculating how soon after sunset the full moon would get up in the east, and whether the gathering clouds would greatly interfere with her lighting of the little island.

With this general hush of the wind—though it still indulged in occasional brief gusts—the river seemed to me to grow blacker, the willows to stand more densely together. The latter, too, kept up a sort of independent movement of their own, rustling among themselves when no wind stirred, and shaking oddly from the roots upward. When common objects in this way become charged with the suggestion of horror, they stimulate the imagination far more than things of unusual appearance; and these bushes, crowding huddled about us, assumed for me in the darkness a bizarre *grotesquerie* of appearance that lent to them somehow the aspect of purposeful and living creatures. Their very ordinariness, I felt, masked what was malignant and hostile to us. The forces of the region drew nearer with the coming of night. They were focusing upon our island, and more particularly upon ourselves. For thus, somehow, in the terms of the imagination, did my really indescribable sensations in this extraordinary place present themselves.

I had slept a good deal in the early afternoon, and had thus recovered somewhat from the exhaustion of a disturbed night, but this only served apparently to render me more susceptible than before to the obsessing spell of the haunting. I fought against it, laughing at my feelings as absurd and childish, with very obvious physiological explanations, yet, in spite of every effort, they gained in strength upon me so that I dreaded the night as a child lost in a forest must dread the approach of darkness.

The canoe we had carefully covered with a waterproof sheet during the day, and the one remaining paddle had been securely tied by the Swede to the base of a tree, lest the wind should rob us of that too. From five o'clock onward I busied myself with the stew-pot and preparations for dinner, it being my turn to cook that night. We had potatoes, onions, bits of bacon fat to add flavor, and a general thick residue from former stews at the bottom of the pot; with black bread broken up into it the result was most excellent, and it was followed by a stew of plums with sugar and a brew of strong tea with dried milk. A good pile of wood lay close at hand, and the absence of wind made my duties easy. My companion sat lazily watching me, dividing his attentions between cleaning his pipe and giving useless advice—an admitted privilege of the off-duty man. He had been very quiet all the afternoon, engaged in re-calking the canoe, strenthening the tent ropes, and fishing for driftwood while I slept. No more talk about undesirable things had passed between us, and I think his only remarks had to do with the gradual destruction of the island, which he declared was now fully a third smaller than when we first landed.

The pot had just begun to bubble when I heard his voice calling to me from the bank, where he had wandered away without my noticing. I ran up.

"Come and listen," he said, "and see what you make of it." He held his hand cupwise to his ear, as so often before.

"*Now* do you hear anything?" he asked, watching me curiously.

We stood there, listening attentively together. At first I heard only the deep note of the water and the hissings rising from its turbulent surface. The willows, for once, were motionless and silent. Then a sound began to reach my ears faintly, a peculiar sound—something like the humming of a distant gong. It seemed to come across to us in the darkness from the waste of swamps and willows opposite. It was repeated at regular intervals, but it was certainly neither the sound of a bell nor the hooting of a distant steamer. I can liken it to nothing so much as to the sound of an immense gong, suspended far up in the sky, repeating incessantly its muffled metallic note, soft and musical, as it was repeatedly struck. My heart quickened as I listened.

"I heard it all day," said my companion. "While you slept this afternoon it came all round the island. I hunted it down, but could never get near enough to see—to localize it correctly. Sometimes it was overhead, and sometimes it seemed under the water. Once or twice, too, I could have sworn it was not outside at all, but *within myself*— you know—the way a sound in the fourth dimension is supposed to come."

I was too much puzzled to pay much attention to his words. I listened carefully, striving to associate it with any known familiar sound I could think of, but without success. It changed in direction, too, coming nearer, and then sinking utterly away into remote distance. I cannot say that it was ominous in quality, because to me it seemed distinctly musical, yet I must admit it set going a distressing feeling that made me wish I had never heard it.

"The wind blowing in those sand-funnels," I said, determined to find an explanation, "or the bushes rubbing together after the storm perhaps."

"It comes off the whole swamp," my friend answered. "It comes from everywhere at once." He ignored my explanations. "It comes from the willow bushes somehow—"

"But now the wind has dropped," I objected. "The willows can hardly make a noise by themselves, can they?"

His answer frightened me, first because I had dreaded it, and secondly, because I knew intuitively it was true.

"It is *because* the wind has dropped we now hear it. It was drowned before. It is the cry, I believe, of the—"

I dashed back to my fire, warned by a sound of bubbling that the stew was in danger, but determined at the same time to escape from further conversation. I was resolute, if possible, to avoid the exchanging of views. I dreaded, too, that he would begin again about the gods, or the elemental forces, or something else disquieting, and I wanted to keep myself well in hand for what might happen later. There was another night to be faced before we escaped from this distressing place, and there was no knowing yet what it might bring forth.

"Come and cut up bread for the pot," I called to him, vigorously stirring the appetizing mixture. That stew-pot held sanity for us both, and the thought made me laugh.

He came over slowly and took the provision sack from the tree, fumbling in its mysterious depths, and then emptying the entire contents upon the ground-sheet at his feet.

"Hurry up!" I cried; "it's boiling."

The Swede burst out into a roar of laughter that startled me. It was forced laughter, not artificial exactly, but mirthless.

"There's nothing here!" he shouted, holding his sides.

"Bread, I mean."

"It's gone. There is no bread. They've taken it!"

I dropped the long spoon and ran up. Everything the sack had contained lay upon the ground-sheet, but there was no loaf.

The whole dead weight of my growing fear fell upon me and shook me. Then I burst out laughing too. It was the only thing to do: and the sound of my own laughter also made me understand his. The strain of physical pressure caused it—this explosion of unnatural laughter in both of us; it was an effort of repressed forces to seek relief; it was a temporary safety valve. And with both of us it ceased quite suddenly.

"How criminally stupid of me!" I cried, still determined to be consistent and find an explanation. "I clean forgot to buy a loaf at Pressburg. That chattering woman put everything out of my head, and I must have left it lying on the counter or—"

"The oatmeal, too, is much less than it was this morning," the Swede interrupted.

Why in the world need he draw attention to it? I thought angrily.

"There's enough for tomorrow," I said, stirring vigorously, "and we can get lots more at Komorn or Gran. In twenty-four hours we shall be miles from here."

"I hope so—to God," he muttered, putting the things back into the sack, "unless we're claimed first as victims for the sacrifice," he added with a foolish laugh. He dragged the sack into the tent, for safety's sake, I suppose, and I heard him mumbling on to himself, but so indistinctly that it seemed quite natural for me to ignore his words.

Our meal was beyond question a gloomy one, and we ate it almost in silence, avoiding one another's eyes, and keeping the fire bright. Then we washed up and prepared for the night, and, once smoking, our minds unoccupied with any definite duties, the apprehension I had felt all day long became more and more acute. It was not then active fear, I think, but the very vagueness of its origin distressed me far more than if I had been able to ticket and face it squarely. The curious sound I have likened to the note of a gong became now almost incessant, and filled the stillness of the night with a faint, continuous ringing rather than a series of distinct notes. At one time it was behind and at another time in front of us. Sometimes I fancied it came from the bushes on our left, and then again from the clumps on our right. More often it hovered directly overhead like the whirring of wings. It was really everywhere at once, behind, in front, at our sides and over our heads, completely surrounding us. The sound really defies description. But nothing within my knowledge is like that ceaseless muffled humming rising off the deserted world of swamps and willows.

We sat smoking in comparative silence, the strain growing every minute greater. The worst feature of the situation seemed to me that we did not know what to expect, and could therefore make no sort of preparation by way of defense. We could anticipate nothing. My explanations made in the sunshine, moreover, now came to haunt me with their foolish and wholly unsatisfactory nature, and it was more and more clear to us that some kind of plain talk with my companion was inevitable, whether I liked it or not. After all, we had to spend the night together, and to sleep in the same tent side by side. I saw that I could not get along much longer without the support of his mind, and for that, of course, plain talk was imperative. As long as possible, however, I postponed this little climax, and tried to ignore or laugh at the occasional sentences he flung into the emptiness.

Some of these sentences, moreover, were confoundedly disquieting to me, coming as they did to corroborate much that I felt myself: corroboration, too—which made it so much more convincing—from a totally different point of view. He composed such curious sentences, and hurled them at me in such an inconsequential sort of way, as though his main line of thought was secret to himself, and these fragments were the bits he found it impossible to digest. He got rid of them by uttering them. Speech relieved him. It was like being sick.

"There are things about us, I'm sure, that make for disorder, disintegration, destruction, our destruction," he said once, while the fire blazed between us. "We've strayed out of a safe line somewhere."

And another time, when the gong sounds had come nearer, ringing much louder than before, and directly over our heads, he said, as though talking to himself:

"I don't think a phonograph would show any record of that. The sound doesn't come to me by the ears at all. The vibrations reach me in another manner altogether, and seem to be within me, which is precisely how a fourth dimensional sound might be supposed to make itself heard."

I purposely made no reply to this, but I sat up a little closer to the fire and peered about me into the darkness. The clouds were massed all over the sky and no trace of moonlight came through. Very still, too, everything was, so that the river and the frogs had things all their own way.

"It has that about it," he went on, "which is utterly out of common experience. It is *unknown*. Only one thing describes it really: it is a non-human sound; I mean a sound outside humanity."

Having rid himself of this indigestible morsel, he lay quiet for a time; but he had so admirably expressed my own feeling that it was a relief to have the thought out, and to have confined it by the limitation of words from dangerous wandering to and fro in the mind.

The solitude of that Danube camping place, can I ever forget it? The feeling of being utterly alone on an empty planet! My thoughts ran incessantly upon cities and the haunts of men. I would have given my soul, as the saying is, for the "feel" of those Bavarian villages we had passed through by the score; for the normal, human commonplaces: peasants drinking beer, tables beneath the trees, hot sunshine, and a ruined castle on the rocks behind the red-roofed church. Even the tourists would have been welcome.

Yet what I felt of dread was no ordinary ghostly fear. It was infinitely greater, stranger, and seemed to arise from some dim ancestral sense of terror more profoundly disturbing than anything I had known or dreamed of. We had "strayed," as the Swede put it, into some region or some set of conditions where the risks were great, yet unintelligible to us; where the frontiers of some unknown world lay close about us. It was a spot held by the dwellers in some outer space, a sort of peephole whence they could spy upon the earth, themselves unseen, a point where the veil between had worn a little thin. As the final result of too long a sojourn here, we should be carried over the border and deprived of what we called "our lives," yet by mental, not physical, processes. In that sense, as he said, we should be the victims of our adventure—a sacrifice.

It took us in different fashion, each according to the measure of his sensitiveness and powers of resistance. I translated it vaguely into a personification of the mightily disturbed elements, investing them with the horror of a deliberate and malefic purpose, resentful of our audacious intrusion into their breeding place; whereas my friend threw it into the unoriginal form at first of a trespass on some ancient shrine, some place where the old gods still held sway, where the emotional forces of former worshippers still clung, and the ancestral portion of him yielded to the old pagan spell.

At any rate, here was a place unpolluted by men, kept clean by the winds from coarsening human influences, a place where spiritual agencies were within reach and aggressive. Never, before or since, have I been so attacked by indescribable suggestions of a "beyond region," of another scheme of life, another evolution not parallel to the human. And in the end our minds would succumb under the weight of the awful spell, and we should be drawn across the frontier into *their* world.

Small things testified to this amazing influence of the place, and now in the silence round the fire they allowed themselves to be noted by the mind. The very atmosphere had proved itself a magnifying medium to distort every indication: the otter rolling in the current, the hurrying boatman making signs, the shifting willows, one and all had been robbed of its natural character, and revealed in something of its other aspect—as it existed across the border in that other region. And this changed aspect I felt was new not merely to me, but to the race. The whole experience whose verge we touched was unknown to humanity at all. It was a new order of experience, and in the true sense of the word *unearthly*.

"It's the deliberate, calculating purpose that reduces one's courage to zero," the Swede said suddenly, as if he had been actually following my thoughts. "Otherwise imagination might count for much. But the paddle, the canoe, the lessening food—"

"Haven't I explained all that once?" I interrupted viciously.

"You have," he answered dryly; "you have indeed."

He made other remarks too, as usual, about what he called the "plain determination to provide a victim"; but, having arranged my thoughts better, I recognized that this was simply the cry of his frightened soul against the knowledge that he was being attacked in a vital part, and that he would be somehow taken or destroyed. The situation called for a courage and calmness of reasoning that neither of us could compass, and I have never before been so clearly conscious of two persons in me—the one that explained everything, and the other that laughed at such foolish explanations, yet was horribly afraid.

Meanwhile, in the pitchy night the fire died down and the wood pile grew small. Neither of us moved to replenish the stock, and the darkness consequently came up very close to our faces. A few feet beyond the circle of firelight it was inky black. Occasionally a stray puff of wind set the willows shivering about us, but apart from this not very welcome sound a deep and depressing silence reigned, broken only by the gurgling of the river and the humming in the air overhead.

We both missed, I think, the shouting company of the winds.

At length, at a moment when a stray puff prolonged itself as though the wind were about to rise again, I reached the point for me of saturation, the point where it was absolutely necessary to find relief in plain speech, or else to betray myself by some hysterical extravagance that must have been far worse in its effect upon both of us. I kicked the fire into a blaze, and turned to my companion abruptly. He looked up with a start.

"I can't disguise it any longer," I said; "I don't like this place, and the darkness, and the noises, and the awful feelings I get. There's something here that beats me utterly. I'm in a blue funk, and that's the plain truth. If the other shore was—different, I swear I'd be inclined to swim for it!"

The Swede's face turned very white beneath the deep tan of sun and wind. He stared straight at me and answered quietly, but his voice betrayed his huge excitement by its unnatural calmness. For the moment, at any rate, he was the strong man of the two. He was the more phlegmatic, for one thing.

"It's not a physical condition we can escape from by running away," he replied, in the tone of a doctor diagnosing some grave disease; "we must sit tight and wait. There are forces close here that could kill a herd of elephants in a second as easily as you or I could squash a fly. Our only chance is to keep perfectly still. Our insignificance perhaps may save us."

I put a dozen questions into my expression of face, but found no words. It was precisely like listening to an accurate description of a disease whose symptoms had puzzled me.

"I mean that so far, although aware of our disturbing presence, they have not *found* us—not 'located' us, as the Americans say," he went on. "They're blundering about like men hunting for a leak of gas. The paddle and canoe and provisions prove that. I think they *feel* us, but cannot actually see us. We must keep our minds quiet—it's our minds they feel. We must control our thoughts, or it's all up with us."

"Death you mean?" I stammered, icy with the horror of his suggestion.

"Worse—by far," he said. "Death, according to one's belief, means either annihilation or release from the limitations of the senses, but it involves no change of character. *You* don't suddenly alter just because the body's gone. But this means a radical alteration, a complete change, a horrible loss of oneself by substitution—far worse than death, and not even annihilation. We happen to have camped in a spot where their region touches ours, where the veil between has worn thin"—horrors! he was using my very own phrase, my actual words—"so that they are aware of our being in their neighborhood."

"But *who* are aware?" I asked.

I forgot the shaking of the willows in the windless calm, the humming overhead, everything except that I was waiting for an answer that I dreaded more than I can possibly explain.

He lowered his voice at once to reply, leaning forward a little over the fire, an indefinable change in his face that made me avoid his eyes and look down upon the ground.

"All my life," he said, "I have been strangely, vividly conscious of another region—not far removed from our own world in one sense, yet wholly different in kind—where great things go on unceasingly, where immense and terrible personalities hurry by, intent on vast purposes compared to which earthly affairs, the rise and fall of nations, the destinies of empires, the fate of armies and continents, are all as dust in the balance; vast purposes, I mean, that deal directly with the soul, and not indirectly with mere expressions of the soul—"

"I suggest just now—" I began, seeking to stop him, feeling as though I was face to face with a madman. But he instantly overbore me with his torrent that *had* to come.

"You think," he said, "it is the spirits of the elements, and I thought perhaps it was the old gods. But I tell you now it is—*neither*. These would be comprehensible entities, for they have relations with men, depending upon them for worship or sacrifice, whereas these beings who are now about us have absolutely nothing to do with mankind, and it is mere chance that their space happens just at this spot to touch our own."

The mere conception, which his words somehow made so convincing, as I listened to them there in the dark stillness of that lonely island, set me shaking a little all over. I found it impossible to control my movements.

"And what do you propose?" I began again.

"A sacrifice, a victim, might save us by distracting them until we could get away," he went on, "just as the wolves stop to devour the dogs and give the sleigh another start. But—I see no chance of any other victim now."

I stared blankly at him. The gleam in his eyes was dreadful. Presently he continued.

"It's the willows, of course. The willows *mask* the others, but the others are feeling about for us. If we let our minds betray our fear, we're lost, lost utterly." He looked at me with an expression so calm, so determined, so sincere, that I no longer had any doubts as to his sanity. He was as sane as any man ever was. "If we can hold out through the night," he added, "we may get off in the daylight unnoticed, or rather, *undiscovered*."

"But you really think a sacrifice would—"

That gong-like humming came down very close over our heads as I spoke, but it was my friend's scared face that really stopped my mouth.

"Hush!" he whispered, holding up his hand. "Do not mention them more than you can help. Do not refer to them by *name*. To name is to reveal: it is the inevitable clue, and our only hope lies in ignoring them, in order that they may ignore us."

"Even in thought?"

He was extraordinarily agitated. "Especially in thought. Our thoughts make spirals in their world. We must keep them *out of our minds* at all costs if possible."

I raked the fire together to prevent the darkness having everything its own way. I never longed for the sun as I longed for it then in the awful blackness of that summer night.

"Were you awake all last night?" he went on suddenly.

"I slept badly a little after dawn," I replied evasively, trying to follow his instructions, which I knew instinctively were true, "but the wind, of course—"

"I know. But the wind won't account for all the noises."

"Then you heard it too?"

"The multiplying countless little footsteps I heard," he said, adding, after a moment's hesitation, "and that other sound—"

"You mean above the tent, and the pressing down upon us of something tremendous, gigantic?"

He nodded significantly.

"It was like the beginning of a sort of inner suffocation?" I said.

"Partly, yes. It seemed to me that the weight of the atmosphere had been altered—had increased enormously, so that we should be crushed."

"And *that*," I went on, determined to have it all out, pointing upward where the gong-like note hummed ceaselessly, rising and falling like wind. "What do you make of that?"

"It's *their* sound," he whispered gravely. "It's the sound of their world, the humming in their region. The division here is so thin that it leaks through somehow. But, if you listen carefully, you'll find it's not above so much as around us. It's in the willows. It's the willows themselves humming, because here the willows have been made symbols of the forces that are against us."

I could not follow exactly what he meant by this, yet the thought and idea in my mind were beyond question the thought and idea in his. I realized what he realized, only with less power of analysis than his. It was on the tip of my tongue to tell him at last about my hallucination of the ascending figures and the moving bushes, when he suddenly thrust his face again close into mine across the firelight and began to speak in a very earnest whisper. He amazed me by his calmness and pluck, his apparent control of the situation. This man I had for years deemed unimaginative, stolid!

"Now listen," he said. "The only thing for us to do is to go on as though nothing had happened, follow our usual habits, go to bed, and so forth; pretend we feel nothing and notice nothing. It is a question wholly of the mind, and the less we think about them the better our chance of escape. Above all, don't *think*, for what you think happens!"

"All right," I managed to reply, simply breathless with his words and the strangeness of it all; "all right, I'll try, but tell me one thing more first. Tell me what you make of those hollows in the ground all about us, those sand-funnels?"

"No!" he cried, forgetting to whisper in his excitement. "I dare not, simply dare not, put the thought into words. If you have not guessed I am glad. Don't try to. *They* have put it into my mind; try your hardest to prevent their putting it into yours."

He sank his voice again to a whisper before he finished, and I did not press him to explain. There was already just about as much horror in me as I could hold. The conversation came to an end, and we smoked our pipes busily in silence.

Then something happened, something unimportant apparently, as the way is when the nerves are in a very great state of tension, and this small thing for a brief space gave me an entirely different point of view. I chanced to look down at my sand-shoe—the sort we used for the canoe—and something to do with the hole at the toe suddenly recalled to me the London shop where I had bought them, the difficulty the man had in fitting me, and other details of the uninteresting but practical operation. At once, in its train, followed a wholesome view of the modern skeptical world I was accustomed to move in at home. I thought of roast beef and ale, motor cars, policemen, brass bands, and a dozen other things that proclaimed the soul of ordinariness or utility. The effect was immediate and astonishing even to myself. Psychologically, I suppose, it was simply a sudden and violent reaction after the strain of living in an atmosphere of things that to the normal consciousness must seem impossible and incredible. But, whatever the cause, it momentarily lifted the spell from my heart, and left me for the short space of a minute feeling free and utterly unafraid. I looked up at my friend opposite.

"You damned old pagan!" I cried, laughing aloud in his face. "You imaginative idiot! You superstitious idolator! You—"

I stopped in the middle, seized anew by the old horror. I tried to smother the sound of my voice as something sacrilegious. The Swede, of course, heard it too—that strange cry overhead in the darkness—and that sudden drop in the air as though something had come nearer.

He had turned ashen white under the tan. He stood bolt upright in front of the fire, stiff as a rod, staring at me.

"After that," he said in a sort of helpless, frantic way, "we must go! We can't stay now; we must strike camp this very instant and go on—down the river."

He was talking, I saw, quite wildly, his words dictated by abject terror—the terror he had resisted so long, but which had caught him at last.

"In the dark?" I exclaimed, shaking with fear after my hysterical outburst, but still realizing our position better than he did. "Sheer madness! The river's in flood, and we've only got a single paddle. Besides, we only go deeper into their country! There's nothing ahead for fifty miles but willows, willows, willows!"

He sat down again in a state of semi-collapse. The positions, by one of those kaleidoscopic changes nature loves, were suddenly reversed, and the control of our forces passed over into my hands. His mind at last had reached the point where it was beginning to weaken.

"What on earth possessed you to do such a thing?" he whispered, with the awe of genuine terror in his voice and face.

I crossed round to his side of the fire. I took both his hands in mine, kneeling down beside him and looking straight into his frightened eyes.

"We'll make one more blaze," I said firmly, "and then turn in for the night. At sunrise we'll be off full speed for Komorn. Now, pull yourself together a bit, and remember your own advice about *not thinking fear!*"

He said no more, and I saw that he would agree and obey. In some measure, too, it was a sort of relief to get up and make an excursion into the darkness for more wood. We kept close together, almost touching, groping among the bushes and along the bank. The humming overhead never ceased, but seemed to me to grow louder as we increased our distance from the fire. It was shivery work!

We were grubbing away in the middle of a thickish clump of willows where some driftwood from a former flood had caught high among the branches, when my body was seized in a grip that made me half drop upon the sand. It was the Swede. He had fallen against me, and was clutching me for support. I heard his breath coming and going in short gasps.

"Look! By my soul!" he whispered, and for the first time in my experience I knew what it was to hear tears of terror in a human voice. He was pointing to the fire, some fifty feet away. I followed the direction of his finger, and I swear my heart missed a beat.

There, in front of the dim glow, *something was moving.*

I saw it through a veil that hung before my eyes like the gauze drop-curtain used at the back of a theater—hazily a little. It was neither a human figure nor an animal. To me it gave the strange impression of being as large as several animals grouped together, like horses, two or three, moving slowly. The Swede, too, got a similar result, though expressing it differently, for he thought it was shaped and sized like a clump of willow bushes, rounded at the top, and moving all over upon its surface—"coiling upon itself like smoke," he said afterward.

"I watched it settle downward through the bushes," he sobbed at me. "Look, by God! It's coming this way! Oh, oh!" He gave a kind of whistling cry. *"They've found us."*

I gave one terrified glance, which just enabled me to see that the shadowy form was swinging toward us through the bushes, and then I collapsed backward with a crash into the branches. These failed, of course, to support my weight, so that with the Swede on the top of me we fell in a struggling heap upon the sand. I really hardly knew what was happening. I was conscious only of a sort of enveloping sensation of icy fear that plucked the nerves out of their fleshly covering, twisted them this way and that, and replaced them quivering. My eyes were tightly shut; something in my throat choked me; a feeling that my consciousness was expanding, extending out into space, swiftly gave way to another feeling that I was losing it altogether, and about to die.

An acute spasm of pain passed through me, and I was aware that the Swede had hold of me in such a way that he hurt me abominably. It was the way he caught at me in falling.

But it was this pain, he declared afterward, that saved me: it caused me to *forget them* and think of something else at the very instant when they were about to find me. It concealed my mind from them at the moment of discovery, yet just in time to evade their terrible seizing of me. He himself, he says, actually swooned at the same moment, and that was what saved him.

I only know that at a later time, how long or short is impossible to say, I found myself scrambling up out of the slippery network of willow branches, and saw my companion standing in front of me holding out a hand to assist me. I stared at him in a dazed way, rubbing the arm he had twisted for me. Nothing came to me to say, somehow.

"I lost consciousness for a moment or two," I heard him say. "That's what saved me. It made me stop thinking about them."

"You nearly broke my arm in two," I said, uttering my only connected thought at the moment. A numbness came over me.

"That's what saved *you*!" he replied. "Between us, we've managed to set them off on a false tack somewhere. The humming has ceased. It's gone—for the moment at any rate!"

A wave of hysterical laughter seized me again, and this time spread to my friend too—great healing gusts of shaking laughter that brought a tremendous sense of relief in their train. We made our way back to the fire and put the wood on so that it blazed at once. Then we saw that the tent had fallen over and lay in a tangled heap upon the ground.

We picked it up, and during the process tripped more than once and caught our feet in sand.

"It's those sand-funnels," exclaimed the Swede, when the tent was up again and the firelight lit up the ground for several yards about us. "And look at the size of them!"

All round the tent and about the fireplace where we had seen the moving shadows there were deep funnel-shaped hollows in the sand, exactly similar to the ones we had already found over the island, only far bigger and deeper, beautifully formed, and wide enough in some instances to admit the whole of my foot and leg.

Neither of us said a word. We both knew that sleep was the safest thing we could do, and to bed we went accordingly without further delay, having first thrown sand on the fire and taken the provision sack and the paddle inside the tent with us. The canoe, too, we propped in such a way at the end of the tent that our feet touched it, and the least motion would disturb and wake us.

In case of emergency, too, we again went to bed in our clothes, ready for a sudden start.

It was my firm intention to lie awake all night and watch, but the exhaustion of nerves and body decreed otherwise, and sleep after a while came over me with a welcome blanket of oblivion. The fact that my companion also slept quickened its approach. At first he fidgeted and constantly sat up, asking me if I "heard this" or "heard that." He tossed about on his cork mattress, and said the tent was moving and the river had risen over the point of the island; but each time I went out to look I returned with the report that all was well, and finally he grew calmer and lay still. Then at length his breathing became regular and I heard unmistakable sounds of snoring—the first and only time in my life when snoring has been a welcome and calming influence.

This, I remember, was the last thought in my mind before dozing off.

A difficulty in breathing woke me, and I found the blanket over my face. But something else besides the blanket was pressing upon me, and my first thought was that my companion had rolled off his mattress on to my own in his sleep. I called to him and sat up, and at the same moment it came to me that the tent was *surrounded*. That sound of multitudinous soft pattering was again audible outside, filling the night with horror.

I called again to him, louder than before. He did not answer, but I missed the sound of his snoring, and also noticed that the flap of the tent door was down. This was the unpardonable sin. I crawled out in the darkness to hook it back securely, and it was then for the first time I realized positively that the Swede was not there. He had gone.

I dashed out in a mad run, seized by a dreadful agitation, and the moment I was out I plunged into a sort of torrent of humming that surrounded me completely and came out of every quarter of the heavens at once. It was that same familiar humming—gone mad! A swarm of great invisible bees might have been about me in the air. The sound seemed to thicken the very atmosphere, and I felt that my lungs worked with difficulty.

But my friend was in danger, and I could not hesitate.

The dawn was just about to break, and a faint whitish light spread upward over the clouds from a thin strip of clear horizon. No wind stirred. I could just make out the bushes and river beyond, and the pale sandy patches. In my excitement I ran frantically to and fro about the island, calling him by name, shouting at the top of my voice the first words that came into my head. But the willows smothered my voice, and the humming muffled it, so that the sound only traveled a few feet round me. I plunged among the bushes, tripping headlong, tumbling over roots, and scraping my face as I tore this way and that among the preventing branches.

Then, quite unexpectedly, I came out upon the island's point and saw a dark figure outlined between the water and the sky. It was the Swede. And already he had one foot in the river! A moment more and he would have taken the plunge.

I threw myself upon him, flinging my arms about his waist and dragging him shoreward with all my strength. Of course he struggled furiously, making a noise all the time just like that cursed humming, and using the most outlandish phrases in his anger about "going *inside* to Them," and "taking the way of the water and the wind," and God only knows what more besides, that I tried in vain to recall afterward, but which turned me sick with horror and amazement as I listened. But in the end I managed to get him into the comparative safety of the tent, and flung him breathless and cursing upon the mattress, where I held him until the fit had passed.

I think the suddenness with which it all went and he grew calm, coinciding as it did with the equally abrupt cessation of the humming and pattering outside—I think this was almost the strangest part of the whole business perhaps. For he just opened his eyes and turned his tired face up to me so that the dawn threw a pale light upon it through the doorway, and said, for all the world just like a frightened child:

"My life, old man—it's my life I owe you. But it's all over now anyhow. They've found a victim in our place!"

Then he dropped back upon his blankets and went to sleep literally under my eyes. He simply collapsed, and began to snore again as healthily as though nothing had happened and he had never tried to offer his own life as a sacrifice by drowning. And when the sunlight woke him three hours later—hours of ceaseless vigil for me—it became so clear to me that he remembered absolutely nothing of what he had attempted to do, that I deemed it wise to hold my peace and ask no dangerous questions.

He woke naturally and easily, as I have said, when the sun was already high in a windless hot sky, and he at once got up and set about the preparation of the fire for breakfast. I followed him anxiously at bathing, but he did not attempt to plunge in, merely dipping his head and making some remark about the extra coldness of the water.

"River's falling at last," he said, "and I'm glad of it."

"The humming has stopped too," I said.

He looked up at me quietly with his normal expression. Evidently he remembered everything except his own attempt at suicide.

"Everything has stopped," he said, "because—"

He hesitated. But I knew some reference to that remark he had made just before he fainted was in his mind, and I was determined to know it.

"Because 'They've found another victim'?" I said, forcing a little laugh.

"Exactly," he answered, "exactly! I feel as positive of it as though—as though—I feel quite safe again, I mean," he finished.

He began to look curiously about him. The sunlight lay in hot patches on the sand. There was no wind. The willows were motionless. He slowly rose to his feet.

"Come," he said; "I think if we look, we shall find it."

He started off on a run, and I followed him. He kept to the banks, poking with a stick among the sandy bays and caves and little back-waters, myself always close on his heels.

"Ah!" he exclaimed presently, "ah!"

The tone of his voice somehow brought back to me a vivid sense of the horror of the last twenty-four hours, and I hurried up to join him. He was pointing with his stick at a large black object that lay half in the water and half on the sand. It appeared to be caught by some twisted willow roots so that the river could not sweep it away. A few hours before the spot must have been under water.

"See," he said quietly, "the victim that made our escape possible!"

And when I peered across his shoulder I saw that his stick rested on the body of a man. He turned it over. It was the corpse of a peasant, and the face was hidden in the sand. Clearly the man had been drowned but a few hours before, and his body must have been swept down upon our island somewhere about the hour of the dawn—*at the very time the fit had passed*.

"We must give it a decent burial, you know."

"I suppose so," I replied. I shuddered a little in spite of myself, for there was something about the appearance of that poor drowned man that turned me cold.

The Swede glanced up sharply at me, an undecipherable expression on his face, and began clambering down the bank. I followed him more leisurely. The current, I noticed, had torn away much of the clothing from the body, so that the neck and part of the chest lay bare.

Halfway down the bank my companion suddenly stopped and held up his hand in warning; but either my foot slipped, or I had gained too much momentum to bring myself quickly to a halt, for I bumped into him and sent him forward with a sort of leap to save himself. We tumbled together on to the hard sand so that our feet splashed into the water. And, before anything could be done, we had collided a little heavily against the corpse.

The Swede uttered a sharp cry. And I sprang back as if I had been shot.

At the moment we touched the body there rose from its surface the loud sound of humming—the sound of several hummings—which passed with a vast commotion as of winged things in the air about us and disappeared upward into the sky, growing fainter and fainter till they finally ceased in the distance. It was exactly as though we had disturbed some living yet invisible creatures at work.

My companion clutched me, and I think I clutched him, but before either of us had time properly to recover from the unexpected shock, we saw that a movement of the current was turning the corpse round so that it became released from the grip of the willow roots. A moment later it had turned completely over, the dead face uppermost, staring at the sky. It lay on the edge of the main stream. In another moment it would be swept away.

The Swede started to save it, shouting again something I did not catch about a "proper burial"—and then abruptly dropped upon his knees on the sand and covered his eyes with his hands. I was beside him in an instant.

I saw what he had seen.

For just as the body swung round to the current the face and the exposed chest turned full toward us, and showed plainly how the skin and flesh were indented with small hollows, beautifully formed, and exactly similar in shape and kind to the sand-funnels that we had found all over the island.

"Their mark!" I heard my companion mutter under his breath. "Their awful mark!"

And when I turned my eyes again from his ghastly face to the river, the current had done its work, and the body had been swept away into midstream and was already beyond our reach and almost out of sight, turning over and over on the waves like an otter.

The Man Who Liked Dickens

by Evelyn Waugh

Like Joseph Conrad and others before him, Evelyn Waugh (1903–1966) knew that we can find our wickedness in the wilderness. Waugh liked to pose painful questions. Here he asks which hurts us most: others' cruelty or our own weakness? This story provided some of the most disturbing material for Waugh's harshest novel, A Handful of Dust.

Although Mr. McMaster had lived in Amazonas for nearly sixty years, no one except a few families of Shiriana Indians was aware of his existence. His house stood in a small savannah, one of those little patches of sand and grass that crop up occasionally in that neighbourhood, three miles or so across, bounded on all sides by forest.

The stream which watered it was not marked on any map; it ran through rapids, always dangerous and at most seasons of the year impassable, to join the upper waters of the River Uraricuera, whose course, though boldly delineated in every school atlas, is still largely conjectural. None of the inhabitants of the district, except Mr. McMaster, had ever heard of the republic of Colombia, Venezuela, Brazil or Bolivia, each of whom had at one time or another claimed its possession.

Mr. McMaster's house was larger than those of his neighbours, but similar in character—a palm-thatch roof, breast-high walls of mud and wattle, and a mud floor. He owned a dozen or so head of puny cattle which grazed in the savannah, a plantation of cassava, some banana and mango trees, a dog, and, unique in the neighbourhood, a single-barrelled, breech-loading shotgun. The few commodities which he employed from the outside world came to him through a long succession of traders, passed from hand to hand, bartered for in a dozen languages at the extreme end of one of the longest threads in the web of commerce that spreads from Manaos into the remote fastness of the forest.

One day, while Mr. McMaster was engaged in filling some cartridges, a Shiriana came to him with the news that a white man was approaching through the forest, alone and very sick. He closed the cartridge and loaded his gun with it, put those that were finished into his pocket and set out in the direction indicated.

The man was already clear of the bush when Mr. McMaster reached him, sitting on the ground, clearly in a bad way. He was without hat or boots, and his clothes were so torn that it was only by the dampness of his body that they adhered to it; his feet were cut and grossly swollen, every exposed surface of skin was scarred by insect and bat bites; his eyes were wild with fever. He was talking to himself in delirium, but stopped when Mr. McMaster approached and addressed him in English.

'I'm tired,' the man said; then: 'Can't go on any farther. My name is Henty and I'm tired. Anderson died. That was a long time ago. I expect you think I'm very odd.'

'I think you are ill, my friend.'

'Just tired. It must be several months since I had anything to eat.'

Mr. McMaster hoisted him to his feet and, supporting him by the arm, led him across the hummocks of grass towards the farm.

'It is a very short way. When we get there I will give you something to make you better.'

'Jolly kind of you.' Presently he said: 'I say, you speak English. I'm English, too. My name is Henty.'

'Well, Mr. Henty, you aren't to bother about anything more. You're ill and you've had a rough journey. I'll take care of you.'

They went very slowly, but at length reached the house.

'Lie there in the hammock. I will fetch something for you.'

Mr. McMaster went into the back room of the house and dragged a tin canister from under a heap of skins. It was full of a mixture of dried leaf and bark. He took a handful and went outside to the fire. When he returned he put one hand behind Henty's head and held up the concoction of herbs in a calabash for him to drink. He sipped, shuddering slightly at the bitterness. At last he finished it. Mr. McMaster threw out the dregs on the floor. Henty lay back in the hammock sobbing quietly. Soon he fell into a deep sleep.

'Ill-fated' was the epithet applied by the Press to the Anderson expedition to the Parima and upper Uraricuera region of Brazil. Every stage of the enterprise from the preliminary arrangements in London to its tragic dissolution in Amazonas was attacked by misfortune. It was due to one of the early set-backs that Paul Henty became connected with it.

He was not by nature an explorer; an even-tempered, good-looking young man of fastidious tastes and enviable possessions, unintellectual, but appreciative of fine architecture and the ballet, well travelled in the more accessible parts of the world, a collector though not a connoisseur, popular among hostesses, revered by his aunts. He was married to a lady of exceptional charm and beauty, and it was she who upset the good order of his life by confessing her affection for another man for the second time in the eight years of their marriage. The first occasion had been a short-lived infatuation with a tennis professional, the second was a captain in the Coldstream Guards, and more serious.

Henty's first thought under the shock of this revelation was to go out and dine alone. He was a member of four clubs, but at three of them he was liable to meet his wife's lover. Accordingly he chose one which he rarely frequented, a semi-intellectual company composed of publishers, barristers, and men of scholarship awaiting election to the Athenaeum.

Here, after dinner, he fell into conversation with Professor Anderson and first heard of the proposed expedition to Brazil. The particular misfortune that was retarding arrangements at the moment was defalcation of the secretary with two thirds of the expedition's capital. The principals were ready—Professor Anderson, Dr. Simmons the anthropologist, Mr. Necher the biologist, Mr. Brough the surveyor, wireless operator and mechanic—the scientific and sporting apparatus was packed up in crates ready to be embarked, the necessary facilities had been stamped and signed by the proper authorities but unless twelve hundred pounds was forthcoming the whole thing would have to be abandoned.

Henty, as had been suggested, was a man of comfortable means; the expedition would last from nine months to a year; he could shut his country house—his wife, he reflected, would want to remain in London near her young man—and cover more than the sum required. There was a glamour about the whole journey which might, he felt, move even his wife's sympathies. There and then, over the club fire, he decided to accompany Professor Anderson.

When he went home that evening he announced to his wife: 'I have decided what I shall do'.

'Yes, darling?'

'You are certain that you no longer love me?'

'*Darling*, you *know*, I *adore* you.'

'But you are certain you love this guardsman, Tony what-ever-his-name-is, more?'

'Oh, yes, *ever* so much more. Quite a different thing altogether.'

'Very well, then. I do not propose to do anything about a divorce for a year. You shall have time to think it over. I am leaving next week for the Uraricuera.'

'Golly, where's that?'

'I am not perfectly sure. Somewhere in Brazil, I think. It is unexplored. I shall be away a year.'

'But darling, how ordinary! Like people in books—big game, I mean, and all that.'

'You have obviously already discovered that I am a very ordinary person.'

'Now, Paul, don't be disagreeable—oh, there's the telephone. It's probably Tony. If it is, d'you mind terribly if I talk to him alone for a bit?'

But in the ten days of preparation that followed she showed greater tenderness, putting off her soldier twice in order to accompany Henty to the shops where he was choosing his equipment and insisting on his purchasing a worsted cummerbund. On his last evening she gave a supper-party for him at the Embassy to which she allowed him to ask any of his friends he liked; he could think of no one except Professor Anderson, who looked oddly dressed, danced tirelessly and was something of a failure with everyone. Next day Mrs. Henty came with her husband to the boat train and presented him with a pale blue, extravagantly soft blanket, in a suede case of the same colour furnished with a zip fastener and monogram. She kissed him good-bye and said, 'Take care of yourself in wherever it is.'

Had she gone as far as Southampton she might have witnessed two dramatic passages. Mr. Brough got no farther than the gangway before he was arrested for debt—a matter of £32; the publicity given to the dangers of the expedition was responsible for the action. Henty settled the account.

The second difficulty was not to be overcome so easily. Mr. Necher's mother was on the ship before them; she carried a missionary journal in which she had just read an account of the Brazilian forests. Nothing would induce her to permit her son's departure; she would remain on board until he came ashore with her. If necessary, she would sail with him, but go into those forests alone he should not. All argument was unavailing with the resolute old lady who eventually, five minutes before the time of embarkation, bore her son off in triumph, leaving the company without a biologist.

Nor was Mr. Brough's adherence long maintained. The ship in which they were travelling was a cruising liner taking passengers on a round voyage. Mr. Brough had not been on board a week and had scarcely accustomed himself to the motion of the ship before he was engaged to be married; he was still engaged, although to a different lady, when they reached Manaos and refused all inducements to proceed farther, borrowing his return fare from Henty and arriving back in South-ampton engaged to the lady of his first choice, whom he immediately married.

In Brazil the officials to whom their credentials were addressed were all out of power. While Henty and Professor Anderson negotiated with the new administrators, Dr. Simmons proceeded up river to Boa Vista where he established a base camp with the greater part of the stores. These were instantly commandeered by the revolutionary garrison, and he himself imprisoned for some days and subjected to various humiliations which so enraged him that, when released, he made promptly for the coast, stopping at Manaos only long enough to inform his colleagues that he insisted on leaving his case personally before the central authorities at Rio.

Thus while they were still a month's journey from the start of their labours, Henty and Professor Anderson found themselves alone and deprived of the greater part of their supplies. The ignominy of immediate return was not to be borne. For a short time they considered the advisability of going into hiding for six months in Madeira or Teneriffe, but even there detection seemed probable; there had been too many photographs in the illustrated papers before they left London. Accordingly, in low spirits, the two explorers at last set out alone for the Uraricuera with little hope of accomplishing anything of any value to anyone.

For seven weeks they paddled through green, humid tunnels of forest. They took a few snapshots of naked, misanthropic Indians, bottled some snakes and later lost them when their canoe capsized in the rapids; they overtaxed their digestions, imbibing nauseous intoxicants at native galas, they were robbed of the last of their sugar by a Guianese prospector. Finally, Professor Anderson fell ill with malignant malaria, chattered feebly for some days in his hammock, lapsed into coma and died, leaving Henty alone with a dozen Maku oarsmen, none of whom spoke a word of any language known to him. They reversed their course and drifted down stream with a minimum of provisions and no mutual confidence.

One day, a week or so after Professor Anderson's death, Henty awoke to find that his boys and his canoe had disappeared during the night, leaving him with only his hammock and pyjamas some two or three hundred miles from the nearest Brazilian habitation. Nature forbade him to remain where he was although there seemed little purpose in moving. He set himself to follow the course of the stream, at first in the hope of meeting a canoe. But presently the whole forest became peopled for him with frantic apparitions, for no conscious reason at all. He plodded on, now wading in the water, now scrambling through the bush.

Vaguely at the back of his mind he had always believed that the jungle was a place full of food, that there was danger of snakes and savages and wild beasts, but not of starvation. But now he observed that this was far from being the case. The jungle consisted solely of immense tree trunks, embedded in a tangle of thorn and vine rope, all far from nutritious. On the first day he suffered hideously. Later he seemed anaesthetized and was chiefly embarrassed by the behaviour of the inhabitants who came out to meet him in footman's livery, carrying his dinner, and then irresponsibly disappeared or raised the covers of their dishes and revealed live tortoises. Many people who knew him in London appeared and ran round him with derisive cries, asking him questions to which he could not possibly know the answers. His wife came, too, and he was pleased to see her, assuming that she had got tired of her guardsman and was there to fetch him back, but she soon disappeared, like all the others.

It was then that he remembered that it was imperative for him to reach Manaos; he redoubled his energy, stumbling against boulders in the stream and getting caught up among the vines. 'But I mustn't waste my breath,' he reflected. Then he forgot that, too, and was conscious of nothing more until he found himself lying in a hammock in Mr. McMaster's house.

His recovery was slow. At first, days of lucidity alternated with delirium, then his temperature dropped and he was conscious even when most ill. The days of fever grew less frequent, finally occurring in the normal system of the tropics between long periods of comparative health. Mr. McMaster dosed him regularly, with herbal remedies.

'It's very nasty,' said Henty, 'but it does do good.'

'There is medicine for everything in the forest,' said Mr. McMaster; 'to make you well and to make you ill. My mother was an Indian and she taught me many of them. I have learned others from time to time from my wives. There are plants to cure you and give you fever, to kill you and send you mad, to keep away snakes, to intoxicate fish so that you can pick them out of the water with your hands like fruit from a tree. There are medicines even I do not know. They said that it is possible to bring dead people back to life after they have begun to stink, but I have not seen it done.'

'But surely you are English?'

'My father was—at least a Barbadian. He came to British Guiana as a missionary. He was married to a white woman but he left her in Guiana to look for gold. Then he took my mother. The Shiriana women are ugly but very devoted. I have had many. Most of the men and women living in this savannah are my children. That is why they obey—for that reason and because I have the gun. My father lived to a great age. It is not twenty years since he died. He was a man of education. Can you read?'

'Yes, of course.'

'It is not everyone who is so fortunate. I cannot.'

Henty laughed apologetically. 'But I suppose you haven't much opportunity here.'

'Oh, yes, that is just it. I have a great many books. I will show you when you are better. Until five years ago there was an Englishman—at least a black man, but he was well educated in Georgetown. He died. He used to read to me every day until he died. You shall read to me when you are better.'

'I shall be delighted to.'

'Yes, you shall read to me,' Mr. McMaster repeated, nodding over the calabash.

• • •

During the early days of his convalescence Henty had little conversation with his host; he lay in the hammock staring up at the thatched roof and thinking about his wife, rehearsing over and over again different incidents in their life together, including her affairs with the tennis professional and the soldier. The days, exactly twelve hours each, passed without distinction. Mr. McMaster retired to sleep at sundown, leaving a little lamp burning—a hand-woven wick drooping from a pot of beef fat—to keep away vampire bats.

The first time that Henty left the house Mr. McMaster took him for a stroll around the farm.

'I will show you the black man's grave,' he said, leading him to a mound between the mango trees. 'He was very kind to me. Every afternoon until he died, for two hours, he used to read to me. I think I will put up a cross—to commemorate his death and your arrival—a pretty idea. Do you believe in God?'

'I've never really thought about it much.'

'You are perfectly right. I have thought about it a *great* deal and I still do not know . . . Dickens did.'

'I suppose so.'

'Oh yes, it is apparent in all his books. You will see.'

That afternoon Mr. McMaster began the construction of a headpiece for the negro's grave. He worked with a large spokeshave in a wood so hard that it grated and rang like metal.

At last when Henty had passed six or seven consecutive days without fever, Mr. McMaster said, 'Now I think you are well enough to see the books.'

At one end of the hut there was a kind of loft formed by a rough platform erected up in the eaves of the roof. Mr. McMaster propped a ladder against it and mounted. Henty followed, still unsteady after his illness. Mr. McMaster sat on the platform and Henty stood at the top of the ladder looking over. There was a heap of small bundles there, tied up with rag, palm leaf and raw hide.

'It has been hard to keep out the worms and ants. Two are practically destroyed. But there is an oil the Indians know how to make that is useful.'

He unwrapped the nearest parcel and handed down a calf-bound book. It was an early American edition of *Bleak House*.

'It does not matter which we take first.'

'You are fond of Dickens?'

'Why, yes, of course. More than fond, far more. You see, they are the only books I have ever heard. My father used to read them and then later the black man . . . and now you. I have heard them all several times by now but I never get tired; there is always more to be learned and noticed, so many characters, so many changes of scene, so many words. . . . I have all Dickens's books except those that the ants devoured. It takes a long time to read them all—more than two years.'

'Well,' said Henty lightly, 'they will well last out my visit.'

'Oh, I hope not. It is delightful to start again. Each time I think I find more to enjoy and admire.'

They took down the first volume of *Bleak House* and that afternoon Henty had his first reading.

He had always rather enjoyed reading aloud and in the first year of marriage had shared several books in this way with his wife, until one day, in one of her rare moments of confidence, she remarked that it was torture to her. Sometimes after that he had thought it might be agreeable to have children to read to. But Mr. McMaster was a unique audience.

The old man sat astride his hammock opposite Henty, fixing him throughout with his eyes, and following the words, soundlessly, with his lips. Often when a new character was introduced he would say, 'Repeat the name, I have forgotten him,' or, 'Yes, yes, I remember her well. She dies, poor woman.' He would frequently interrupt with questions; not as Henty would have imagined about the circumstances of the story—such things as the procedure of the Lord Chancellor's Court or the social conventions of the time, though they must have been unintelligible, did not concern him—but always about the characters. 'Now, why does she say that? Does she really mean it? Did she feel faint because of the heat of the fire or of something in that paper?' He laughed loudly at all the jokes and at some passages which did not seem humorous to Henty, asking him to repeat them two or three times; and later at the description of the sufferings of the outcasts in 'Tom-all-alone' tears ran down his cheeks into his beard. His comments on the story were usually simple. 'I think that Dedlock is a very proud man,' or, 'Mrs Jellyby does not take enough care of her children.' Henty enjoyed the readings almost as much as he did.

At the end of the first day the old man said, 'You read beautifully, with a far better accent than the black man. And you explain better. It is almost as though my father were here again.' And always at the end of a session he thanked his guest courteously. 'I enjoyed that very much. It was an extremely distressing chapter. But, if I remember rightly, it will all turn out well.'

By the time that they were well into the second volume, however, the novelty of the old man's delight had begun to wane, and Henty was feeling strong enough to be restless. He touched more than once on the subject of his departure, asking about canoes and rains and the possibility of finding guides. But Mr. McMaster seemed obtuse and paid no attention to these hints.

One day, running his thumb through the pages of *Bleak House* that remained to be read, Henty said, 'We still have a lot to get through. I hope I shall be able to finish it before I go.'

'Oh, yes,' said Mr. McMaster. 'Do not disturb yourself about that. You will have time to finish it, My friend.'

For the first time Henty noticed something slightly menacing in his host's manner. That evening at supper, a brief meal of farine and dried beef eaten just before sundown, Henty renewed the subject.

'You know, Mr. McMaster, the time has come when I must be thinking about getting back to civilization. I have already imposed myself on your hospitality for too long.'

Mr. McMaster bent over his plate, crunching mouthfuls of farine, but made no reply.

'How soon do you think I shall be able to get a boat? . . . I said how soon do you think I shall be able to get a boat? I appreciate all your kindness to me more than I can say, but . . .'

'My friend, any kindness I may have shown is amply repaid by your reading of Dickens. Do not let us mention the subject again.'

'Well, I'm very glad you have enjoyed it. I have, too. But I really must be thinking of getting back . . .'

'Yes,' said Mr. McMaster. 'The black man was like that. He thought of it all the time. But he died here . . .'

Twice during the next day Henty opened the subject but his host was evasive. Finally he said, 'Forgive me, Mr. McMaster, but I really must press the point. When can I get a boat?'

'There is no boat.'

'Well, the Indians can build one.'

'You must wait for the rains. There is not enough water in the river now.'

'How long will that be?'

'A month . . . two months . . .'

They had finished *Bleak House* and were nearing the end of *Dombey and Son* when the rain came.

'Now it is time to make preparations to go.'

'Oh, that is impossible. The Indians will not make a boat during the rainy season—it is one of their superstitions.'

'You might have told me.'

'Did I not mention it? I forgot.'

Next morning Henty went out alone while his host was busy, and, looking as aimless as he could, strolled across the savannah to the group of Indian houses. There were four or five Shirianas sitting in one of the doorways. They did not look up as he approached them. He addressed them in the few words of Maku he had acquired during the journey but they made no sign whether they understood him or not. Then he drew a sketch of a canoe in the sand, he went through some vague motions of carpentry, pointed from them to him, then made motions of giving something to them and scratched out the outlines of a gun and hat and a few other recognizable articles of trade. One of the women giggled, but no one gave any sign of comprehension, and he went away unsatisfied.

At their midday meal Mr. McMaster said: 'Mr Henty, the Indians tell me you have been trying to speak with them. It is easier that you say anything you wish through me. You realize, do you not, that they would do nothing without my authority. They regard themselves, quite rightly in most cases, as my children.'

'Well, as a matter of fact, I was asking them about a canoe.'

'So they gave me to understand . . . and now if you have finished your meal perhaps we might have another chapter. I am quite absorbed in the book.'

They finished *Dombey and Son*; nearly a year had passed since Henty had left England, and his gloomy foreboding of permanent exile became suddenly acute when, between the pages of *Martin Chuzzlewit*, he found a document written in pencil in irregular characters.

Year 1919.

I James McMaster of Brazil do swear to Barnabas Washington of Georgetown that if he finish this book in fact Martin Chuzzlewit I will let him go away back as soon as finished.

There followed a heavy pencil X, and after it: *Mr. McMaster made this mark signed Barnabas Washington.*

'Mr. McMaster,' said Henty, 'I must speak frankly. You saved my life, and when I get back to civilization I will reward you to the best of my ability. I will give you anything within reason. But at present you are keeping me here against my will. I demand to be released.'

'But, my friend, what is keeping you? You are under no restraint. Go when you like.'

'You know very well that I can't get away without your help.'

'In that case you must humour an old man. Read me another chapter.'

'Mr. McMaster, I swear by anything you like that when I get to Manaos I will find someone to take my place. I will pay a man to read to you all day.'

'But I have no need of another man. You read so well.'

'I have read for the last time.'

'I hope not,' said Mr. McMaster politely.

That evening at supper only one plate of dried meat and farine was brought in and Mr. McMaster ate alone. Henty lay without speaking, staring at the thatch.

Next day at noon a single plate was put before Mr. McMaster, but with it lay his gun, cocked, on his knee, as he ate. Henty resumed the reading of *Martin Chuzzlewit* where it had been interrupted.

Weeks passed hopelessly. They read *Nicholas Nickleby* and *Little Dorrit* and *Oliver Twist*. Then a stranger arrived in the savannah, a half-caste prospector, one of that lonely order of men who wander for a lifetime through the forest, tracing the little streams, sifting the gravel and, ounce by ounce, filling the little leather sack of gold dust, more often than not dying of exposure and starvation with five hundred dollars' worth of gold hung round their necks. Mr. McMaster was vexed at his arrival, gave him farine and *passo* and sent him on his journey within an hour of his arrival, but in that hour Henty had time to scribble his name on a slip of paper and put it into the man's hand.

From now on there was hope. The days followed their unvarying routine; coffee at sunrise, a morning of inaction while Mr. McMaster pottered about on the business of the farm, farine and *passo* at noon, Dickens in the afternoon, farine and *passo* and sometimes some fruit for supper, silence from sunset to dawn with the small wick glowing in the beef fat and the palm thatch overhead dimly discernible: but Henty lived in quiet confidence and expectation.

Some time, this year or the next, the prospector would arrive at a Brazilian village with news of his discovery. The disasters to the

Anderson expedition would not have passed unnoticed. Henty could imagine the headlines that must have appeared in the popular Press; even now probably there were search parties working over the country he had crossed; any day English voices might sound over the savannah and a dozen friendly adventurers come crashing through the bush. Even as he was reading, while his lips mechanically followed the printed pages, his mind wandered away from his eager, crazy host opposite, and he began to narrate to himself incidents of his home-coming—the gradual re-encounters with civilization; he shaved and bought new clothes at Manaos, telegraphed for money, received wires of congratulation; he enjoyed the leisurely river journey to Belem, the big liner to Europe; savoured good claret and fresh meat and spring vegetables; he was shy at meeting his wife and uncertain how to address her . . . '*Darling*, you've been much longer than you said. I quite thought you were lost . . .'

And then Mr. McMaster interrupted. 'May I trouble you to read that passage again? It is one I particularly enjoy.'

The weeks passed; there was no sign of rescue, but Henty endured the day for hope of what might happen on the morrow; he even felt a slight stirring of cordiality towards his gaoler and was therefore quite willing to join him when, one evening after a long conference with an Indian neighbour, he proposed a celebration.

'It is one of the local feast days,' he explained, 'and they have been making *piwari*. You may not like it, but you should try some. We will go across to this man's home tonight.'

Accordingly after supper they joined a party of Indians that were assembled round the fire in one of the huts at the other side of the savannah. They were singing in an apathetic, monotonous manner and passing a large calabash of liquid from mouth to mouth. Separate bowls were brought for Henty and Mr. McMaster, and they were given hammocks to sit in.

'You must drink it all without lowering the cup. That is the etiquette.'

Henty gulped the dark liquid, trying not to taste it. But it was not unpleasant, hard and muddy on the palate like most of the beverages he had been offered in Brazil, but with a flavour of honey and brown bread. He leant back in the hammock feeling unusually contented.

Perhaps at that very moment the search party was in camp a few hours' journey from them. Meanwhile he was warm and drowsy. The cadence of song rose and fell interminably, liturgically. Another calabash of piwari was offered him and he handed it back empty. He lay full length watching the play of shadows on the thatch as the Shirianas began to dance. Then he shut his eyes and thought of England and his wife and fell asleep.

He awoke, still in the Indian hut, with the impression that he had outslept his usual hour. By the position of the sun be knew it was late afternoon. No one else was about. He looked for his watch and found to his surprise that it was not on his wrist. He had left it in the house, he supposed, before coming to the party.

'I must have been tight last night,' he reflected. 'Treacherous drink, that.' He had a headache and feared a recurrence of fever. He found when he set his feet to the ground that he stood with difficulty; his walk was unsteady and his mind confused as it had been during the first weeks of his convalescence. On the way across the savannah he was obliged to stop more than once, shutting his eyes and breathing deeply. When he reached the house he found Mr. McMaster sitting there.

'Ah, my friend, you are late for the reading this afternoon. There is scarcely another half-hour of light. How do you feel?'

'Rotten. That drink doesn't seem to agree with me.'

'I will give you something to make you better. The forest has remedies for everything; to make you awake and to make you sleep.'

'You haven't seen my watch anywhere?'

'You have missed it?'

'Yes. I thought I was wearing it. I say, I've never slept so long.'

'Not since you were a baby. Do you know how long? Two days.'

'Nonsense. I can't have.'

'Yes, indeed. It is a long time. It is a pity because you missed our guests.'

'Guests?'

'Why, yes. I have been quite gay while you were asleep. Three men from outside. Englishmen. It is a pity you missed them. A pity for them, too, as they particularly wished to see you. But what could I do? You were so sound asleep. They had come all the way to find you, so—I thought you would not mind—as you could not greet them yourself I gave them a little souvenir, your watch. They wanted something to take home to your wife who is offering a great reward for news of you. They were very pleased with it. And they took some photographs of the little cross I put up to commemorate your coming. They were pleased with that, too. They were very easily pleased. But I do not suppose they will visit us again, our life here is so retired . . . no pleasures except reading . . . I do not suppose we shall ever have visitors again . . . well, well, I will get you some medicine to make you feel better. Your head aches, does it not . . . We will not have any Dickens to-day . . . but tomorrow, and the day after that, and the day after that. Let us read *Little Dorrit* again. There are passages in that book I can never hear without the temptation to weep.'

a c k n o w l e d g m e n t s

Many people made this anthology.

At Thunder's Mouth Press and Avalon Publishing Group: Neil Ortenberg and Susan Reich offered vital support and counsel. Dan O'Connor and Ghadah Alrawi also were indispensable.

At Balliett & Fitzgerald Inc.:

Designer Sue Canavan is an artist. Production editor Maria Fernandez skillfully oversaw production with patience, foresight and a wonderful courtesy. Proofreader Kathryn Daniels did meticulous and skillful work on this book as well as on three previous Adrenaline titles: *High, Rough Water* and *The War*. Kristen Couse found some wonderful photographs. Thanks also to Mike Walters and Simon Sullivan.

At the Thomas Memorial Library in Cape Elizabeth, Maine: The librarians cheerfully worked to locate and borrow books from across the country. Their help was more important than they know.

At the Writing Company:

Shawneric Hachey did superb work gathering books, permissions and facts. Meghan Murphy helped copyedit and check text. Mark Klimek, Nate Hardcastle, Mike Miliard and Taylor Smith cheerfully took up slack on other projects while I read books for this one.

Among friends and family:

My wife Jennifer Schwamm Willis helped gather materials and find and choose selections. She lent her rock-solid judgement to many important decisions.

My esteemed friend and colleague Will Balliett made it happen and made it a pleasure. I could not wish for a better collaborator.

Finally, I am grateful to the writers whose work appears in this book.

Excerpt from *In Trouble Again* by Redmond O'Hanlon, U.S. rights: copyright © 1988 by Redmond O'Hanlon, used by permission of Grove/Atlantic, Inc.; World rights excluding U.S.: copyright © 1988 by Redmond O'Hanlon, reprinted by permission of The Peters Fraser and Dunlop Group Limited. ❖ Excerpt from *Savages* by Joe Kane, copyright © 1995 by Joe Kane. U.S. rights: Reprinted by permission of Alfred A. Knopf Inc.; Canadian rights: Published in Canada by Douglas & McIntyre. Reprinted by permission of publisher. ❖ "Down the River" by Edward Abbey, excerpted from *Desert Solitaire*. Reprinted by permission of Don Congdon Associates, Inc. Copyright © 1968 by Edward Abbey, renewed 1996 by Clarke Abbey. ❖ Excerpt from *Deborah: A Wilderness Narrative*, copyright © 1991 by David Roberts, included with permission of the publisher from The *Early Climbs: Deborah and the Mountain of My Fear* by David Roberts, published by The Mountaineers, Seattle, WA. ❖ "Pearyland" by Barry Holstun Lopez, excerpted from *Field Notes*, copyright © 1994 by Barry Holstun Lopez. Reprinted by permission of Alfred A. Knopf, a division of Random House, Inc. ❖ Excerpt from *Young Men & Fire* by Norman Maclean, copyright © 1992 by the University of Chicago Press. Reprinted by permission of the University of Chicago Press. ❖ Excerpt from *Arabian Sands* by Sir Wilfred Thesiger, copyright © 1959 by Sir Wilfred Thesiger. Reprinted by permission of Curtis Brown Ltd. ❖ Excerpt from *A Walk in the Woods* by Bill Bryson. Copyright © 1997 by Bill Bryson. U.S. rights: Used by permission of Broadway Books, a division of Random House; Canadian and world rights: Used by permission of Jed Mattes Inc., New York. All rights reserved. ❖ Excerpt from *Deliverance* by James Dickey, copyright © 1970 by James Dickey. Renewed 1998 by Christopher Dickey, Kevin Dickey, and Bronwen Dickey. Used by permission of Dell Publishing, a division of Random House, Inc. ❖ "The Man Who Liked Dickens" by Evelyn Waugh. Reprinted by permission of The Peters Fraser and Dunlop Group Limited on behalf of: The Estate of Evelyn Waugh, copyright © 1988.

bibliography

The selections used in this anthology were taken from the editions listed below. In some cases, other editions may be easier to find. Hard to find or out-of-print titles often can be acquired through inter-library loan services. Internet sources also may be able to locate these books.

Abbey, Edward. *Desert Solitaire*. New York: Simon & Schuster, 1968. (For "Down the River".)

The Book of Fantasy. Jorge Luis Borges, editor. New York: Viking Press, 1988. (For "The Man Who Liked Dickens" by Evelyn Waugh.)

Bryson, Bill. *A Walk in the Woods*. New York: Broadway Books, 1998.

Dickey, James. *Deliverance*. New York: Houghton Mifflin, 1970.

Famous Ghost Stories. Bennett A. Cerf, editor. New York: Random House, Inc., 1944. (For "The Willows" by Algernon Blackwood.)

Kane, Joe. *Savages*. New York: Alfred A. Knopf, 1995.

London, Jack. *Novels & Stories*. New York: Viking Press, 1982. (For "To Build A Fire".)

Lopez, Barry. *Field Notes*. New York: Avon Books, 1994. (For "Pearyland".)

MacLean, Norman. *Young Men & Fire*. Chicago: University of Chicago Press, 1992.

O'Hanlon, Redmond. *In Trouble Again*. New York: Vintage Books, 1990.

Roberts, David. *The Early Climbs: Deborah and the Mountain of My Fear*. Seattle, WA: The Mountaineers, 1991.

Thesiger, Sir Wilfred. *Arabian Sands*. New York: E.P. Dutton, 1959.

Tomlinson, H.M. *The Sea and the Jungle*. New York: Time Life Books, 1964.